Explorations in Diversity

Examining Privilege and Oppression in a Multicultural Society

SECOND EDITION

SHARON K. ANDERSON
Colorado State University

VALERIE A. MIDDLETON
University of Northern Colorado

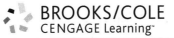
BROOKS/COLE
CENGAGE Learning™

Australia • Brazil • Japan • Korea • Mexico • Singapore • Spain • United Kingdom • United States

BROOKS/COLE
CENGAGE Learning™

Explorations in Diversity: Examining Privilege and Oppression in a Multicultural Society, 2nd Edition

Sharon K. Anderson and Valerie A. Middleton

Publisher/Executive Editor: Linda Schreiber-Ganster

Discipline Acquisitions Editor: Seth Dobrin

Senior Assistant Editor: Arwen Petty

Editorial Assistant: Rachel McDonald

Media Editor: Dennis Fitzgerald

Senior Marketing Manager: Trent Whatcott

Marketing Coordinator: Darlene Macanan

Senior Marketing Communications Manager: Tami Strang

Content Project Management: Pre-PressPMG

Senior Art Director: Caryl Gorska

Production Technology Analyst: Lori Johnson

Print Buyer: Paula Vang

Rights Specialist, Text: Roberta Broyer

Production Service: Pre-PressPMG

Rights Specialist, Image: Leitha Etheridge-Sims

Cover Designer: Brittney Singletary

Compositor: Pre-PressPMG

For product information and technology assistance, contact us at **Cengage Learning Customer & Sales Support, 1-800-354-9706**

For permission to use material from this text or product, submit all requests online at **www.cengage.com/permissions**. Further permissions questions can be emailed to **permissionrequest@cengage.com**.

Library of Congress Control Number: 2010924242

ISBN-13: 978-0-8400-3215-7

ISBN-10: 0-8400-3215-3

Brooks/Cole
Cengage Learning
20 Davis Drive, Belmont, CA 94002
USA

Cengage Learning is a leading provider of customized learning solutions with office locations around the globe, including Singapore, the United Kingdom, Australia, Mexico, Brazil, and Japan. Locate your local office at **international.cengage.com/region**.

Cengage Learning products are represented in Canada by Nelson Education, Ltd.

For your course and learning solutions, visit **www.cengage.com**.

Purchase any of our products at your local college store or at our preferred online store **www.CengageBrain.com**.

Printed in the United States of America
2 3 4 5 6 7 14 13 12 11 10

*To my parents (Joanne and Lawrence), who are one in a million; to my wonderful son,
Bobby, and awesome daughter, Taya;
and to God, who gives me all my worthwhile ideas.*
Sharon

Keeping thoughts of you on my mind helped me to persevere—
God, Ma, Kia, Mudea, Tink, Doreen, Bobby, Taya, Family.
Rest in Peace: Dwight, Kajka, and Kody
Valerie

Contents

Preface

VALERIE A. MIDDLETON AND
SHARON K. ANDERSON

VAL'S STORY

Relying on eight years of public school teaching experience in the Chicago area, I smiled confidently upon entering my first university classroom as a teacher educator, in spite of the fact that nearly every student in the room sat before me with mouth agape. I turned my back to them to write identifying information on the board while I subtly checked to make sure I was buttoned and zipped. When I realized that I was appropriately secured, I assumed that the shocked expressions were a result of my being a Black female in a classroom of all White students. At my about face, the students had corrected their posture and were awaiting my delineation of the syllabus for a course on diversity. That was the first time I taught a university course. Similar scenarios exist every semester, but lend themselves to teaching about issues of diversity, privilege, and oppression since my first position as an assistant professor in the School of Education at Colorado State University and in my present position as a tenured professor at the University of Northern Colorado, Greeley.

My previous teaching experiences were in Chicago area K–12 public school settings where students came from a variety of racial, ethnic, religious, and socioeconomic backgrounds. In contrast, my university experience has been teaching predominantly White, Christian, middle-class graduate and undergraduate students training to be teachers, counselors, social workers, and the like. As a Black American, female college professor, I am somewhat of an anomaly. Typically, I am the only teacher of color many of my students have had, the only Black teacher they have had, or the only Black professor they have had. As a result, I find I must carefully and purposefully establish a level of credibility and authority that would typically come with the position, as it does for many of my White American male counterparts—a privilege they automatically have. An additional privilege they have is being called by the distinguished title of "Dr." Ninety percent of the time, in face-to-face, e-mail, or phone interactions, students address me by my first name or when trying to be polite call me Miss, Mrs., or Ms. Although these titles are not "offensive" to me, what does offend me is that none of my male counterparts are called Mr., but are given the title of Dr. or professor, whether or not they have earned it.

These are the kinds of conversations I would have with Sharon, my friend and coeditor. We are both university faculty—one Black and one White, working in predominately White university settings with predominately White undergraduate and graduate students enrolled in education or counseling programs. Most of our students come from monoracial, White suburban or rural settings in Colorado or other states across the country, whereas few come from areas such as Denver, Chicago, or Los Angeles. In my current position as secondary education director at UNC, which is situated in a town with a significant number of Latino and Somali families, the student population is still predominately White. This speaks to a situation that is also impacted by privilege.

Within the context of teaching about multiculturalism, many of our students say they support issues of diversity and multiculturalism; however, closer inquiry reveals that they mean "I am not a racist." They then go on to share scenarios of how they have a Black or Mexican friend, have dated someone outside of their ethnicity, listen to rap music, or attend Native American Pow Wows. When the burden of proof regarding the validity of their claims is placed at the forefront, many students become agitated, defensive, or resistant. However, rather than shy away from these reactions, I believe that they are necessary and critical steps towards deconstructing and reconstructing a belief system that supports multicultural understanding.

Sharon and I have had many conversations about these aforementioned reactions and their connection to privilege. In the *Introduction: An Awakening to Privilege*, Sharon shares her own story, which addresses such reactions in the context of her life. It is our hope that this book contributes to the resources on privilege, diversity, and oppression by encouraging readers to look within themselves—rather than claim "I'm not ..." and place the blame elsewhere.

EMERGENT NARRATIVES:
HOW THE BOOK WAS DEVELOPED

This book was originally conceived as a resource for individuals in various helping professions, such as counseling, social work, psychology, and education, and was originally titled *Explorations in Privilege, Oppression, and Diversity*. We chose this title to highlight the elusive nature of privilege, its resulting oppression, and many of the diversity of statuses in which it is manifested. With this second edition, we have expanded the content and modified the title in order to draw attention to the practicality and necessity of the text for a broader audience; that is, any individual or group personally or professionally interested in understanding and uprooting privilege can benefit from reading this book. *Explorations in Diversity: Examining Privilege and Oppression in a Multicultural Society* assumes that its readers have a general understanding of the concept of privilege and are seeking to explore some of the myriad ways it is expressed. However, for those who are somewhat new to the concept, privilege is generally described as an invisible, weightless knapsack of special provisions—unearned assets of which one is conditioned to be oblivious (McIntosh, P. 1989, July/August. *White Privilege: Unpacking the Invisible Knapsack*. Peace and Freedom 10–12). Regardless of whether you are new to the concept or have vast knowledge and experience, the stories in this book will provide you with the opportunity to learn, grow, and expand your thinking about privilege.

The process by which the first edition took shape was emergent. That is, although a fairly structured and descriptive call for papers went out, the manuscripts that came back were varied in style and different from what we had imagined, but nevertheless thought-provoking in content. We thought it important to be as inclusive as possible, knowing firsthand about the "publish or perish" paradigm of higher education. As a result, we worked through our differences over the goal of the book, what should be included or not included, and what to do about manuscripts that did not "specifically" fit the focus (that is, "Is this privilege or something else?"). We also wanted to provide balance and equity, but were restricted by the types of submissions we received. In the end, we tried to provide for the best representation of privilege categories we could with the manuscripts we received. Although limited in number, the power of the stories surpassed the quantity in their ability to inform and transform readers.

EXPLORATIONS IN DIVERSITY: EXAMINING PRIVILEGE AND OPPRESSION IN A MULTICULTURAL SOCIETY

Approximately two years after *Explorations in Privilege, Oppression, and Diversity* (2005) had been in circulation, Sharon called a group together to discuss things learned from using the book in various courses, positive and constructive comments heard about the book, and additional topics we wished covered. From those conversations, several ideas were generated; however, the outcome was condensed into two doable projects: an analysis of the stories in the first edition resulting in (at the time of this printing) an unpublished manuscript titled, *The Journey to Understanding Privilege: A Meta-Narrative Approach* and a desire to produce a second edition of Explorations.

With a contact from the publisher and the desire already in place, we developed a plan for the second edition. This second edition of Explorations adds the voices of some who have used the text and desired to have their story added individually and to the collective of experiences addressing issues of privilege, oppression, and diversity. In adding new voices and stories to this edition, our initial process was duplicated in that we sent out another fairly structured and descriptive call for papers focused on areas in which there were gaps or limited contributions. As a result, Part I of this edition, *Stories of Privilege*, includes chapters on white privilege, socioeconomic privilege, able-bodied privilege, an expanded section on heterosexual privilege which includes cisgender privilege and marriage, and concludes with chapters on male privilege and sexism. Part II, *Are We There Yet? ... Not Quite* includes a piece that examines the processes the authors share in Explorations (2005) regarding their efforts to understand and address issues of privilege and oppression in both the personal and professional spheres of their lives. The contributors' experiences are analyzed and the commonalities are shared via a journey metaphor that might inform a framework for individuals coming to understand their own privilege. As researchers, we were interested in understanding: How do agents in the majority, be it race, religion, class, gender, ability, or sexual orientation, come to understand their privilege statuses that result in the oppression of others? Are there defining elements (experiences and/or conversations) that help people progress beyond defensiveness and toward understanding? Is there a common journey to understanding? And finally, is there a state of full understanding? *Part III* includes *Stories of Assumed Privilege—Racism, Heterosexism, and Ageism* with ageism as a newly included topic. The stories of assumed privilege address situations in which the chapter authors are members of an oppressed group, but are assumed to be members of a privileged group. These situations present challenges that address privilege and oppression in a different way than dominant status privilege as each author adds more layers to the ways privilege and oppression are expressed. *Part IV* includes *Stories of Internalized Oppression, Acculturation, and Assimilation and the Complexities of Identity*. Authors in this section speak to the "benefits" and pitfalls associated with navigating a system that rewards sameness and hierarchy rather than diversity, multiplicity, and equity. The stories in this section share commonalities with the stories in Parts I and III, but add the complexity associated with fitting in or gaining acceptance by "buying in to the oppression or being blinded by the privileges." *Part V, International Perspectives: Stories of Privilege, Acculturation, and Assimilation* is a new section addressing international perspectives on privilege and including a chapter focused on intersectionality. While many of the chapters in the text speak to intersectionality, the chapters in this section add focus to the topic and provide an opportunity to look at privilege and oppression both within and outside of the United States. *Part VI, Stories of Personal Compassion and Being Allies*, brings a strong ending to the book by adding to the aforementioned stories and reinforcing the ways in which we all have our roles in uprooting privilege and oppression and gives concrete suggestions on how to do so.

The authors of each chapter represent real people involved in their struggles with privilege. Each chapter represents the authors' voices and their own way of sharing their stories. The authors use various means to describe their own positions relative to ability, socioeconomic class, gender, race, ethnicity, religion, sexual orientation, gender identity, etc. Although it is recognized by all of the authors that the concepts discussed are socially, politically, and ideologically constructed, it is also recognized that these are the categories by which we name ourselves and others, and the categories that make the meaning of the narratives clear and accessible to the reader. The authors speak to the psychological costs of privilege rather than its benefits, as well as constructive methods of working through the dissonance that occurs when privilege is realized, acknowledged, and the process of dismantling begins. Finally, the authors address key components of the dismantling process and key ingredients to transformational learning.

In closing, we believe that we selected accessible stories that allow for challenging the thinking around the issues informing the transformative process of our students, ourselves, and others. We hope you join us in laughing, crying, being angry, and gaining hope as you journey with us through our lives and add your own in uprooting privilege, fighting oppression, and affirming diversity in your personal and professional lives.

ACKNOWLEDGMENTS

We would like to thank all of our contributors for their willingness to share their stories and their hard work in making this book become a reality. You have been an awesome group to work with. Thank You!

We would also like to thank the following reviewers who carefully read the first edition: Barry Feldman, MSW, PH.D., University of New Hampshire; Deborah McGriff, University of Wyoming; Beth Rienzi, California State University, Bakersfield; and Thomas Scofield, University of Nebraska, Kearney. We also appreciate the valuable suggestions offered for this second edition by the following reviewers: Wendy Campbell, Winthrop College; Margaret Elbow, Texas Tech University; Saliwe Kawewe, Southern Illinois University; and Joy S. Whitman, DePaul University.

About the Contributors

Sharon K. Anderson Sharon grew up on a farm/ranch in Wyoming. Being the youngest of three, she has fond memories of playing football, softball, and basketball with her older brothers, helping her mom with indoor responsibilities and occasionally getting to drive a tractor with her dad, and attending a very small public school that held K–12 grades in the same building.

After graduating from high school, she attended the University of Wyoming and received her B.A. in English education in 1978. She taught junior high for one year and then returned to the University to work on a master's in counseling. She then worked for the TRIO programs at UW. This is where her first experiences with people really different from her began. Sharon worked with TRIO for several years, and then decided in 1988 to pursue her doctorate in Counseling Psychology through the University of Denver. She graduated in 1993 and obtained her current faculty position at Colorado State University in 1994. As an associate professor, she teaches professional ethics, practicum, and internship classes in a master's program.

On the personal side, Sharon is a single mom of two awesome children, Bobby and Taya. She spends a lot of her free time with them playing outside, watching children's movies, and reading them stories. She loves to travel and see new scenery, as well as spend time in the Rocky Mountains.

Valerie A. Middleton Valerie A. Middleton, Ph.D., is a tenured professor at the University of Northern Colorado teaching and researching the topics of diversity and privilege and educational methodology utilizing service-learning, professional development school partnerships, and international education delivery systems. She holds a bachelor's degree in Special Education from Illinois State University, a master's degree in Special Needs from Colorado State University, and a doctorate in Teacher Education and Staff Development from Colorado State University. Previously, she taught students in grades K–12 in Chicago area public schools as well as graduate and undergraduate students at Colorado State University and Northern Arizona University.

James H. Banning   James H. Banning, PhD, is a professor in the School of Education at Colorado State University. Jim teaches qualitative research courses and campus ecology. He also teaches environmental psychology for CSU's Department of Psychology. Jim received his MA and PhD from the University of Colorado-Boulder in 1965 in the field of clinical psychology. Dr. Banning has authored books, book chapters, and numerous journal articles on the campus environment often focusing on issues of campus diversity. Jim's special interest is in visual research associated with cultural artifacts.

Allan Barsky   Allan Edward Barsky, the third of four sons, was born and raised in Regina, Saskatchewan, the "Queen City" of the Canadian Prairies. Regina, a city of 200,000 people in an agricultural province, had a small but tight-knit Jewish community whose cultural life centered around its orthodox synagogue. Growing up as part of a religious minority, Allan learned about the challenges of dealing with various forms of bigotry and the importance of pride in oneself and one's heritage. Allan was instilled with social democratic values, where people worked together for the common good, as Saskatchewan was the birthplace of universal health care, farming cooperatives, and no-fault automobile insurance.

At 18 years old, Allan moved east to study business at Queen's University at Kingston, Ontario. He studied law at the University of Toronto and was called to the Bar of Ontario. Although law and business education provided Allan with useful life and career skills, Allan headed back to school for a course of studies that provided an outlet for his interest in fostering social justice. Allan received his MSW from Yeshiva University at New York City, where he worked with heroin abusers in the Bronx and with families in conflict with the law in Brooklyn. Allan received his Ph.D. in Social Work from the University of Toronto where his doctoral dissertation looked at the process of mediation in helping families and child protective services work out plans to ensure children were free from abuse and neglect.

Allan's academic career has spanned three universities—Ryerson University in Toronto, University of Calgary in Alberta, and now, Florida Atlantic University in Boca Raton. Allan's teaching and research interests include human diversity, conflict resolution, professional ethics, and addictions. His book credits include *Social Work Ethics and Values* (2010, Oxford), *Conflict Resolution for the Helping Professions* (2007, Brooks/Cole), *Alcohol, Other Drugs, and Addictions* (2006, Brooks/Cole), and *Clinicians in Court* (2002, Guilford). Since 2006, Dr. Barsky has been faculty advisor for a group of 35 to 80 students who go to the state capitol in Tallahassee each year to meet with legislators and advocate for social justice.

Allan and his husband, Greg, were legally married in Canada in 2003, although the people of Florida voted (62%) in 2008 to amend the state constitution to deny same-sex couples the 2,000+ rights and privileges of marriage. Ironically, they live in a relatively progressive area of south Florida, where they are generally accepted as a "real couple" by their neighbors and community organizations. Allan and Greg have a seven-year old daughter who proudly describes herself as her parents' wedding present, forever.

Allison Cashwell   Allison Cashwell grew up in the quaint town of Mount Airy, North Carolina, hometown of actor Andy Griffith, and better known as the inspiration for the fictional TV town of "Mayberry." After graduating from the University of North Carolina at Chapel Hill with a B.A. in psychology in 1992, she relocated to Crested Butte, Colorado, where she was for two years the artistic director of the Crested Butte Mountain Theatre, Colorado's longest-running community theatre. She received a master's degree in education and human resource studies from Colorado State University in 1999.

Allison is a Licensed Professional Counselor, Certified Addictions Counselor, and an Approved Domestic Violence Offender Treatment Provider for the state of Colorado. Since 1998, her work in the helping professions has focused on educating nonvoluntary clientele in the areas of addictions and domestic violence. A strong believer in co-creating solutions in a therapeutic setting, her theoretical orientation is Solution-Focused Therapy. She strives to takes this philosophy into the classroom as well as home from work each day.

Allison is a professor of psychology at Front Range Community College in Fort Collins, Colorado. She teaches introductory psychology, human growth and development, and stress management. A proponent of primary prevention, her teachings in the classroom include therapeutic touch as well as didactic discussions. Her motto is "Conflict is inevitable; violence is not."

Additionally, Allison teaches aerobics and weight-training group fitness classes three days per week at the Fort Collins Club. In the summertime, she works as an experiential counselor/ropes course facilitator for Hands On Resources, LLC. She enjoys hiking, camping, and exploring the majestic Rocky Mountain region she now calls home.

Ruth Chao   Ruth Chao was born and raised in Keelung, the "rain harbor" in Taiwan. Keelung is a city and a harbor that has rain almost the whole year and is well known for fresh seafood and local foods. While growing up, Ruth's homemaker mother would go to the food market to buy fresh fish caught just a few hours before dawn. Ruth's father is a retired sailor, who used to work as an engineer on board ships for 30 years. She has two elder brothers and two elder sisters who were all her best support in childhood.

Taiwan is a country with diverse cultures. It used to be governed by Japan for 50 years before World War II, then by Chiang Kai Shek and KMT. Taiwan blends Western/American thoughts and foods (e.g., McDonalds, Starbucks, Subway) with its native culture.

Since she was quite young, Ruth experienced diverse cultures in life. Her father, who used to work as ship engineer overseas, always brought her American toys and chocolates. These exotic toys were the envy of her classmates. When in college, she changed her major from literature to psychology so as to understand human mind. She came to the United States to obtain her Ph.D. in

Counseling Psychology from the University of Missouri–Columbia. Being culturally different from others has inspired her reflection as she counsels clients who are almost always culturally different from her (e.g., White or non-Chinese). Being culturally different is one thing, whereas how one consciously reflects on cultural difference is quite another. She proceeds from the former to the latter and enjoys the latter.

Ruth is now teaching at the Counseling Psychology program, University of Denver. She has 60 publications and presentations to her credit. Her articles include "Integrating Culture and Attachment" and "Toward an Integrative Curriculum," both published in the American Psychologist. Some of the book chapters include "Well-being and Resilience: Another Look at African American Psychology" (in press) and "The Role of Ethnic Identity, Gender Roles, and Multicultural Training in College Counselors' Multicultural Counseling Competence: A Mediation Model" (in press, *Journal of College Counseling*).

Ruth enjoys travels around the world. She has been to Finland, Denmark, German, New Zealand, China, and Japan. She loves cooking and tasting different fine foods.

Dibya Choudhuri   Dibya Choudhuri is currently an Associate Professor at Eastern Michigan University. She received a Ph.D. in Counselor Education, with a specialization in Multicultural Counseling from Syracuse University, and an M.S. in counseling from the University of Vermont. She teaches cross-cultural counseling, helping skills, counseling theories, and group counseling courses.

She is licensed as a Professional Counselor in Michigan, and is a national certified counselor and approved clinical supervisor. She is a member of the American Counseling Association, the Association of Multicultural Counseling and Development, and the Association for Counselor Education & Supervision. She has served on the Editorial boards of the *Journal of Counseling and Development, Journal of Multicultural Counseling and Diversity, and Ethnic and Minority Psychology*. Her research interests are in qualitative approaches to understanding the experience of clients, pedagogical issues in teaching multicultural counseling and counselor supervision, and in international issues in counseling.

Dibya worked as a counselor with international students for five years as well as with refugee and immigrant clients through a community mental-health agency. She continues to see clients on a pro bono basis, specializing in trauma and culture shock. She also worked through university multicultural affairs in coordinating student programs for ALANA students as well as providing counseling services. Dibya grew up in India, an army brat who traveled constantly leading a nomadic experience across sixteen schools. She came to the United States for her undergraduate work and ended up staying. Dibya brings multicultural issues to her daily experience as an immigrant, as well as in her intercultural marriage and parenting a multiracial child. Her activities are a mix of sedentary and active: reading, writing, and dance. The public library of every town she has lived in knows her well.

Kelly Costello   Kelly is the Director of Victim Services at the Colorado Anti-Violence Program, a statewide organization that works to eliminate violence within and against lesbian, gay, bisexual, transgender and queer (LGBTQ) communities. He primarily oversees a 24-hour crisis hotline, provides limited case management, and coordinates volunteers. He also provides training for various audiences including, but not limited to, community members, health-care professionals, law enforcement, students, and service providers. Kelly also has a long history of community activism and organizing. Since moving to Denver in 2003, he has invested much time and energy into coordinating the Denver Zine Library, which currently includes a lending collection of over 9,000 zines (independently published media), as a co-founder. His interest in promoting underground media is rooted in a commitment to ensuring access for voices not heard in mainstream media. In 2005, Kelly worked with a co-founder to create The Tranny Roadshow, a national tour consisting of all self-identified transgender performance artists. The tour continues to be successful in its mission to both educate and entertain within and outside of LGBTQ communities.

Deborah L. Cox   Deborah L. Cox is a licensed psychologist and associate professor of counseling at Southwest Missouri State University, where she is also a member of the gender studies faculty. She directs research teams and teaches graduate courses in multicultural counseling, family therapy, and basic counseling skills. Having grown up in a fundamentalist Christian community in the southern United States, Deborah feels particularly grateful for the feminist training she received in graduate school; training that allowed her to question traditional assumptions about things such as cultural difference, good versus evil, and gender or sex roles. She received a Ph.D. in counseling psychology from Texas Woman's University in 1996 and has extensive clinical experience including individual; couples; and family therapy in mental-health agencies, private practice, and in the Dallas Public Schools. Cox is coauthor of *Women's Anger: Clinical and Developmental Perspectives* (1999, Brunner-Mazel) and *The Anger Advantage* (2003, Broadway). Her formal research program involves emotional development, anger, cultural beauty issues for women and men, and gender socialization. Deborah values models of teaching and psychotherapy that involve a focus on emotion. She considers it a personal ambition to raise social consciousness in her students and facilitate emotion consciousness in both clients and students. She resides in Springfield with her colleague and partner, Joseph Hulgus, and their son, A.J.

James A. Cummings   James Cummings grew up in the small town of Aitkin, in the heart of Minnesota's lake country. Growing up with five older siblings, he enjoyed many of the outdoor activities his home area offered, such as hunting, fishing, boating and biking. After graduating from high school in 1988, he attended Bemidji State University and obtained bachelor's degrees in history and secondary education. He completed a master's program in counseling at the University of North Dakota. After working as a school counselor in the quiet farming town of Finley, North Dakota, he has been Dean of Students in at the Fridley High School in the Twin Cities metropolitan area for the past five years while he completed an Education Specialist degree and principal's license from the University of St. Thomas.

Cummings and his wife are proud parents of three children—Megan, 12; Ryan, 11; and Ellie, 6. He and his family enjoy time together watching movies, playing board games, ice-skating, ice-fishing, swimming and visiting relatives. Cummings is still an avid outdoorsman who also enjoys cooking, computers and singing.

Helen Deines Helen Deines is Professor Emeritus in the school of social work at Spalding University in Louisville, KY. She earned an A.B. in history from Stanford University, then an M.Ed. (counseling in higher education) from Oregon State, M.S.S.W. from the University of Louisville, and Ed.D. (educational leadership) from Spalding University.

Deines continues to be active in her profession, working on a consultation and training team that promotes anti-racist, anti-classist social work practice. Helen volunteers with Kentucky's Race, Community, and Child Welfare Initiative as well as a number of programs for persons who are homeless. She also pursues a longstanding interest in the relationship between spirituality, religion, and the promotion of social and economic justice, most recently publishing a study of the Catholic Worker movement as a model of solidarity in the helping relationship.

Helen gratefully acknowledges the contribution of Linda Chatmon, MSSW, Director of First Neighborhood Place, in Louisville, KY—the colleague who reminded her that she always had a choice about naming her racial identity.

Edward A. Delgado-Romero Edward A. Delgado-Romero is an Associate Professor and Director of Training in the Counseling Psychology program at the University of Georgia. He is the president of the National Latina/o Psychological Association (NLPA) and a Fellow of the American Psychological Association in both the Society for the Psychological Study of Ethnic Minority Psychology and the Society of Counseling Psychology. Ed is on several editorial boards including the *Hispanic Journal of Higher Education* and *The Counseling Psychologist*.

Ed teaches Advanced Multicultural Counseling, Internship and Consultation, as well as supervises doctoral students in research and clinical work. He is a licensed psychologist in Georgia. Ed has published extensively and been a keynote speaker for several conferences including the Winter Roundtable. Ed's research interests include Latino/a psychology, multicultural counseling competence, ethics and investigating race, and racism in psychotherapy process.

Ed graduated from the University of Notre Dame with a Ph.D. in Counseling Psychology. He spent his internship year at Michigan State University. From 1997–2002 he was Assistant Director for Clinical Services at the University of Florida Counseling Center. He was the advisor of the UF Colombian Student Association from 1997–2002. He was an Assistant Professor in Counseling Psychology at Indiana University from 2002-2005.

Ed is married to Dr. Amy Heesacker, who is also a Counseling Psychologist and a Notre Dame graduate, and they have three children: Javier, Isabel and Guillermo. Ed owes a debt of thanks to his mother Isabel Delgado Alonso who immigrated to the United States in the hopes of giving her family a better life.

Deborah Megivern Foster   Deborah Megivern Foster, Ph.D., is an academic enrichment specialist for the TRiO Student Support Services Program at Metropolitan State University in Saint Paul, Minnesota. TRiO programs are federally- funded educational opportunity programs serving low-income and first-generation college students, as well as, students with disabilities. Dr. Foster attributes her own journey from poverty to PhD to the tremendous services she received from TRiO through Upward Bound and Student Support Services. In addition to her work with TRiO, Dr. Foster does professional speaking on poverty, mental illness, and diversity.

Dr. Foster earned her undergraduate degree at Luther College in Decorah, Iowa, and her master's degrees in social work and psychology from the University of Michigan in Ann Arbor. Prior to entering graduate school, she worked as a residential counselor in community mental health and as a probation officer in adult corrections. In 2001, Dr. Foster completed her Ph.D. in a joint degree in social work and psychology at the University of Michigan following completion of her dissertation, which focused on the college experiences of students who have a mental illness. She completed a two-year position as a postdoctoral research fellow with the National Institute of Mental Health's Center for Mental Health Services Research at Washington University in Saint Louis, Missouri, followed by two years as an assistant professor. Dr. Foster taught social policy, mental-health policy, and human diversity at the George Warren Brown School of Social Work during her time as an assistant professor. Her courses focused on social justice, and the application of multiculturalism to public policy and social problem resolution.

Dr. Foster is married and has a stepson (one stepson is deceased). The sister that Dr. Foster assisted in parenting completed her Masters in Social Work and works with seniors with dementia, while the brother she raised is currently active duty in Afghanistan as part of the United States Army.

Rich Furman   Rich Furman, MSW, PhD, is Associate Professor and Director of Social Work at the University of Washington, Tacoma. Rich is the author of over 100 articles, books, and book chapters. His most recent books are *Social Work Practice with Latinos: Key Issues and Emerging Themes, An Experiential Approach to Groupwork, Navigating Human Service Organizations* and *Practical Tips for Publishing Scholarly Articles.* His forthcoming books include *Transnational Social work* and *Social Work Practice with Men at-Risk,* both to be published in 2010 by Colombia University Press. Rich's main areas of research are social work practice with transnational Latino populations, men at risk and masculinities, and the use of the arts and humanities in social work practice, research and education. He has conducted research, practiced, volunteered or taught throughout Latin America. A qualitative methodologist, Rich is dedicated to innovations in expressive and creative approaches to research. His practice background includes ten years experience in direct practice and administration.

Genaro Gonzalez   Genaro Gonzalez was born in McAllen, Texas, into a family of farm workers. After two years in the Honors Program at Pan American College, he transferred to California when his activism in the local Chicano movement jeopardized his scholarship status. After receiving his B.A. in Psychology from Pomona College, he obtained his Ph.D. in Social Psychology and Personality from the University of California at Santa Cruz in 1982.

In addition to his publications in psychology, Genaro has published four books of fiction with Arte Publico Press (University of Houston). These include a collection of short stories, *Only Sons*, and three novels: *Rainbow's End, The Quixote Cult, and A So-Called Vacation*. A second collection of short fiction, *The Unearthing*, is currently under review at another university press.

Genaro's interest in psychology centers on cultural issues and narrative psychology. He has taught at the Texas Governors School at U.T. Austin; at The Wichita State University's Minority Studies Program; and at the University of the Americas in Puebla, Mexico, a position that allowed him to enhance his fluency in Spanish and his knowledge of Mexican culture. Genaro is currently a Professor of Psychology at the University of Texas–Pan American, the same institution where years earlier he thought it best to leave. His courses include Social Psychology, Systems and Theories, Cross-Cultural Psychology, and Personal Relationships.

In addition to working on his garden, Genaro likes to spend time in his backyard with his dogs, stagazing and practicing archery.

Barbara Gormley   Barbara Gormley was raised in a homogeneous suburb of Detroit in the 1960s and 1970s and was a member of a large, politically active Irish Catholic community. She provided services to violent families in a rural setting for 12 years before returning to school to get her doctorate. She received her Ph.D. in Counseling Psychology from Michigan State University in 2002 after completing a clinical internship at Harvard Medical School. Currently, Dr. Gormley is a National Institute of Mental Health Postdoctoral Fellow in the Clinical Services Research Training Program in the Department of Psychiatry at the University of California–San Francisco, and work on this chapter was partially supported by Grant T32 MH18261.

Marya Howell-Carter   Marya Howell-Carter is a New York State Licensed Clinical Psychologist. She currently serves as Assistant Director for Clinical Services of Counseling, Career Development, and Placement and an Adjunct Professor in the Department of Psychology, at the College of New Rochelle in New Rochelle, New York. She received her doctorate from Northwestern University in Counseling Psychology. After completing her dissertation, Marya began a faculty position at the University of Saint Francis in Fort Wayne, Indiana. At Saint Francis, she was the Director of the Master's Program in General Psychology. After a change in her husband's employment necessitated relocation to New York, Marya's interest in a position in which she could utilize and expand her clinical skills, conduct clinical research, and use these experiences to inform her instruction, led her to select a position at the counseling center of The College of New Rochelle, in the fall of 2002.

Marya was raised in Detroit, Michigan—her mother is of German descent and from a large, rural, farm family and her father is African-American and was raised an only child in urban-industrialized Detroit. Marya's experience of being both a member of the White community in a dominantly African-American city and being a member of the Black community in a dominantly White nation where racism pervades belief and behavior sparks her professional interest in investigating issues of diversity, culture, and the nature of group membership and exclusion. She has selected professional opportunities that challenge her ethnocentric thinking by infusing her understanding of race, mental health, and group membership with the dynamics of economic diversity, skin-color privilege, and cultural bias in the helping professions. She attempts to bring this broad perspective to her treatment, research, and teaching.

Marya is married to a music-industry executive and is the mother of two children—one a budding performer, the other a gymnast (or perhaps daredevil)-in-training. She finds that neither her education nor her professional experiences were adequate preparation for motherhood, but that motherhood has been an invaluable source of knowledge and illustration for both teaching and clinical practice.

Saliwe M. Kawewe B.S.W., M.S.W., Ph.D. Dr. Kawewe is a Professor of Social Work with over 30 years of university teaching, research, and service experience. She has been at Southern Illinois University, School of Social Work, since 1996. She earned her B.S.W. from the University of Zambia in 1974; an M.S.W. from George Warren Brown School of Social Work, Washington University in St. Louis in 1979; and a Ph.D. in Social Work from the School of Social Service, Saint Louis University in 1985. Dr. Kawewe has a diverse background experience in social work practice, policy, planning, administration, and child welfare in Zambia, Zimbabwe, and the United States.

Dr. Kawewe has published over 45 scholarly articles and is a consulting editor/editorial board member for several professional journals. Dr. Kawewe has attended over 50 conferences and made over 60 national and international professional presentations in the United States, Asia, Europe, and Africa. Her research focuses on the Third World women and children, particularly in sub-Sahara Africa; international social development; international social work HIV/AIDS; family and child welfare; cultural and human diversity, gender disempowerment: especially women's and children's rights and social justice; and globalization and economic structural adjustment policies and programs. At her current institution Dr. Kawewe teaches Ethnic Diversity and Social Work Practice, Child Welfare Policy and Program Issues, Program Evaluation Research, Field Practicum Seminars I & II, Social Work Practice with Groups, Social Welfare Policy Development and Analysis, and Perspectives on Human Behavior and Social Environment.

Carol L. Langer Carol Langer is a lifelong resident of Nebraska. She grew up on a small farm near Dawson, a town so small that people joked: "Blink, and you'll miss it." She attended a consolidated high school, graduating in 1967 with 28 other young people. She attended Peru State College, an institution whose original and primary mission was teacher education. After graduation, she taught high school for several years. She and her family relocated to a larger town in Nebraska, and after her husband's death, Langer returned to school and received her master's degree in social work in 1985. She was a school social worker and a medical social worker for a number of years. She began teaching college courses in early 1986, and as a result, began work on her doctorate in sociology. Langer completed her doctorate in 2000 and moved to her current position at the University of Nebraska, Omaha, in 2002. She is currently an assistant professor teaching a variety of social work courses, including generalist practice, social work with American Indian families, and human behavior in the social environment.

Langer has three married sons—Jason, Justin and Jeremy—and two grandchildren, David and Alexis. She travels frequently, preferring the Southwest for lengthy stays. Her ongoing commitment to Native American populations is her passion. Reading, writing, and spending time in nature occupy her leisure time.

Becky Liddle   Becky Liddle spent 14 years in the Department of Counseling and Counseling Psychology at Auburn University, where she taught masters and doctoral students in counseling-related fields. Her favorite course was Counseling Diverse Populations. It was rewarding to watch the dawning of awareness of oppression and privilege in a group of Alabamians who had typically never had the opportunity to talk directly about race, class, or sexual orientation. Challenging students enough to provoke growth without provoking defensiveness is a delicate balance, but one with great rewards. It is a joy to watch good-hearted but naïve students move from mere tolerance of diversity to becoming allies in the struggle against multiple oppressions.

Becky received her bachelor's degree from Oberlin College. Throughout her time in Alabama, Oberlin remained a touchstone for her, a reminder that there are whole communities working together effectively for social justice. Becky holds an M.Ed. in Counselor Education from James Madison University and a Ph.D. in Counseling Psychology from the University of North Carolina. After 14 years at Auburn University, she followed her wife, Kathy Liddle, to Canada. Becky now teaches part-time at the University of Toronto and maintains a full-time private practice in counseling psychology, specializing in serving the lesbian, gay, bisexual, and transgender (LGBT) communities. She has served on the editorial boards of *Journal of Counseling Psychology, Psychology of Women Quarterly, Journal of Lesbian Studies,* and *Counselor Education and Supervision,* and has published extensively on LGBT issues.

Kaying Lo   Kaying Lo grew up in Wisconsin and currently resides in Minnesota. She has a master's degree in marriage and family therapy and currently practices with a nonprofit mental health agency. Her graduate studies have included topics of immigration, assimilation, and gender classification. She has aspirations to continue her education and teach at the collegiate level. Kaying is working to expand her professional experience before returning for her doctorate degree.

Being the oldest daughter in her family, Kaying seeks to define herself in both the mainstream and Hmong culture. During most of her childhood, she grew up with two brothers in a single-parent home. Her biological father died in Thailand. As a refugee growing up in America, Kaying has faced the many challenges of poverty, prejudice, isolation, discrimination, acculturation, privilege, loss, and redefinition. Kaying's history influences her commitment to defining herself and how she relates to others in a culture of privilege and bias.

Colleen Loomis Colleen Loomis spent most of her youth barefoot and swimming in Florida lakes, springs, and the Atlantic Ocean. At home with alligators, water moccasins, and jellyfish, Colleen's sense of adventure developed early and continues in both personal and professional aspects of her life.

Colleen is recognized as a "Trailblazing Woman" in community psychology by the Society for Community Research and Action. An associate professor of psychology at Wilfrid Laurier University in Ontario, Canada, Colleen's research examines the meaning of *sense of community* and its relation to preventing alienation and promoting social responsibility. She also investigates how sense of community relates to positive and negative educational (e.g., literacy and numeracy) and health consequences for youth in the United States, Canada, and Switzerland. She has published on these and related subjects, including self-help groups, gender and power, socioeconomic class, mentoring, and bilingual education in the United States. In 1994, Colleen completed a B.A. in psychology at the University of Tulsa. She earned her Ph.D. in human services psychology from the University of Maryland Baltimore County in May 2001 and was a Postdoctoral Scholar at Stanford University Medical Centers for the following two years.

Loving solitude and companionship, Colleen takes long walks, enjoys sharing an evening with friends over dinner and conversation, watches independent films, reads, and travels. She says, "I want to go anywhere I haven't been, and there are many places where I would go again." She focuses on the journey as well as the destination. Often she is found near water, whether a fountain, ocean, lake, or mountain stream. At the publishing of the first edition of *Explorations*, Colleen began taking piano lessons for the first time in her life.

David MacPhee David MacPhee is a professor in Human Development and Family Studies at Colorado State University. His research and teaching focus on parenting, risk and resilience, and effective prevention programs. Related to diversity issues, he has been actively involved in work on feminist issues, including CSU's Women's Studies Program; the Multicultural Curriculum Infusion Project, which has become a national model for teaching about diversity; how best to recruit and retain underrepresented students into the STEM disciplines; in research on families from diverse cultures.

Although he grew up in a fairly homogenous culture in Idaho, David has traveled, studied, and worked throughout the United States (particularly the South and Southeast), Belize, and Australia, all of which deepened his appreciation for diverse cultures. Being the father of a daughter also has brought into relief issues of gender development.

Matthew R. Mock Matthew was born in Santa Monica, California, as one of seven children. He grew up in the west Los Angeles community (one of few Chinese families). He remembers being very Chinese while in the family home and almost anything but Chinese outside the home. His father financially supported the family as a postal carrier for 50 years until he retired and his mother worked very hard tending to the needs of the children, all the while making her own cultural adjustments and adaptations. He has memories of how his family oftentimes had very little in terms of economic resources but a lot in terms of sibling richness and interactions.

An academic scholarship took Matthew to Providence, Rhode Island, to attend Brown University in Providence, Rhode Island. While in school, he wrote short stories and poetry and followed his heart to work as a teacher with children in special education. He received a B.A. with a major in psychology and a minor in special education.

Matthew moved to Berkeley, California (where he has since lived), to attend graduate school. While in school, he worked as the mental health coordinator at an Asian-American organization. This crystallized his developing awareness of his own identity and significance in addressing all of the differences and cultural shock that he had experienced in his life up to that time. He received his Ph.D. from the California School of Professional Psychology, Berkeley/Alameda.

Matthew holds multiple professional roles: Professor and Director of the Cross-Cultural Program in Psychology at John F. Kennedy University in Orinda, California; Director of the Family, Youth, Children's and Multicultural Services for the City of Berkeley; and runs a private clinical and consulting practice in Berkeley.

Matthew still bicycles, writes professionally and personally, and travels, oftentimes as an invited speaker, consultant, and trainer nationally and internationally. He loves to teach and write and to break stereotypes by demonstrating to his audiences that he is one example of a "passionate, Asian-American man"! Most importantly, Matthew has an 18-year-old, "full-focus" daughter who is "our gift to life, our jewel" who gently reminds him about social justice and gender issues on a daily basis.

Christina Paguyo Christina Paguyo is a doctoral student in the School of Education at the University of Colorado at Boulder. Her academic studies are grounded in policy analysis, quantitative and qualitative research methodology. Her current projects include analyzing policies that affect university recruitment and retention programs and understanding the relationship between language, culture, development, and pedagogies of empowerment. Passionate about issues related to equity, she is a member of the American Educational Research Association and one of the co-founders of Racial Initiatives for Students and Educators (RISE), a student-led effort to foster critical discussions about race and racism in academic scholarship. She currently lives in Fort Collins, Colorado with her partner of 10 years and two dogs.

Jackie Peila-Shuster, M. Ed. Jackie is an adjunct instructor in the College of Applied Human Sciences at Colorado State University. She is also working on her Ph.D. with a specialization that focuses on the areas of counselor education, career counseling, and adult development and aging. Jackie completed her master's degree in 2004 with a specialization in counseling and career development. Prior to that, she worked as an occupational therapist where she developed her affinity for the aging population. Jackie has an innate passion for facilitating the success, growth, and development of others in their educational, career, and personal lives. She also loves spending time with her family, fly-fishing and being a faithful CSU Ram fan.

Jessica Pettitt Jess currently travels from campus to campus as a social justice trainer, facilitator, consultant, and keynote speaker. Her work is highly interactive and directly addresses our collective responsibility in confronting systems of oppression. She deals with tough subjects directly and holds space for progressive ideas regarding white privilege, sexuality, trans advocacy, and a growing sense of entitlement. After working for 10 years in Student Affairs around the country, Jess brings a national perspective to making change on college campuses.

She has a M.Ed. from the University of South Carolina; graduated from Hendrix College in Conway, Arkansas; and hails from Texas. Currently, Jess lives with her husband and two dogs in northern California and is represented by CAMPUSPEAK.com. To continue the conversation, visit www.jessicapettitt.com.

Paul Priester Paul Priester is an assistant professor in the Department of Educational Psychology at the University of Wisconsin-Milwaukee. He completed a master's degree in rehabilitation counseling at the University of Iowa and a Ph.D. in counseling psychology at Loyola University, Chicago. Dr. Priester's research interests include the substance abuse counseling process, 12-step-based recovery from addictions, the integration of spiritual/religious issues in psychotherapy, meta-analysis as a research tool, and the cross-cultural counseling process. He has a wife (Kathy), three kids (Caiti, 16; Paul, 10; and Margie, 8), and a black and tan coonhound (Buddy, 90 pounds). His hobbies include morel mushroom hunting, gardening, old cars that don't run, fantasy football, and taking his kids fishing. His dream is to run a small farm, growing heirloom apples and berries.

Damien W. Riggs, Ph.D. Damien is a lecturer in the School of Social Work at Flinders University, South Australia.

His background is in critical psychology and gender studies, and he also works as a family and relationship counselor for Relationships Australia. Damien's approach to counseling draws upon narrative, psychoanalytic, and feminist approaches with an emphasis on the relational nature of subjectivity. Damien has increasingly been involved in working with children and young people and hopes to develop this in working with LGBT youth.

Damien's research interests include critical race and whiteness studies, LGBT psychology, and family and parenting studies. Largely as a result of his work at the intersections of these areas, Damien holds a somewhat ambivalent position about the current status of LGBT rights in Western cultures. Specifically, his own politics on LGBT issues in Australia are centrally concerned with recognizing the histories xxvi ABOUT THE CONTRIBUTORS

of colonization that continue to shape the nation. Whilst for the sake of his children and others he is committed to a praxis that emphasizes the deleterious effects of heteropatriarchy, he nonetheless seeks to place that praxis in a relationship to an ongoing critique of racial privilege.

Cherice Sommer   Cherice Sommer received her M.S. in counseling from Southwest Missouri State University in 2003 and has an extensive background in feminist and gender issues. Currently she is in private counseling practice, where her work includes individual, couples, and group therapy, as well as treatment of sexual offenders. In addition, she has presented at multiple conferences on topics including sexuality, stress management, and domestic violence. Her areas of interest at this time involve lesbian identity maintenance and gender socialization. In addition, Cherice feels an urgency and personal responsibility to raise awareness of the connection of all living things in her work, and of the power of creating a safe world for all to share. She and her partner, Sandi Hart, spend their time nurturing creativity and guiding their two teenage boys in finding their own unique paths.

Heather Trepal, Ph.D., LPC-S   Heather Trepal received her M.Ed. in Community Counseling from Cleveland State University. She graduated in December of 2003 with her Ph.D. in Counseling and Human Development Services from Kent State University. She is licensed as a Professional Counselor and board approved supervisor in the state of Texas. She is an Assistant Professor and serves as the Graduate Advisor of Record for the master's programs in the Department of Counseling at the University of Texas at San Antonio. She is also the Associate Editor for the Theory and Practice sections of the *Journal of Mental Health Counseling*. She received a national award during the 2009 American Counseling Association convention in Charlotte. She is the past recipient of the 2009 *Professional Leadership Award* from the Association for Counselor Education and Supervision and the 2006 *Professional Leadership Award* from the Association for Creativity in Counseling as well as the 2005 *Outstanding Research Award* from Chi Sigma Iota International. Dr. Trepal currently serves as the President-Elect for the Association for Creativity in Counseling (ACC), a division of the American Counseling Association. She has over 30 publications in the areas of self-injurious behavior, relationships/relational development, gender issues in counseling, counselor preparation, supervision, and the use of technology in counseling and counselor training.

Ma. Teresa Tuason   Ma. Teresa Tuason is currently an associate professor in the Psychology Department of the University of North Florida in Jacksonville, Florida. Teresa (or Tes, as she is fondly called by family, friends, and colleagues) came to the United States for her graduate degree. She was born and raised in the Philippines.

Her first time to live outside of the Philippines was when she came to the University at Albany, State University of New York for her Ph.D. During this time she really experienced being different (i.e., as a Catholic, heterosexual, poor, Asian woman). After completing her dissertation, she went to do her internship and postdoctoral fellowship at the University of Utah, Salt Lake City, Utah. It was here that she experienced the nurturance and generosity of her Caucasian American supervisors and colleagues and learned how White people can be multiculturally competent and sensitive, too.

As part of her love for the Philippines and her emotional obligation to share what she had learned here in the United States, Tes went back to the Philippines. She taught at the Psychology Department of the Ateneo de Manila University and was Clinical Director of the Ateneo Wellness Center. Within eight months she realized that the country's economic and political instability and the institution's inability to welcome what she taught were inhibiting her commitment to her country. It became clear that she could help her country in service and advocacy more from the outside. She then applied and received a counseling center job in Illinois. Tes is now teaching at the University of North Florida and lives with her husband and 5 yr old son in Jacksonville, Florida.

Her research interests has two foci, one in counseling minority populations and the other in cultural psychology. Her research interests express her advocacy as a psychologist – specifically in addressing a) social issues such as poverty and inequities, and social justice issues related to counseling minority populations, and b) conducting research that is respectful and appreciative of culture given our global community, specifically of the populations of developing countries such as the Philippines.

In her free time, she exercises through zumba, sings and dances to karaoke, experiments on her cooking, meditates, plays with her son and reads him stories, and visits her family and her husband's family on opposite sides of the world.

N. Eugene Walls, Ph.D. Eugene is an Assistant Professor in the Graduate School of Social Work at the University of Denver where he teaches courses on multicultural social work practice, research methods, and disrupting privilege through anti-oppressive practice. He completed a master's degree in social work at the University of Texas at Austin and a master's degree and doctorate in sociology at the University of Notre Dame. His research interests include modern forms of prejudice; issues of lesbian, gay, bisexual, and transgender youth; and multicultural social work education, particularly around issues of privilege. He and his partner, David Fronczak, live in Denver where they enjoy square dancing, raising their two long-haired Chihuahuas (Missy and Chuleta), and frequent hiking treks in the Rocky Mountains.

Suzanne Weatherman Suzanne Weatherman is a Lecturer in the Gender Studies program and the Freshman Orientation program at Southwest Missouri State University. She received a master's degree in counseling from SMSU in 2000. She is currently working as part of a multidisciplinary federal grant project aimed at implementing emotional intelligence curriculum into the education system. Suzanne, who is also an artist, makes glass beads that she incorporates into her jewelry designs.

She received her B.S. in agriculture at the University of Missouri in 1976 and her M.S. in counseling from SMSU in 2000. Suzanne's current interests involve gathering women of difference together to discover their mutual concerns for social justice. She hopes to someday provide a permanent gathering space for women in the Ozarks region.

David H. Whitcomb David Whitcomb grew up in small, picturesque towns in Connecticut, at the edge of the New York City metropolis. The oldest of three sons, he comes from a musical family where singing, musical instruments, and a rich variety of recorded music resounded throughout the home. In addition to exploring Connecticut, summers were spent hiking and canoeing in New York's Adirondack Mountains and swimming in the Atlantic waters of Nantucket—while winters were filled with ice skating and downhill skiing.

Even though his interest in psychology began in high school, Whitcomb's career took a circuitous route, from being an exchange student in Peru, interning in mental health, community theater, and public radio positions, and several years of working before starting a doctoral program in counseling psychology. Whitcomb's career has included residential care and vocational instruction for individuals with multiple disabilities; vocational counseling for welfare-to-work clients; crisis counseling at several hospitals; outpatient substance abuse counseling; individual and group counseling for gay and bisexual men; psychological assessments for pre-adoptive children; and a predoctoral internship at the University of Maryland Counseling Center.

Whitcomb once lived in a rustic home in the Berkshires that he helped build "from scratch." He remains equally attracted to big city life and a slower rural pace and enjoys travel adventures with his partner of five years. Since 1998, he has been on the faculty at the University of North Dakota, where he directs the master's program in counseling, teaches several courses, and generates research from social justice projects such as HIV prevention and discrimination based on sexual orientation and gender identity. Currently, Whitcomb maintains a small clinical practice, is on the Executive Committee of the Society of the Psychological Study of Men and Masculinity and is a Past Chair of the Section for Lesbian, Gay and Bisexual Awareness within the Society of Counseling Psychology.

Joy S. Whitman, Ph.D. Joy is a licensed Clinical Professional Counselor and Associate Professor of Education in the Human Services and Counseling Program at DePaul University. There she directs the program and serves as Associate Chair in the Department of Counseling and Special Education. She has a doctorate degree in counseling psychology and a master's degree in counseling and human relations. In addition to teaching at DePaul, she serves in the American Counseling Association as the Governing Council Representative for the division and Association for Lesbian, Gay, Bisexual, and Transgender Issues in Counseling and is past president of this division. In the community, she volunteers with Illinois Safe Schools Alliance and offers her time to help make schools safer for LGBT students and faculty. Her research focus is also on LGBT issues, specifically on training counselors to provide affirmative therapeutic treatment to LGBT clients, and she has written and presented on this issue throughout her career. Her commitment to educating others about affirmative treatment of LGBT people is her passion. She also maintains a small private practice, and in her spare time, she is learning to play the banjo.

Dr. Heidi A. Zetzer   Dr. Heidi A. Zetzer is the Director of the Hosford Counseling & Psychological Services Clinic in the Department of Counseling, Clinical, & School Psychology at the University of California, Santa Barbara. The Hosford Clinic provides evidence-based culturally-responsive mental health services to members of the Santa Barbara community. Zetzer teaches practicum and supervision courses, supervises graduate student clinicians, provides psychotherapy to community clients, and is engaged in two research projects: *Evaluating Counseling Techniques in Cross Cultural Counseling with Mexican Americans* and *Building Cultural Competence through Individual and Organizational Multicultural Identity Development*. Zetzer is Past-President of the Santa Barbara County Psychological Association.

Zetzer was a core faculty member in the Graduate Psychology Program at Antioch University, Santa Barbara from 1996 to 2006. During that time, she served as the Director of Clinical Training, Clinical Traineeship Director, and Coordinator of the Professional Development and Career Counseling Program. She taught Multicultural Awareness, Multicultural Clinical Skills, Feminist Theories of Psychology, Psychopathology, and Psychological Assessment. While serving on the Antioch faculty, Zetzer co-authored a handbook called *Build the Field and They Will Come: Multicultural Organizational Development for Mental Health Agencies*. The handbook was the culmination of a four-year qualitative study of two agencies. To access: http://www.calendow.org/uploadedFiles/build_the_field.pdf

✳

Stories of Privilege
Introduction to Part I

Reading, critically examining, and using self-reflection prompted by the "coming to consciousness" stories of others is a way to come to terms with one's own beliefs and actions. This book is a catalyst for that process. It is divided into topic area sections which contain chapters written by individuals or pairs of authors. Part I explores issues of privilege, oppression, and diversity predominantly in the context of the experiences of those who identify and/or are identified by a particular dominant culture status, regardless of the other statuses they possess. Part I addresses the following privileged statuses and oppression labels via five sections: *White Privilege (Racism), Socioeconomic Privilege (Classism), Able-bodied Privilege (Ableism), Heterosexual and Cisgender Privilege (Heterosexism and Cisgenderism)*, and *Male Privilege (Sexism)*. In the chapters within these sections, the authors share their personal histories and their journeys toward recognizing and acknowledging their privilege. In instances in which the authors address more than one privileged status, the chapter has been placed in the section that represents the most prominently described journey.

Privilege is elusive in nature and presents itself in a variety of ways; however, the outcome of it results in the oppression of others. This text assumes that its readers have a general understanding of the concept of privilege and are seeking to explore some of the myriad ways it is expressed. Privilege is generally described as an invisible, weightless knapsack of special provisions—unearned assets of which one is often oblivious (McIntosh, 1989). Discussions of privilege aimed at surfacing believes about diversity generally impact individuals in the same way they bring to the surface their fear of being labeled a racist. Denial and resistance often are manifested in statements such as "I've had to work hard for everything

I have," "I grew up poor and/or I'm just a poor college student," "Anybody can achieve if they just work hard enough," or "Both of us help around the house." The focus of this book is moving individuals beyond defensiveness and clichés and toward truer self-relative beliefs about race, class, gender, ability, religion, language, sexual orientation, and gender identity through reading and reflecting on the struggles and transformations of others.

The collection of narratives in Part I is designed to help readers understand that privilege has many faces and many statuses, and individuals are subject to it as either agents of discrimination, targets of discrimination, or both. Agent statuses groups (i.e., White, male, heterosexual, able-bodied) benefit from the inequality of privilege while target groups (i.e., People of Color, female, homosexual, people with disabilities) are oppressed. This oppression often occurs unknowingly, by well-meaning friends and colleagues.

Stories of White Privilege begins with *An Awakening to Privilege, Oppression, and Discrimination: Sharon's Story* . . . begins in the introduction of this book and starts the reader on the journey to understanding white privilege and the impetus for the co-creation of *Explorations in Privilege, Oppression, and Diversity* (2005). *Val's Story*, in the Preface, sets the stage for the need to expose the issue of privilege within the context of teaching about diversity and multiculturalism. Readers get a brief look at how white privilege manifests for faculty of color in the classroom and in relationships with White colleagues.

Sharon's story delves into the ways oppression is manifested by White faculty against students of color as well as how privilege is denied and oppression is excused in interactions with friends and colleagues of color. Sharon also reflects on how she came to understand issues of privilege and her continuous journey and struggles to be an ally in support of diverse others.

Zetzer follows with her story titled *Whiteout* by giving a clear introduction to the concepts of White identity development and white privilege and the mixed messages received when she states, "the explicit message was that we are all created equal and the civil rights movement was a good thing. The implicit message was that Whites just happen to be better than Blacks at certain things." In an effort to uncover such messages, she addresses the value of dialog as a constructive response to multicultural conflict and introduces multicultural dialog as a key ingredient to transformational learning.

In *Supposed to Know Better*, Megivern discusses her difficulty in accepting a basic element of social justice learning—the struggle to acknowledge her own privileges because of the intersection of being White and growing up poor. Her story strikes at the core of the "bootstrap" mentality which falsely suggests that everyone can succeed if they only work hard enough.

Furman describes what it is like to identify in one way (Jewish) while being perceived and treated by others as White. *In White Male Privilege in the Context of My Life*, he describes the conflict his dominant status appearance brings to the forefront regardless of his efforts to use his privileged status in positive ways.

Loomis single-handedly takes us on a journey of *Understanding and Experiencing Class Privilege* through her foray from lower class to working-class poor to middle class, in the section on *Stories of Socioeconomic Privilege*. In this chapter, she discusses the hidden rules of class and how various aspects of her life circumstance influence her understanding of class privilege.

Stories of Able-Bodied Privilege are brought to the forefront when Lo states, ". . . it had never occurred to me that [people with physical disabilities] could hold the same type of parties as everyone else." In *Seeing Through Another Lens*, Lo takes us into a world where able-bodied people are not the norm, Priester forces us to look at our own thoughts and *Dirty Secrets* about the privilege of being able-bodied specifically when Priester thinks, "It could be worse, I could be in a wheelchair." Also of great importance is the use of person first/affirming language and seeing people with disabilities in everyday situations. These stories reinforce the personhood of people with disabilities, the daily situations that may be taken for granted by the privilege of able-bodiedness, and what it means to be an ally.

Heterosexual privilege, cisgender privilege, gender identity, heterosexism, and homophobia are explored in the fourth subsection addressing privilege. This subsection addresses topics in which many people in our society prefer a "don't ask, don't tell" policy—a term which in its own label is oppressive. The stories in this section are filled with incidents of overt and systematic oppression in a time period where much of humanity professes the need for equity and equality regarding groups previously mentioned. *Stories of Heterosexual and Cisgender Privilege* delves readers of all sexual identities into arenas they may not have been aware of or thought about in a particular way. Cashwell begins *Increasing Our Awareness of Heterosexism and Homophobia* by introducing us to some of the terminology needed to untangle terms that are often used interchangeably and randomly. Sommer, Weatherman, and Cox discuss assumed heterosexuality and the importance of including LGBTQ issues in courses addressing multicultural issues in their chapter, *Reflections on Heterosexual Privilege*. Whitman adds a new chapter to this section with *How I Became a Counseling Professional Lesbian* and brings to the forefront the question of whether or not her status as a self-proclaimed professional lesbian is a privileged status. Walls and Costello join as new contributors with *Exploring Cisgender Privilege* along with Pettitt who introduces us to *The New Frontier* of marriage and transgender identities.

Sexism remains a societal challenge as evidenced by the gender constraints for both men and women and those who identify as neither. Trepal opens the section on *Sexism* with her poignant article, *Men Can't be Raped*, in which she looks at the misnomer, but also addresses the social construction of gender that includes specific and limiting role expectations. In this section, Trepal asks us to ask ourselves whether or not we believe men can be raped when the question would have an obvious answer if the person in question is a woman. Whitcomb and Cummings follow up on the issue of role expectations in *Exploring Male Privilege* by looking at the changing face of male privilege. They share a variety of experiences in which they are privy to observing sexism perpetrated against women in the workplace and as a male who decides to "stay home with the kids." Langer closes out the section with *How I Got My Wings: Growing Up Female in the 1950's* by taking us through four decades and allowing us to reflect on how far we have come (or not).

1

✳

An Awakening to Privilege, Oppression, and Discrimination
Sharon's Story

SHARON K. ANDERSON AND
VALERIE A. MIDDLETON

A few years ago, a friend told me about an experience she had had at a fast-food restaurant. My friend, an African American woman, was in the front of the line, ready to order, when the cashier looked right past her and asked the next person in line what she would like. I had a hard time believing my friend's story, but I listened to her as though I did. Behind my attentive facade, however, I was thinking, "I'm sure you're mistaken. People aren't that rude. I'll bet she thought you were still deciding on your order."

My blindness to White privilege and other privileged statuses most certainly originates in my social and cultural background. I was born into a family of White European descent and middle-class income, and I was raised in a White, rural community. All of my extended family is White. I attended a school in which almost all students and faculty were White. The people who attended my country church were White. When I look back on my childhood, I don't recall hearing my parents make derogatory remarks about other ethnic groups, nor do I recall any discussions about inequality, discrimination, or privilege. I suspect that my family's view was one that espoused "if people work hard enough, they can achieve, no matter what their skin color or cultural differences." Inadvertently, I was taught not to see my advantage as a White, middle-class person.

5

I carried this thinking with me into my early adulthood and college environment, where it manifested itself in a belief that almost everyone in the United States spoke or should speak English, could gain entry into college if he or she just tried hard enough, and that "discrimination" was just a word that "angry people of color" used to push their weight around. I was oblivious to the fact that having white skin, speaking standard American English, being able-bodied, and supporting a Christian belief system were all "unearned assets" (McIntosh, 2000) that afforded me entry into places and opportunities less available or not available to everyone. As I reflect, my worldview was not challenged in my college classes or other higher-education contexts.

COMING INTO CONTACT

After earning my master's degree, I began working for Upward Bound and Educational Talent Search programs. While employed in these programs, I provided services to students from different ethnic groups (Asian, Hispanic, African American, and Native American), and I worked alongside colleagues who represented these groups as well. This was the first time I had genuine and sustained contact with people whose skin color was different from mine. My obliviousness was challenged, and I started to realize how truly ignorant I was of the obstacles people of color face in achieving their goals. However, I still did not understand the significance of their home culture and consequent expectations. For instance, the Native American students in our Upward Bound program often requested leave from our summer session to participate in Pow Wows and other cultural events. When I became the director of the program, I honored the students' requests to be gone for a week or more; but, inside my head and heart, I questioned and disliked the disruption. I did not understand the meaning or the importance of Pow Wows or why our students had to miss school for such events. Sometimes, these students would leave for the week and then not want to come back to finish out the summer session. In response, I settled on the premise that the students were "less able" to adjust and were missing out on a good thing—six weeks on a university campus with good teachers and an awesome residential staff.

Elizabeth Minnich articulates the thinking in which I was grounded this way: ". . . whites are taught to think of their lives as morally neutral, normative, and average, and also ideal, so that when we work to benefit others, this is seen as work that will allow 'them' to be more like 'us'" (cited in McIntosh, 2000, p. 32). As the program director, I could have taken the opportunity to look at our program for ways to make it more culturally sensitive and welcoming. Instead, I wanted the students of color to fit into the program; that is, I wanted "them" to be more like "us." When my students of color talked about discrimination, oppression, and feelings of alienation—the consequences of systems based on privilege, *I didn't really see it—the reality of their experiences.*

INTELLECTUALIZING

After 7 years of working with Upward Bound, I quit my job and attended graduate school to obtain a Ph.D. in Counseling Psychology. One of my fellow students was a gentleman who identifies himself as Chicano. He introduced me to multicultural literature in psychology and counseling. He shared his concerns about the inequality of mental-health services for people of color, and how people of color typically preferred to counsel with someone from their own culture. I found this perspective insulting and thought, "Aren't White counselors good enough for these people?" Intellectually, I was able to take in the information from the multicultural literature and the concerns about the inequality of mental-health services, but when his perspective and experience challenged my view of the "normative, average, or ideal," in which a White counselor might not be viewed as "good enough," I became disconcerted and defensive. I continued to listen to his stories of discrimination, gross misunderstanding, oppression, and profiling by Whites in authority, *but I didn't really hear him—once again, I didn't "get it."*

DEFLECTING COGNITIVE DISSONANCE

After I had completed my doctorate and had spent a year in the Midwest as a staff psychologist at a university counseling center, I received a faculty appointment at Colorado State University, where I developed a friendship with Val, my coeditor. Our friendship brought together many differences. Val is Black; I am White. She was born and raised in a city; I was born and raised on a farm. She experiences oppression and discrimination because of her skin color; I experience privilege (a term I use in retrospect) because of my skin color.

As I previously mentioned, I had been told stories by my students, colleagues, and friends of color without truly accepting the validity of their articulated experiences. Eventually, I was challenged to feed my intellectual hunger for understanding multicultural issues, and I accepted Val's invitation to attend a "Women of Color" conference.

Upon our arrival at the conference, I experienced the uncomfortable feeling of being one of a few White women in attendance. I began to wonder whether I had made a mistake in coming. I wasn't a woman of color, and I assumed others would wonder why I was there. I truly didn't think or feel I should be welcomed, and I wondered what I was going to face or be a target for.

As the sessions progressed, I became enlightened, but also dissonant. I became particularly irritated during one session when the women of color expressed anger and hurt toward White women. I felt like a target and wondered why I wasn't positively recognized for my presence, as a White woman, at the conference. Val encouraged me to listen and stay emotionally and psychologically present, even though I wanted to run away by mentally/emotionally disconnecting and focusing on other thoughts or feelings.

During that time and later, Val and I would have what I call "difficult dialogues." She wanted me to truly listen to the stories of oppression and discrimination, and I wanted to deflect the issues by claiming Whites are treated poorly, too. I didn't want to see my own privilege as a White person and the invisibility of others who represented minority cultures. *I just didn't really want to "get it."*

CRITICAL INCIDENT: "HOW CAN I HELP YOU?"

As our friendship and work relationship progressed, so did our level of dialogue. We would occasionally meet for lunch to discuss ideas relative to teaching our predominately White population of students about issues of diversity and privilege. When Val and I had ended one such business lunch at a nearby restaurant, we decided to check into the possibility of using that restaurant as a meeting place for future business activities that would include more of our colleagues. Val approached the receptionist, a White woman, to inquire about the cost and availability of the facility. The receptionist craned her neck to look around Val, and then asked me, "How can I help you?" As this scene played out before me, so did a flashback of the scenario I used to open this introduction.

In that instant, my privilege failed to blind me in a way that had previously kept me from "getting it." I saw how my white skin made me visible and others invisible. I saw why the Native American students I worked with in Upward Bound might not want to come back from a Pow Wow or Sun Dance ceremony to a summer school session on a university campus that was insensitive to their cultural values. I saw why a person of color might want to work with a counselor of color. I saw how being recognized is an event that I experience and expect as natural, and how not being recognized is disrespectful, discriminatory, and oppressive. I saw how what I experience and expect in everyday life is an unearned privilege. I saw why I needed to be a believer—one who believes the stories of inequity shared by friends, students, and colleagues of color. Although I can't truly understand the experiences of people of color, the sum of my past experiences, united with critical incidents such as this, helps me to see that privilege exists and that I am one of its beneficiaries.

CREATING THIS BOOK

Following this eye-opening experience, I began to explore the literature on multicultural issues in psychology and counseling (for example, Helms & Cook, 1999; Pedersen, Draguns, Lonner, & Trimble, 2002; D. W. Sue & Sue, 2003), looking for evidence of what is needed to help privileged individuals "see it," "believe it," and most importantly "get it"—the discrimination and oppression others experience because we are potentially blind to our own points of privilege. This body of literature seemed to be missing the personal stories often so essential to understanding the concept of privilege, the impact of privilege on one's professional and personal interactions with others, the process of acknowledging one's own privilege, and the subsequent journey involved in changing one's beliefs and behaviors.

I discussed this gap in the literature with my coeditor, Val. She gave me literature from the teacher preparation field to read. We talked some more, and the idea that emerged was that we would ask professionals in the helping fields to share their personal stories about how they recognized their own privileged statuses, and how that recognition has changed them personally and professionally. We believe that students in training programs need to read about other professionals like themselves who have additionally come to acknowledge their privileged statuses associated with being White, male, heterosexual, able-bodied, Christian, and/or economically advantaged, and who have integrated this acknowledgment into their practice and/or teaching.

With this idea on paper and a book contract in hand, we sent out a call for papers, asking people to tell us about their journeys toward understanding their own privilege and the subsequent impact on their professional roles. We received numerous submissions covering a broad range of issues such as ableism, anti-Semitism, classism, heterosexism, racism, and sexism. Author after author shared stories of injustice, inequality, and privilege, in which they or their colleagues, friends, students, and partners experienced the "phenomenon of invisibility" or other ramifications of the aforementioned "–isms." Their stories of personal and professional struggles and triumphs in recognizing and addressing issues of their own privilege and the prejudice and discrimination experienced by others provide opportunities for readers to explore these concepts from many perspectives—a necessary exercise, since we have observed in our classes that acknowledgment of privilege in one area (for example, racism) does not automatically transfer to recognition and understanding in other areas (for example, heterosexism, anti-Semitism).

As you, our readers, explore the topics in this book, we ask that you be open-minded and sensitive, for the sharing of these stories has not come without cost. Feelings of vulnerability, guilt, shame, embarrassment, and the like have all been part of the process of bringing this important topic into view in this way. In preparing this introductory chapter, I personally became aware of my vulnerability and feelings of shame about my own journey. My lack of understanding and sensitivity seems abhorrent. However, I also recognize the value of disclosure in furthering my journey and the journey of others. It is with this understanding and extreme appreciation that we wish to acknowledge and thank all of the authors for their honesty, their willingness to be vulnerable, and their valuable contribution to this book.

REFERENCES

Helms, J. E., & Cook, D. A. (1999). *Using race and culture in counseling and psychotherapy: Theory and process.* Boston: Allyn and Bacon.

McIntosh, P. (2000). White privilege and male privilege: A personal account of coming to see correspondences through work in women's studies. In A. Minas (Ed.), *Gender basics: Feminist perspectives on women and men* (2nd ed.) (pp. 30–38). Belmont, CA: Wadsworth/Thomas Learning, Inc.

Pedersen, P. B., Draguns, J. G., Lonner, W. J., & Trimble, J.E. (2002). *Counseling across cultures* (5th ed.). Thousand Oaks: Sage Publications.

Sue, D.W., & Sue, D. (2003). *Counseling the culturally diverse: Theory and practice* (4th Ed.). New York: John Wiley & Sons.

2

✳

White Out

Privilege and Its Problems

HEIDI A. ZETZER

IDENTITY AND THE POLITICS OF LOCATION

I am an educated, employed, White, heterosexual, 40-something woman who is 5 feet, 7 inches tall and weighs 114 pounds. I go to church (occasionally). I have a husband, and two sons, ages 16 and 19. I grew up in the '60s with an irreverent, hippie artist father and a sympathetic, conventional artist mother. I attended integrated public schools in the Cleveland suburbs with lots of Christians and Jews. I lived in the midst of racist jokes and interracial relationships. Like many of my White contemporaries, I was raised to see myself as a color-blind individual living in a cultural mosaic.

I come from a flock of aversive racists (Dovidio, Gaertner, Kawakami, & Hodson, 2002). No one I knew would ever admit to racist thoughts or actions, notions of White superiority, or fear of "the other," but the subtext was often there. The explicit message was that we are all created equal and the Civil Rights Movement was a good thing. The implicit message was that Whites just happen to be better than Blacks at certain things, and Affirmative Action is a questionable thing. Praise for Black achievements belied the expectation of none. Concerns for safety, housing prices, and miscegenation were characteristic of the private conversations that White families had with one another. White privilege was far outside anyone's consciousness, while fear of being called a racist was well inside it. The psychological discordance between the text and the subtext was very confusing. How could I be free of prejudice and filled with prejudicial thoughts? How could I be color-blind and react so viscerally to cultural differences? How could my Black friends and White friends be so similar and yet so different?

As a graduate student in Counseling Psychology in the mid-80s, I participated in a variety of cross-cultural counseling courses and diversity workshops offered by prominent psychology programs at the cutting edge of multiculturalism. These experiences helped me comprehend the discord. They led to a tremendous growth in my intellectual understanding of cultural differences, but on a deeper level, I was left unchanged. In the language of the Multicultural Change Intervention Matrix (Pope, 1993 as cited by Reynolds, 1997), I experienced first-order, but not second-order, change. For individuals, first-order change is characterized by increased awareness, knowledge, or skills, whereas second-order change results in a paradigm shift. I entered graduate school as a naive "well-meaning white person" (WMWP) (Wolfe, 1995), and I exited it as a knowledgeable one; but I still did not fully and deeply comprehend the impact of daily racism on people of color and the part that WMWP (like me) play in its perpetuation.

It was not until I became a university professor and joined a diverse team of multicultural counseling educators that my perceptions of the world and myself began to change. I started a journey that is endless and essential. I finally understand what my colleagues of color, LGBTQ students, working-class and Jewish friends, and large-bodied companions have been telling me: that there are no breaks from the work of living in a multicultural community. Oppression is real, and seeking social justice for oneself and others, is a difficult job. Once, while speaking to a colleague, I said that I was weary of the resistance that I encountered while teaching a multicultural awareness course to graduate psychology students. She wanted to support me and offered, "Well, you won't have to deal with it when the quarter is over!" That might have been true if I were to have retreated into my privilege, but I have come to the conclusion that the comfort of privilege is not worth its price. The cost to oneself and one's friends is too great.

The purpose of this article is a) to describe a critical incident in my multicultural development, an incident that highlights some of the relational and psychological costs of racism and white privilege, and illustrates the value of dialogue as a constructive response to multicultural conflict; and b) to introduce multicultural dialogue as a key ingredient to transformational learning—the kind that sinks into our bones and is remembered.

EDUCATOR AS STUDENT: WHITE RACIAL IDENTITY DEVELOPMENT AND TRANSFORMATIONAL LEARNING

Models of White racial identity development (WRID) (Carter, 1997; Helms, 1995; Rowe, Bennet, & Atkinson, 1994) provide educators with benchmarks for their students' growth. But what if I apply one of these models to myself? I agree with the basic premises of these models, which assume that "No child is born wanting to be racist!" (D. W. Sue & Sue, 2003, p. 254), and that there is no protection from breathing the "smog" of cultural racism (Tatum, 1997, p. 6). White people benefit from institutional and individual manifestations of racism, however indirectly or unintentionally, and this creates a dilemma for fair-minded White folks. How can I see myself as a just person when I willingly participate in a system that is inherently unfair? This dilemma has motivated my WRID.

If I apply D. W. Sue and Sue's (2003) five-stage process model of WRID to myself, I can track my evolution from the Conformity Phase in childhood, high school, and college; to the Dissonance Phase of graduate school; to the Resistance and Immersion Phase of my early career, to now. Now, I see myself in the Introspective Phase, and, curiously, this phase describes perfectly my motivation for writing this chapter. I am in an existential crisis, disconnected, isolated, and confused. I am roiling around in a developmental eddy, asking, "What does it mean to be White [at my institution]? Who am I in relation to my whiteness [as a parent, educator, and administrator]?" And "Who am I as a racial/cultural being [who embraces principles of social justice]" (D. W. Sue & Sue, 2003, p. 257)?

Sometimes I feel like I am in a "White-out"—lost in a blizzard of white privilege and unable to discern my next step. Personally, what I lack is contact with White folks who are expanding or questioning their worldviews. I often feel isolated and alone. I feel supported by my White, heterosexual, middle-class colleagues, but few are actively involved in moving themselves or the institution in the direction of multiculturalism. We do not connect with one another very easily. My insights into myself as a heterosexual White woman are often painful. I am aware that the further I go in my development, the less I cry for myself (feeling shame for my mistakes) and the more I cry for humanity (feeling sadness for the acts of violence or indifference that we intentionally or unintentionally perpetrate on one another).

I see how the tears of my wounded ego used to silence the voices of my colleagues of color. My colleagues took steps to relieve my hurt feelings by quieting their own frustration or disdain to take care of me. I have learned that I can listen to their accusations and their requests for accountability, and search for the ways that I contributed to their concerns. In the past, I would respond instantly and automatically. I gave myself only two choices. I could swallow their accusations whole or reject them outright. Now, I am getting better at allowing myself time to reflect on their words before leaping to a response.

What brought me to this place? Like Ponterotto (1998) and Kiselica (1998), the reason I have matured as a multicultural being is through relationships with colleagues. One of the greatest surges in my multicultural development can be attributed to my collaboration with three diverse colleagues: Juliet Betita (Pilipina American), Keith Mar (Chinese American), and Muriel Shockley (African American). (Naturally, we have multiple identities, but for the purpose of this narrative, our racial/cultural identities are the most salient.) We sat around my kitchen table with the intention of revising Antioch University's Multicultural Awareness course, but we serendipitously discovered that our reciprocal disclosures about oppression and privilege, of all types, were more powerful and more meaningful than the literature we planned to provide our students.

The topics of our meetings flowed spontaneously between course design and personal revelations about race, class, gender, and sexual orientation. We revealed our vulnerabilities gradually. Keith, Muriel, and Juliet described how they felt when someone made a racist comment, treated them differently because of their appearance, or ignored their racial identities. I disclosed my fear of difference, or of being seen as racist. We also identified and examined various sources of privilege. For example, Keith holds male privilege, Muriel has class privilege, Juliet possesses heterosexual privilege, and I have white privilege, just to name a few. The multiplicity of our identities became undeniable. Periodically we confronted each other with respect and compassion. We learned to tolerate the discomfort of our differences, which allowed us to gain valuable insight into each other's perspectives.

Over the course of two years, we transformed these focused conversations into a new approach to multicultural counselor training, which we call Multicultural Dialogue (MCD) (Betita, Mar, Shockley, & Zetzer, 2001; Zetzer, Shockley, Mar, & Betita, 2000). We define MCD as an authentic conversation about what it means to walk in the world as a member of a multicultural group. The purpose of MCD is for people to hear each other's stories and perspectives so that they can learn from each other and grow in ways that promote their racial/cultural identity development (RCID or WRID) (adapted from Swindler, 1983). We modified Swindler's 10 principles of interreligious dialogue (1983, p.1) for use in our classrooms.[1] The principles are guideposts for students to use as they listen and respond to each other's experiences of and perspectives on oppression and privilege. For example, three of the principles call for students to allow each other to self-define, to abandon "hard-and-fast assumptions" about "the other," and to aim to experience the other's culture from "within." We have observed that MCD nurtures the presence of Rogers' (1957) core conditions in our classrooms and leads to broadened perspectives on oppression, privilege, and multiculturalism.

The notion of dialogue as an interpersonal enzyme is not new (Bohm, 1996; Isaacs, 1999; Patterson, Grenney, McMillan, & Switzler, 2000). Even its application to diversity training has been done before (W. G. Stephan & Stephan, 2001; Wilcox, 2000). But we did one thing very differently. Keith, Muriel, Juliet, and I started the course with a three-hour demonstration of MCD. This was an exciting teaching strategy for me. The four of us sat in a "fishbowl" with 60 students seated around us, and we provided them with our own version of *The Color of Fear* (Wah & Hunter, 1994). For example, during one of our dialogue demonstrations, I confessed that I felt guilty for being White. Muriel replied that she saw White guilt as an impediment to change, and that she wished that I would just get over it and move myself to action. I felt relief at hearing this because I thought that I was *supposed* to feel guilty when confronted with my racism or white privilege. Muriel's comment made me realize that my guilt was paralyzing me. My shame prevented me from empathizing with people of color and stymied me from

---

1. The author is indebted to Dr. Jim Malarkey, from The McGregor School of Antioch University, for introducing her to Swindler's principles of interreligious dialogue.

striving for social justice. After the demonstration, students were invited to ask questions and make comments.

The MCD demonstration was followed by instructor-facilitated dialogue throughout the remainder of the quarter. Our hope was that MCD would raise *student* consciousness. For me, however, the most powerful result has been my own transformation. Now, I am absolutely certain that I will never be the same. I have a fuller understanding of my racial identity and privilege, and a renewed vision of myself as an agent of social change.

For me, social change depends on genuine participation. It means engaging in reciprocal self-disclosure as often as I can. It means sharing knowledge and experiences of culture, oppression, and privilege with colleagues, friends, lovers, family members, students, and clients. It means paying attention to race, gender, class, sexual orientation, ability, and other aspects of identity that are meaningful to us. It means wondering what my appearance says to the other person. It means asking for feedback and contemplating it before I respond. This kind of dialogue is both draining and exhilarating.

THE COST IS IN THE CRUX: A CRITICAL INCIDENT AND MULTICULTURAL DIALOGUE

My perspective on this critical incident has changed dramatically over time. Multicultural dialogue and personal reflection led me to three important insights. Each insight produced a "disorienting dilemma" (Mezirow, 1991) for me and challenged my ability to receive feedback that is incommensurate with my well-meaning White identity.

Several years ago, I was part of a multisite faculty conference-design team, and I was responsible for facilitating the opening session on leadership. The purpose of the session was to describe what motivates someone to serve as a leader. A participant mentioned moral indignation as a driving force. I thought this was a productive avenue for elaboration, so I invited more responses on this topic; but my inquiry was met with blank looks. My anxiety started to rise, and I feared that I had gotten off track. I felt I needed help. So in a room comprising mostly White people, I looked to an African American colleague, who was also on the design team, and asked her to talk about how anger motivates her work in the field of social justice. I hadn't known her for long, but I had already had several conversations with her about her passion for this work, and I thought that her comments might deepen the discourse. Her facial expression told me instantly that she was angry with me. She politely declined to speak. There was a long, awkward pause. I found myself thinking, "Please say something! Please help me out!" She looked away from me and didn't say anything more.

First Insight

I was surprised by her reticence—baffled, really. What could I have done wrong? I was relieved when the large-group discussion ended and I could stop facilitating and start reflecting on my actions and her response. My realization of wrongdoing was sudden and distressing. I experienced that sinking, awful feeling associated with failing to grasp the situation until it's too late and wanting desperately to take it all back. My initial understanding of this critical incident was that I had failed to step outside of myself and consider the situation in which I was prompting my colleague to speak. It was unsafe. At the time, the atmosphere on her campus was rife with racial conflict, and my colleague was serving as the sole source of support for African American students. She was politically vulnerable. I knew this when I addressed her, but I lacked the sense to situate her in that context. I was blinded by my own needs and unconscious of the privilege afforded to me as a White woman in that setting. I was free to speak without someone attributing my attitudes to my race. I could be seen as an individual and not a representative of a racial/ethnic group. I could assume that my perspective would not be challenged because of my race/ethnicity. I arrived at the conference unhampered by a history of endless questions about my race or racial perspective that are part of being a "racial/ethnic minority" in the United States (Johnson, 2001; Kivel, 1996).

I felt tears in my eyes. My distress stemmed from my dismay over my own ineptitude and my fear of the impending confrontation. At a minimum, I had broken any sense of trust that might have existed between us. I had identified myself to her as a conscientious White person, and I had proven myself to be an unconscious privileged White person. I tried to talk to her right after the morning session, but she refused. She was visibly perturbed. Others asked me, "What happened? What's wrong?" None of the White people I talked to seemed to know what was awry.

We did not talk until later in the day. My colleague was furious with me. We sat in the presence of other team members and engaged in a dialogue about my actions and her response. The conversation was extremely difficult and extremely valuable. Both of us made explicit efforts to understand and articulate each other's perspectives. As we spoke, we saw the institution's role in building the context for what happened between us. The lack of faculty diversity and absence of support for African American students were two factors that made the campus climate stressful (at the time, the Multicultural Affairs Office was without personnel). I gained a fuller understanding of what I had done and the impact my white privilege had on someone I admired.

Second Insight

I had been in these situations before and had resisted taking responsibility for the unintended impact of my behavior. I used to leap to my own defense. This time, I knew that it was vital for me to *reflect on my actions first*. This stance allowed me to hear some of what my colleague had to say. However, it was not until a full year later, after an e-mail exchange, that I gained some deeper insight into my behavior. My colleague wrote:

Heidi,

One of the elements that I think is very important when peeling back the onion (so to speak) as it relates to unlearning issues of oppression and privilege is the false sense of superiority that whites adopt/construct in their relationships with persons of color. I believe that is what you experienced with me, stay with me on this ... the more you learn about how oppression operates, you learn that anger is a natural state in the unlearning process. However, liberation can be achieved through cognitive dissonance, which is also a natural stage that can be achieved in the unlearning oppression process. Oppression work is a journey, and the work feeds into the quality of our lives as human beings.

After first resisting and then contemplating this e-mail, I reached a deeper level of understanding. I came to realize that I had assumed too much. Not about her willingness to speak or what she would have to say. I assumed that I could *define her contribution.* I assumed that I was *entitled* to do that. This was more than a facilitator's mistake; this was a *White* facilitator's mistake, and, of course, it was my mistake. Certainly, I aim to avoid making the mistake again. In the past, I might have vowed to stop participating altogether—to avoid the risk and stay away from multicultural situations in which conflict might occur. However, I will not change and grow unless I maintain my commitment to "difficult dialogues" (Sue, Bingham, Porche-Burke, & Vasquez, 1999). I understand that I am unfinished in my multicultural development, and, as a result, I am committed to increasing my multicultural competence (Sue, Arredondo, & McDavis, 1995). This requires participation in a multicultural community, which in turn necessitates that I recognize my fallibility, own it, learn from it, and remain open to another person's experiences of me. I also understand that I have a responsibility to behave differently next time.

Third Insight

I recently requested feedback on this chapter from my colleague. I feel grateful to her for continuing to dialogue with me about historical events. My latest insight is the most painful one. I did not understand this until now, but it's clear that I ignored my colleague's right to confidentiality when I used my political location to elicit the disclosure of experiences and viewpoints, which she had shared *privately and in the context of the conference design team.* This is a disturbing realization for me and a perfect illustration of the way in which unexamined white privilege destroys trust in multicultural relationships. I had privileged my needs over her rights without even realizing it. This latent insight gives me an opportunity to behave differently in the future and to move in the direction of increased congruence between my actions and my identity as a WMWP.

ANALYSIS

The costs of racism and white privilege for people of color are evident on macro and micro levels (Neville, Worthington, & Spierman, 2001). On a macro level, there are tremendous structural-economic disparities in our society (D'Andrea &

Daniels, 2001; D. W. Sue & Sue, 2003). The legacies of historical oppression are evident in modern-day inequities (Collins, 2000; Takaki, 1993) and have yet to be completely undone. On a micro level, there is increasing awareness and understanding of the physical and psychological impact of racism for people of color (R. Clark, Anderson, Clark, & Williams, 1999; Contrada, et al., 2000; Lowe, et al., 2000; Thompson & Neville, 1999).

The costs of racism and white privilege for White folks, however, are less obvious. On a macro level, there is an astonishing loss of productivity, which affects the quality of life for everyone (Neville, et al., 2001). On a micro level, the costs include, but are not limited to, loss of connection to one's ancestors, condemnation for affiliating with "those people," discomfort with people of color, and witnessing or participating in oppressive practices (Kivel, 1996). Spanierman, Heppner, and Neville (2002, p. 3) identified three overlapping domains in which Whites may experience the costs of racism: The costs of racism to Whites may be cognitive (for example, distorted perceptions of reality, lack of knowledge of others, confusion regarding the coexistence of democracy and racial inequality), affective (for example, fear of others, anger, and guilt), or behavioral (for example, having relationships exclusively with other Whites, censoring oneself to avoid a perceived tension, being rejected by other Whites when challenging racism).

The varied dimensions of the costs of racism to Whites will be referred to collectively as psychosocial costs. Spanierman, et al. (2002) devised an instrument designed to measure these costs, the Psychosocial Costs of Racism to Whites Scale (PCRW). In my view, the costs associated with each of these domains converge at the crux of multicultural relationships.

One way that racism and white privilege affect multicultural relationships is through the periodic resurrection of racist double-binds. According to Mahmoud (1998), racist double-binds are perpetrated when a person with more power or privilege torments a less powerful person by conveying contradictory overt and covert messages, which leave the respondent with no cost-free alternatives. If the respondent confronts the instigator of the double-bind by identifying the contradictory messages, the instigator is likely to play the victim and accuse the respondent of being hostile, argumentative, or hypersensitive.

A typical example of this occurs when students of color are asked by their instructors to offer the Black/Latino/Indian/Asian person's perspective on a particular issue. The students risk appearing uncooperative or overly sensitive if they do not comply, but abiding by the request violates their integrity. The faculty person is using her or his position to define the student's contribution, and students of color must accept this definition or risk being silenced or censured for their resistance. Other double-binds are expressed in White-proffered statements such as "I don't see you as Mexican/Indian/Black. You aren't like the rest of them." People of color are left with two choices: a) deny one's own identity and be seen as 'good'; or b) own one's identity and be seen as bad.

I exercised my power and privilege in my attempt to define my colleague's contribution to the discussion on leadership. The *overt* message looked like an innocent invitation to speak, but the covert message was "Walk into this

minefield because *I* need your help and *my* needs (or the needs of the organization) supersede yours." Granted, I did not consciously concoct this situation, but
I did initiate the dilemma. My colleague had two poor choices: a) comply with
my request and disclose privately held observations and opinions, which would
have the effect of reinforcing white privilege, or b) resist my request, which entailed the risk of appearing uncooperative or overly sensitive.

Mahmoud (1998) argues that narcissism is behind the double-bind, and
I have to agree. I asked my colleague to speak because I was worried about embarrassing myself. Later, I could not accept my colleague's reaction to me because it
would damage my well-meaning White identity. The risks to me both during and
after this critical incident were strictly *personal*. I could either a) take a close look
at myself and feel empathic remorse for hurting someone, or b) defend against
this insight. The risk for my colleague was *personal and political*. She could decline
to speak, or she could speak up. Both of these options were confounded with
individual and institutional ramifications.

Oppression and privilege flow beneath the surface of multicultural relationships like an underground river. All parties are aware of it on one level or another. Every so often, the river rises and we have an opportunity to witness its
impact and change its course. The critical incident I just described provided me
with multiple revelations. I realized that I am likely to persist in putting my multicultural relationships at risk if I do not unpack my invisible backpack of privilege (McIntosh, 1989) and engage in antiracist actions. I also realized that it is
getting harder to live in a state of incongruence. The dissonance between my
well-meaning White identity and the impact of my behavior is like mental tin-
nitus. I am in a chronic state of discomfort.

Other White people in the United States are in a similar state. Winant
(1997) refers to this as racial dualism (p. 41). The Civil Rights Movement and
related reforms have

> … partially transformed white racial consciousness. Obviously they did
> not destroy the deep structures of white privilege, but they did make
> counterclaims on behalf of the racially excluded and subordinated. As a
> result white identities have been displaced and refigured: they are now
> contradictory, as well as confused and anxiety-ridden, to an unprece-
> dented extent.

The incommensurability of racialism and democracy (Myrdal, 1962 [1944] as
cited by Winant, 1997) creates cognitive dissonance and emotional distress for
WMWP.

As I have matured as a person, I have come to realize that I am dependent
on the positive appraisals of people of color. Somehow, if I am deemed a "good
White person," I can relax my vigilance and breathe a sigh of relief. This is faulty
thinking. At my age, my self-regard stems primarily from my *self-appraisal* and
not the appraisal of others. Even if I got preapproval as a "good White person,"
I would still make the mistakes that I do. I would still struggle with cultural de-
lusions produced by privilege, and I would still unintentionally trample on the
rights of my colleagues and friends. I cannot leap over my own development and

arrive at a place where it's easy all the time. A White student in one of my classes expressed this wish eloquently: "I just want to *be*." I often find myself wishing for this kind of comfort; but I know, deep down, that I need to find my voice and work toward greater congruence between how I see myself as a WMWP and how I behave in the world. If I am lucky, then my colleagues will be patient with me when I blunder.

The critical incident I described illuminates "the recursive relationship between structural and ideological racism" (Neville, et al., 2001, p. 260). My colleague and I work in a university system that is progressive and "well-meaning" but incomplete in its own multicultural organizational development (Sue, et al., 1998). Social justice requires transformation of institutions as well as individuals. If privilege is what allows an individual or an organization to "just be," then this freedom is not earned, but instead owned as an entitlement.

CONCLUSION: ALLIES, ADVOCATES, AND ACTIVISTS

In the past, I used my counseling and facilitation skills to avoid authentic engagement with people of color. I was afraid of revealing a hidden bias, a stereotype, or a prejudice. I would ask open-ended questions and use politically correct terms as a way to minimize the chance that I might say something offensive. I understand now that, rather than increasing my trustworthiness, I greatly reduced it by appearing fake. I expected people of color to reveal themselves to me, while I displayed little of myself.

I now realize that if I avoid in-depth, forthright dialogues about oppression and privilege, I lose the opportunity to form meaningful relationships with colleagues and students who are different from me. If I dampen the expression of my colleague's observations of oppressive attitudes or practices in my workplace, then everyone loses the opportunity to be understood or to engage in understanding. As an instructor and colleague, I have learned the value of trading privileged comfort for the reward of real dialogue across difference. I have learned that my students will be more courageous in their communication with each other if I participate as well as facilitate, if I model authenticity, if I self-correct, and if I repeatedly demonstrate that the development of multicultural counseling competence is a life-long process of deconstructing early learning and staying open to the experiences of others.

I find walking the talk and displaying my imperfections extremely challenging, but multicultural dialogue requires just that. Interpersonal multicultural conflicts are unavoidable and part of living in a pluralistic society. These critical incidents beg for a dialogic response. When I unintentionally say something that reveals a stereotype, prejudice, or privilege, I am suddenly faced with behavioral choices, nearly all of which coincide with the ways in which White folks in higher education tend to respond (D'Andrea & Daniels, 1999): I can aggressively defend myself (anger), passively retreat (generalized apathy), or distance myself from the discussion (intellectual detachment). My personal goal, however, is to grow more tolerant of my own discomfort and maintain a level of engagement that will lead to intrapersonal insight and interpersonal détente or resolution. I am deeply honored and sincerely grateful for the moments of multicultural immediacy that I have had with colleagues who are different from me. It is through these relationships that I have grown to recognize the cost of white privilege.

I am experiencing a painful and delightful merger of my real and ideal self. The process has involved letting go of unrealistic self-impressions (for example, I am without prejudice) and of accepting my imperfections (for example, the critical incident described here). My multicultural experiences remind me of the psychotherapeutic process of change (Highlen & Hill, 1984). I continuously cycle forward and back in a spiral of progress that brings me closer to my colleagues and my authentic self.

Speaking and behaving authentically is about finding one's voice. Feminist educators have said this for many years. An oppressive society divides us, silences us. It privileges a few and marginalizes many. Unity through diversity is a well-worn adage, but the theme has more than one meaning. During the past several years, I have experienced a unity of persons and a unity of *self* that is priceless.

Finding one's voice is a metaphor for integrating the disparate parts of oneself and the disparate parts of one's community. Finding one's voice is the first step in creating individual and institutional change. Ongoing dialogue is one way to build the alliances that are needed to transform people and systems and turn intention into action.

DISCUSSION QUESTIONS

1. In what ways are you oppressed? In what ways are you privileged?

2. One-half of the conference design team thought my actions were not worth condemning. The other half thought my behavior was reprehensible. What do you think?

3. Do you think that I am speaking from a place of "white guilt" and/or "political correctness"? How do you contrast these phenomena with ethical growth and development? Do you think that I was not "honest enough" in my interpretation of this critical incident, and that my perspective is still limited by my white privilege? How?

4. If you are a White person, how would you feel if someone asked you to talk about your anger regarding oppression and privilege in a room full of your friends or colleagues? Have you ever tried doing that? If yes, what happened? If no, why not?

5. Have you had similar experiences? How did you resolve them in your own mind? How did you resolve them interpersonally?

6. Have you ever been confronted by someone who experienced your actions as oppressive? In what ways did you respond defensively? In what ways did you respond openly and with a willingness to learn?

7. What does it mean to engage someone in multicultural dialogue? What are your barriers to multicultural dialogue? How can you overcome them?

8. Where are you in your racial/cultural or white racial identity development? How might your status in your own racial/cultural identity development or White racial identity development affect your perceptions of this narrative?

9. What have you learned about yourself by reading this narrative?

REFERENCES

Betita, J., Mar, K., Shockley, M., & Zetzer, H. (November, 2001). Challenging racism, privilege, & oppression: Building bridges through multicultural dialogue. Workshop presented at The Multicultural Center, University of California, Santa Barbara.

Bohm, D. (1996). *On dialogue*. NY: Routledge.

Carter, R. T. (1997). Is white a race? Expressions of white racial identity. In M. Fine, L. Weis, L. C. Powell, & L. M. Wong (Eds.), *Off white: Readings on race, power, and society* (pp. 198–209). NY: Routledge.

Clark, R., Anderson, N. B., Clark, V. R., & Williams, D. R. (1999). Racism as a stressor for African Americans, *The American Psychologist, 54*, 805–816.

Contrada, R. J., Ashmore, R. D., Gary, M. L., Coups, E., Egeth, J. D., Sewell, A., et al. (2000). Ethnicity-related sources of stress and their effects on well-being, *Current Directions in Psychological Science, 9*, 136–139.

Collins, P. H. (2000). *Black feminist thought: Knowledge, Consciousness, and the Politics of Empowerment* (2nd ed.). NY: Routledge.

D'Andrea, M., & Daniels, J. (1999). Understanding the different psychological dispositions of white racism: A comprehensive model for counselor educators and practitioners. In M.S. Kiselica (Ed.), *Confronting prejudice and racism during multicultural training*. Alexandria, VA: American Counseling Association.

D'Andrea, M., & Daniels, J. (2001). Expanding our thinking about white racism: Facing the challenge of multicultural counseling in the 21st century. In J. G. Ponterotto, J. M. Casas, L. A. Suzuki, & C. M. Alexander (Eds.), *Handbook of multicultural counseling* (2nd ed.) (pp. 289–310). Thousand Oaks, CA: Sage.

Dovidio, J. F., Gaertner, S. L., Kawakami, K., Hodson, G. (2002). Why can't we just get along? Interpersonal bias and interracial distrust. *Cultural Diversity & Ethnic Minority Psychology, 8*, 88–102.

Helms, J. E. (1995). An update of Helm's white and people of color racial identity models. In J. G. Ponterotto, J. M. Casas, L. A. Suzuki, & C. M. Alexander (Eds.), *Handbook of multicultural counseling* (pp. 181–191). Thousand Oaks, CA: Sage.

Highlen, P. S., & Hill, C. E. (1984). Factors affecting client change in individual counseling: Current status and theoretical speculation. In S. D. Brown & R. W. Lent (Eds.), *Handbook of counseling psychology*, 334–396. NY: Wiley.

Isaacs, W. (1999). *Dialogue and the art of thinking together: A pioneering approach to communicating in business and in life*. NY: Random House.

Johnson, A. G. (2001). *Privilege, power, and difference*. Boston: McGraw-Hill.

Kiselica, M. S. (1998). Preparing Anglos for the challenges and joys of multiculturalism. *The Counseling Psychologist, 26,* 5–21.

Kivel, P. (1996). *Uprooting racism: How white people can work for racial justice*. Gabriola Island, British Columbia: New Society Publishers.

Lowe, S. M., Chang, Y., Chapman, B., Dettinger, S., Henze, K., Latta, R., et al. (August, 2000). Hearing voices: Coping with racism among Asian Americans. Paper presented as part of a symposium at the Annual Meeting of the American Psychological Association, San Francisco, CA.

Mahmoud, V. M. (1998). The double binds of racism. In M. McGoldrick (Ed.), *Re-Visioning family therapy: Race, culture, and practice* (pp. 255–267). NY: Guilford Press.

McIntosh, Peggy (1989, July/August). White privilege: Unpacking the invisible knapsack. *Peace and Freedom,* 8–10.

Mezirow, J. (1991). *Transformative dimensions of adult learning*. San Francisco: Jossey-Bass.

Neville, H. A., Worthington, R. L., Spanierman, L. B. (2001). Race, power, and multicultural counseling psychology. In J. G. Ponterotto, J. M. Casas, L. A. Suzuki, & C. M. Alexander (Eds.), *Handbook of multicultural counseling* (2nd ed.) (pp. 257–288). Thousand Oaks, CA: Sage.

Patterson, K., Grenny, J., McMillan, R., & Switzler, A. (2000). *Better than duct tape: Dialogue tools for getting results and getting along*. Plano, TX: Pritchett, Rummler-Brache.

Ponterotto, J. G. (1998). Charting a course for research in a multicultural counseling training program. *The Counseling Psychologist, 26,* 43–68.

Reynolds, A. L. (1997). Using the Multicultural Change Intervention Matrix (MCIM) as a multicultural counseling training model. In D. Pope-Davis & H. L. K. Coleman (Eds.), *Multicultural aspects of counseling series: Vol. 7. Multicultural counseling competencies: Assessment, education, and training, and supervision* (pp. 209–226). Thousand Oaks: Sage.

Rogers, C. R. (1957). The necessary and sufficient conditions of therapeutic personality change. *Journal of Consulting Psychology, 21,* 95–103.

Rowe, W., Bennett, S., & Atkinson, D. R. (1994). White racial identity models: A critique and alternative proposal. *The Counseling Psychologist, 22,* 120–146.

Spanierman, L. B., Heppner, M. J., & Neville, H. A. (August, 2002). Psychosocial Costs of Racism to Whites Scale: Measuring the construct. Poster presented at the Annual Convention of the American Psychological Association, Chicago, IL.

Stephan, W. G., & Stephan, C. W. (2001). *Improving intergroup relations*. Thousand Oaks: Sage Publications.

Sue, S., Arredondo, P., & McDavis, R. (1995). Multicultural counseling competencies and standards: A call to the profession. In J. G. Ponterotto, J. M. Casas, L. A. Suzuki, & C. M. Alexander (Eds.), *Handbook of multicultural counseling* (pp. 624–643). Thousand Oaks, CA: Sage.

Sue, D. W., Bingham, R., Porche-Burke, L., & Vasquez, M. (1999). The diversification of psychology: A multicultural revolution. *The American Psychologist, 54,* 1061–1069.

Sue, D. W., Carter, R. T., Casas, J. M., Fouad, N. A., Ivey, A. E., Jensen, M., LaFromboise, T., Manese, J. E., Ponterotto, J. G., & Vasquez-Nutall, E. (1998).

Multicultural counseling competencies: Individual & organizational development. Thousand Oaks: Sage Publications.

Sue, D. W., & Sue, D. (2003). *Counseling the culturally diverse: Theory to practice* (4th ed.). NY: Wiley.

Swindler, L. (1983). The dialogue decalogue: Ground rules for interreligious, interideological dialogue. *The Journal of Ecumenical Studies, 20,* 1–4.

Takaki, R. (1993). *In a different mirror: A history of multicultural America.* Boston: Little Brown & Co.

Tatum, B. (1997). *Why are all the black kids sitting together in the cafeteria? And other conversations about race.* NY: Basic Books.

Thompson, C. E., & Neville, H. A. (1999). Racism, mental health, and mental health practice. *The Counseling Psychologist, 27,* 155–223.

Wah, L. M. (Producer and Director), & Hunter, M. (Co-Producer). (1994). The color of fear [video recording]. Available from Stir-Fry Productions, Oakland, CA.

Wilcox, D. (2000). Deliberative dialogue: A different kind of talk, another way to act. Paper presented at The Summit on Blacks in Higher Education, American Association for Higher Education Black Caucus, Savannah State University, Savannah, Georgia.

Winant, H. (1997). Behind blue eyes: Whiteness and contemporary U.S. racial politics. In M. Fine, L. Weis, L. C. Powell, & L. M. Wong (Eds.), *Off white: Readings on race, power, and society* (pp. 40–56). NY: Routledge.

Wolfe, N. (1995). The racism of well-meaning white people. In M. Golden & S. R. Shreve, *Skin deep: Black and white women write about race* (pp. 37–46). NY: Doubleday.

Zetzer, H. A., Shockley, M. E., Mar, K., & Betita, J. V. (2000, Aug.). Dismantling resistance with self-disclosure: Dialogue as innovation in multicultural training. In J. N. Valdez (Chair), Overcoming resistance, achieving transformation: Innovations in teaching multicultural counseling skills. Symposium conducted at the Annual Meeting of the American Psychological Association, Washington, D.C.

AUTHOR'S NOTE

Heidi A. Zetzer, Ph.D., Core Faculty, Graduate Psychology Program, Antioch University, Santa Barbara.

I would like to express my appreciation to Sharon Anderson and Valerie Middleton for their editorial comments. Special praise is due to Richard Whitney and Michael Loewy for their valuable feedback during the construction of this narrative. I feel especially grateful to Juliet Betita, Keith Mar, Muriel Shockley, A. J. Thoroughgood, and Jesse Valdez for their contributions to my multicultural development. Portions of this chapter were presented at the 109th Annual Convention of the American Psychological Association, San Francisco, California, August, 2001.

Correspondence concerning this chapter should be addressed to Heidi A. Zetzer, Ph.D., Director, Hosford Counseling & Psychological Services Clinic, Department of Counseling, Clinical, & School Psychology, 1151 Education Building, University of California, Santa Barbara, CA 93106-9490. Electronic mail may be sent via Internet to hzetzer@education.ucsb.edu.

3

✳

Supposed to Know Better

On Accepting Privilege

DEBORAH MEGIVERN FOSTER

INTRODUCTION

During my studies as a doctoral student in social work and psychology, I volunteered to become a facilitator for a graduate-level multicultural dialogue class focusing on dimensions of oppression, privilege, and diversity. At first, I justified taking on extra work because I would soon be teaching graduate students about multicultural and social justice–oriented approaches to mental-health practice and policy—a tremendous responsibility, considering I had witnessed mental-health providers who were ill-prepared to work with diverse clientele. My second justification for taking a minor leadership role in this class was more compelling and significant to me. I was having a great deal of trouble accepting a basic element of social-justice learning—the struggle to acknowledge my own privileges.

UNDERSTANDING AND EXPERIENCING WHITE PRIVILEGE: DEBORAH'S STORY

Even after nearly 8 years in a graduate social-work program—in an environment in which discussion of oppression and privilege occurred frequently—I still had trouble with the idea that I had personally benefited from many advantages. It was not that I cognitively denied my privileges, particularly those gleaned from being White. My challenge was the intersection of being White and growing up poor. I struggled with feeling privileged when I could not get over feeling deprived; I could easily make a direct connection between current miseries and lifelong disadvantages. Educating others around me who just didn't get economic or class oppression drew my focus away from my white privilege.

ROOTS OF AN IDENTITY

Although I am a White, heterosexual woman, the identity most salient throughout my life was "poor trash"—a welfare child. Many life experiences reinforce the importance of this identity over the more privileged identities I enjoy. Both of my parents suffered from psychiatric illnesses. My mother received disability payments, and my father was employed as a janitor, which meant minimal income. Economic struggles within my family led to bouts with homelessness, daily reliance on the Salvation Army for meals, and dependence on charity from public and private sources. Lack of food and heat led child-protective services to remove my siblings and me from my parents to be placed in foster care. We were eventually returned to our parents but the strain of family separation and poverty led my parents to divorce shortly thereafter. My mother became a single parent to six children, while my father moved into a roach-infested, single-room-occupancy hotel.

The neighborhood in which we were being raised was dangerous and dilapidated. Indeed, the rampant negative influences likely contributed significantly to the fact that three of my younger siblings were mandated to services within the juvenile justice system, and two of them became drug dependent. Eventually, one of my brothers committed suicide. I will always be convinced that poverty and our childhood life circumstances played the largest role in his death.

My departure from this life of poverty at the age of 17 was the result of support from family and friends, an extensive series of governmental interventions (ranging from Head Start to Project Upward Bound), and a natural inclination toward academia. As I was driven off to college, I felt relieved to have escaped that life of dispossession. Unfortunately the feeling was short-lived, for it was during college and graduate school that I discovered the seemingly permanent effects of my economic history. My identity, the essence of who I am, had been shaped by adapting to long-term poverty. The majority of my classmates came from middle-class to upper-middle-class families. There were daily reminders of our differences.

In political science and economics classes, my privileged college classmates degraded welfare recipients. I was too frightened of social exclusion to speak up. Instead, I silently sat in isolation, absorbing the significant social distance between us. Outside of class, many acquaintances were frustrated with my seeming unwillingness to spend more time with them in social activities and less time at work. They did not understand that, for me, work was not a choice.

My full-time work schedule throughout college did not allow much time for socializing. Whether I was serving other students food at the school's cafeteria during the day or taking their orders at the popular local restaurant in the evening, I would overhear college classmates complaining about reductions in their allowances from $500 a month to $250. They did not have to pay their college expenses, and they even got an allowance. They did not need to work. I fantasized about what that would be like. It was hard not to feel bitter as my own course work often got behind in a heavy workweek. Chronic fatigue also made me prone to headaches, stomach pain, and colds.

The burden of poverty lingered tangibly as well, because each life step I took continued to be plagued by economic hardship. During graduate school, I found myself in the role of parent when I obtained custody of my two youngest siblings, accumulating more than $125,000 in student-loan debt while attempting to raise them on a graduate student's stipend and other meager employment. It was under these circumstances of relative deprivation that I studied oppression and privilege in my graduate classes and learned extensively about white privilege. Certainly, it felt to me as though my entire life had been defined by deprivation. If there were white privileges to be recognized, I could not see them. In my mind, what on earth good had it done to be White? It had not spared me hunger, frostbite, lice, poor medical care, ridicule, violence, or trauma. This feeling of deprivation was especially true in academia because the vast majority of graduate students, including students of color, had spent their lives in material comfort and security.

THE EMBERS OF TRANSFORMATION

Eventually, I gained an intellectual, if not intuitive, understanding of privilege through my graduate program. Vowing to continue work on my own issues of privilege, I decided to become a co-facilitator with a well-regarded lead instructor, Dr. Michael Spencer. Dr. Spencer offers multicultural dialogue groups as a major means for learning about social justice, oppression, and privilege in his Contemporary Cultures in the United States class at the University of Michigan. I maintained the goal of focusing on my privileged identities, but I often felt ambivalent. On the one hand, I felt guilt and defensiveness at being blamed for my culpability in race oppression, as class members of color described their experiences. On the other hand, I felt envy and bitterness toward those individuals who had been economically privileged throughout their lives. I craved their basic privilege of getting fundamental needs met and the sense of security that elicited.

About mid-semester, I was asked by Dr. Spencer to give a presentation on classism and poverty. He knew this was an area I knew a lot about. As I presented general information to the class, I shared specific details from my personal experiences to give fellow students a sense of how economic labeling and stigmatization make an impact. At one point, I showed the class a Child Protective Services document that declared *me* guilty of child neglect when I left two of my siblings in the house while I went to rescue another younger sibling being beaten by kids at the local park. I was 12 years old at the time. We discussed whether the "guilty" verdict would have occurred for a middle-class family under the same circumstances, and most class members agreed that it likely would not have.

The presentation stirred a mix of emotions in me. To share the lack of power, the deprivation, and the humiliation was empowering. Nonetheless, the stigma of poverty and child neglect, even though I was only 12 years old at the time, still stung. I felt I had performed a duty to other poor people by telling our story, but the cost was shame that took weeks to shake off.

At the end of the presentation, an African American graduate student I respected a great deal approached me. She told me honestly, "I feel bad for you; but to be blunt, by the end of your talk, I was still thinking, 'So what? You're still White.' I guess I think that being White makes a big difference." Her words stung; her expression seemed defiant and accusatory. It felt as though my oppression was deniable, because I was White. The weight of race oppression was her burden. To me, it seemed as if she could not see my burden of class oppression or her own class privilege as long as her awareness stayed entirely within race oppression.

It dawned on me, eventually, that I was not going to be able to own my white privilege until I let go of enough of my own oppression to really listen and internalize the privilege. My classmate's comment was a precipitant to the gradual coherence and redirection of my conflicting thoughts and feelings. There we had been, both in pain from dealing with the ramifications of oppression, yet we had been at odds.

When I recollected that exchange later on, the importance of accepting my white privilege finally became clear to me on an emotional level. I was unwilling to move beyond my oppression, how could I expect anyone else to do as much? This meant I was going to have to really attend to all of the daily instances in which my race advantaged me. If I applied for an apartment, I knew any rejection would be because I didn't have enough credit. In my community, police officers chronically stop my neighbors for "Driving While Black," while I cruise by without significant worry of harassment. I did not have to question whether my race was a factor. I had personally witnessed millions of examples of white privilege as I grew up in a predominantly African American neighborhood; but I had not focused on these. As I became more willing to explore the totality of my life circumstances, I became more conscious of my privileged identity and not just my oppressed identity.

During this period of awakening and transformation, I was fortunate to have the guidance of authors such as June Jordan (2001), who taught me that oppressed people have to examine their privileges just as often as they grapple with their oppression. Jordan (2001), an African American woman, described an interaction with a White, female student who declared her (Jordan) to be "lucky" for having lived with oppression. From the student's perspective, dealing with oppression gave Jordan a cause or purpose to her life. Alternatively, this student felt she was "just a housewife and mother," and thus, a "nobody" (p. 39). Jordan used this experience to reflect on the ramifications of gender, race, and class oppression. In that exchange, she saw that this student did not see others' oppression as her own cause or her purpose. There was no unity between them as they struggled against gender and race oppression.

Later in her essay, Jordan (2001) writes about an African woman and an Irish woman joining in solidarity to solve a problem, "It was not who they both were but what they both know and what they were both preparing to do about what they know that was going to make them both free at last" (p. 44). This was the lesson. Without understanding my white privilege—privilege being the constant companion to oppression—I could not "know" or work against either class or race oppression. If I didn't fully know what others with whom I wanted solidarity experienced, we would be unable to be free of our respective oppressions together.

THE REPEATING PROCESS OF SELF-EXAMINATION: CONCLUSIONS AND LESSONS LEARNED

Examining one's own privileged status is a constant process. I have had to continually revisit my tasks as a member of oppressing groups. Freire (1970) called this repeated process of self-examination "critical consciousness." Specifically, I have to repeatedly remind myself that I cannot expect others to examine their economic privileges if I am not willing to work on owning my white privilege. I knew the vexation that came from waiting for others to accept their class advantages; that economically secure people took for granted their safe neighborhoods, regular meals, and designer clothes always seemed to make poverty worse.

So I planned to appreciate my white privilege, notice it, and then work to extend these privileges to others. For example, not long ago, I was riding on a city train. A beautiful African American child, about 4 years old, was smiling and talking to passengers. When this little girl and her mother exited the train, a White man with all of the markers of being from a lower-class background made a derogatory comment about the young girl's hair, which had been combed out to a full Afro. I winced to hear his insensitive and disparaging views. He was part of the system of white oppression, a blatant racist asserting cultural dominance based on skin privilege. Only a few moments later, an aging African American male trudged up the aisle of the train carrying a mop and a bucket. He looked weary, confined to cleaning up the mess made by other people on train cars.

This story is relevant in my transformation because my previous instincts would have been to overlook the obvious signs of race oppression. In the past, I would have mentally felt united with the poverty of the janitor, feeling connected to him by the fact that I had scrubbed my share of toilets, and because my father has been a janitor most of his life. I would not have focused on what I had in common with the lower-class White person, or how I personally benefited from systemic oppression based on race. However, this time, I understood in that moment the privilege of being White, and I reminded myself how my race had almost certainly played a beneficial role in my escape from poverty. How many people had just assumed, in part because I am White, that I was bright and easily educated? How often had my "merits" been recognized where they may have been overlooked if I had darker skin? In that moment, I recognized that I was exceptionally blessed to be riding to a sports event on the train, enjoying my free time, having the funds to pay for leisure, and possessing the capabilities to avoid doing the kind of work that would put that immutable wearied look on my face.

More and more, I recognize that I am fortunate to have had experiences with being disadvantaged. The circumstances of my life have allowed me to develop an empathy that has resulted in deeper interpersonal relationships with others. The weight of oppression has alerted me to the need to participate actively in efforts to change societal injustices. I have come to consider much of what is white privilege as a set of basic rights all people should be entitled to. I am working, through social and political action, dialogue in the classes I teach, and constant reexamination of my self-awareness, to challenge the oppression-privilege dichotomy. There is a certain gift in feeling as if, just maybe, I might be a part of the solution.

DISCUSSION QUESTIONS

1. How does the complication of overlapping identities affect this author's struggle to identify her race privilege?

2. Describe in your own words the author's transformation in identity. Then, consider your own social identities and try to identify any transformative experiences related to oppression and privilege from your own life.

3. How might this author interact differently with a client from a different race now versus before her self-exploration?

4. The author states that white privilege is mostly a set of basic rights that all people should be entitled to receive. First, give examples of white privilege that go beyond basic rights. How would White individuals relinquish an unearned privilege of this nature?

5. In what ways does this author demonstrate the importance of "critical consciousness" and continual self-reflection as a critical component of cultural competence for mental-health practice?

6. The author repeatedly describes feelings of marginalization related to her mixed identity of being both poor and White. She laments the lack of community, based on class, in higher education. In what ways might multicultural education transform colleges and universities into environments in which people collaborate across nontraditional social-identity groups?

7. How might a student from outside the United States view the dynamics of class and race in the United States after reading this author's story?

REFERENCES

Freire, P. (1970). *Pedagogy of the oppressed.* New York: Continuum.

Goodman, D. (1995). Difficult dialogues: Enhancing discussions about diversity, *College Teaching, 43*(2), 47–52.

Jordan, J. (2001). Report from the Bahamas. In M. Andersen & P. Hill Collins (Eds.). *Race, class, and gender: An anthology* (4th ed.) (pp. 35–44). Belmont, CA: Wadsworth Publishing.

McIntosh, P. (2001). White privilege and male privilege: A personal account of coming to see correspondences through work in women's studies (1988). In M. Andersen & P. Hill Collins (Eds.). *Race, class, and gender: An anthology* (4th ed.) (pp. 95–105). Belmont, CA: Wadsworth Publishing.

Miner, B. (2001). Taking multicultural, antiracist education seriously: An interview with Enid Lee. In M. Andersen & P. Hill Collins (Eds.). *Race, class, and gender: An anthology* (4th ed.) (pp. 556–562). Belmont, CA: Wadsworth Publishing.

Reed, B., Newman, P., Suarez, Z., & Lewis, E. (1997). Interpersonal practice beyond diversity and toward social justice: The importance of critical consciousness. In C. Garvin & B. Seabury (Eds.). *Interpersonal practice in social work: Promoting competence and social justice* (2nd ed.) (pp. 44–77). Boston: Allyn & Bacon.

Wade, J. C. (1993). Institutional racism: An analysis of the mental health system, *American Journal of Orthopsychiatry, 63*(4), 536–44.

4

✳

White Male Privilege in the Context of My Life

RICH FURMAN

UNDERSTANDING AND EXPERIENCING WHITE PRIVILEGE: RICH'S STORY

I am White and male, but also Jewish. As a White male, I have often been presumed to possess certain positive attributes before I have exhibited them. That is, I am usually presumed competent, intelligent, and skillful s based solely upon my physical type, manner of speech, and experiences that may or may not have occurred.

At times, thinking about my own white privilege is difficult. This is largely because, although I have white skin, in many ways I do not consider myself White, but Jewish. Non-Jews rarely understand what I mean by this without some explanation. All my life it has been clear to me that I do not think or feel as the majority of White males do—I tend to be more emotional, more willing to engage in debate and conflict, and more animated. Many Jews experience a dual identity crisis by sometimes being able to pass as members of the dominant society while simultaneously hiding a portion of their identity that is often celebrated in other venues. Both the ability and inability to hide one's identity makes one painfully aware of the costs and benefits of the ability to assimilate. The following stories illustrate this phenomenon.

STORY ONE

My days before I embarked upon my graduate-school experience were full of hope and awe. I imagined I was on the precipice of an epic adventure into a new, mystical, multicultural land where experiences of difference were cherished and commonalties were the foundation of mutual sharing. Perhaps such naiveté is commonplace among the soon-to-be-initiated. Regardless, my fantasy of finding a place in our United States where multiculturalism was a simple, easy-to-take-for-granted norm was soon to be discarded. It has been many years since, yet I remember my first day of graduate school as if it were yesterday.

The welcoming party was typical of such events: the basic finger foods, short speeches from administrators, and second-year student leaders assigned to both inform and assure us anxious neophytes. What struck me as ironic, sad, and bizarre was how the students broke into small groupings based almost entirely upon ethnicity, gender, and race. Certainly, in a school with a social-work curriculum, people would be able to transcend traditional barriers. After about an hour, I decided to approach a group of African American women to say "hello." In my usual fearless and, in retrospect, painfully oblivious manner, I walked over to the group and stated, "Hi, my name is Rich. I am shocked that we are all talking only to those of the same race or sex, so I thought I would try to desegregate the party." Two of the women smiled brightly and laughed. Another scolded me fiercely, "Segregation is what White men have done to us historically. I am *choosing* to talk to my sisters here. This is not segregation. Have a nice day."

At first, my reaction was utter shame. Clearly, not only had I committed a grave error, but also, in that moment, I felt responsible for hundreds of years of racism and oppression. In that moment, I was no better than a whip-cracking southern slaveholder. Because I had not worked through this issue previously, I was not able to simply apologize for my gaffe and rectify the situation. Instead, I had to endlessly ruminate about the incident, shifting blame onto the young woman, myself, or both of us.

STORY TWO

One year after graduate school, I obtained a position working as the clinical coordinator in a residential treatment program for adolescents with emotional disabilities. My responsibilities included developing treatment plans for the residents, providing therapy, and conducting family visits. I was also responsible for helping the line-level counselors implement the treatment plan and be "clinical" in their approach. All and all, I did a good job. It was curious though that I was in a supervisory position over much more experienced yet less educated workers, most of whom were African Americans. Being aware of my difference as the only White person in the building much of the time was not difficult; some of the children made me painfully aware. One day a child told me that I did not care about him because I was "just some [blank, blank] White guy who was there to keep Black people down." Not having worked through my white privilege, I responded defensively. I assured him that he was wrong, that I did care. Exasperated, he shrugged his shoulders and stomped off.

STORY THREE

As I originally was typing the previous stories, I was sitting in a café in a trendy area of Los Angeles. The café was full of people reading, studying, and talking. An African American man walked in with a backpack, similar to the one that was lying on my table. He laid it down on a table next to a young White woman and took out books and paper to write, just as I had done several minutes earlier. As the young woman got up to use the bathroom, she asked *me* to watch her things. Just a half-hour before, however, she had left her things on the table unguarded as she used the bathroom. The only thing in the scenario that was different now was the presence of the African American man about the same distance away from her as I was.

At the instant she asked me to watch her things, I became painfully aware of what had happened and wondered whether my African American counterpart was also conscious of the situation. I struggled with how to respond in the moment. After a split second had passed, in which all these things raced through my mind, I told the young woman that I would not be able to watch her things because I was just about to go to the bathroom myself. As soon as I said this, she organized her things, placed them into her bag, and walked to the bathroom with her bag in tow.

In the bathroom myself, I wondered whether there was something for me to do in this situation to challenge my white privilege. Was it enough merely to refuse to be party to such racism, or was something else required? Because I did not have a relationship with the woman, I decided to do nothing. I went back to my table and I sat down. I felt powerless and angry. I wished I could find the words to speak to the man about the situation, but how could I talk about such things with a stranger when I had problems doing so even with those with whom I was close?

FROM THEORY TO PRACTICE: REFLECTION ON
WHITE PRIVILEGE

White male privilege has distinct costs. As the recipient of benefits bestowed upon me solely due to the color of my skin, I sometimes experience resentment from others that I find baffling and unfounded. When I don't understand the essence of my white privilege, I become reactive or shut down. My encounter with the group of African American women illustrates how white privilege, and my lack of understanding of the phenomenon, cut off communication. A proper analysis would have revealed that both our behaviors could in some way be understood as a natural by-product of years of white privilege and its legacy of anger and resentment. I lost a valuable opportunity to learn from her experiences, and a valuable opportunity to relate to her as an equal by never speaking to her about the situation. In fact, I never spoke to her again. Feeling too conflicted and ashamed, I was unable to work through these difficult feelings.

In the second scenario, I again cut off communication by invalidating the feelings of the youth who told me in earnest what he was feeling. While he might have been wrong about me, he was expressing his real feelings about a society that devalues him, a society that considers it more likely that he will go to prison than to college. Had I validated his anger and expressed my desire to understand his experience, we might have been able to create a dialogue. I might have been a far more effective therapist to him personally had I worked through my own guilt and shame, which caused me to react defensively. Although in both instances I cut off communication, after the second experience, I had embarked on a higher level of ethno-relative development and was better able to reflect on how I might use my privileged status to validate and encourage this disenfranchised youth.

The more I work to understand my white privilege, the more I come to some kind of acceptance of it and continue to learn how I wish to deal with my privileges and paradoxes. When in this frame of mind, I am freer to choose my responses, as the following conclusion to the third story illustrates.

I became wrapped up in my contemplation about challenging the thinking of the woman who asked me to watch her things while she went to the restroom. It took me awhile to become aware enough to try to understand how the African American man might be feeling if he was aware of the situation. Words such as *discounted*, *devalued*, and *dehumanized* scrolled across my consciousness.

I decided that while I would not bring up the situation directly, I would challenge the behavior that I had witnessed by attempting to make some kind of human connection with him. I excused myself for interrupting and asked him what he was reading. It was a book of poetry, one of my great passions, so we talked about writing and poetry. When the young woman returned from the bathroom, she reclaimed her seat between the two of us. In order not to be rude by talking around her, I asked my new acquaintance if I could join him. He was pleased to accept, and we continued our conversation. Fifteen minutes later, the young woman gathered her things to leave. I bid her a nice day and smiled at her, holding eye contact for several seconds too long as she walked out the door. Did she understand what I was trying to say to her? I will never know, but I felt better for attempting to communicate with her on some level.

CONCLUSIONS AND LESSONS LEARNED

One of the most important things I have learned in regard to privilege and other issues pertaining to the -isms is that humility and self-forgiveness are essential. We must accept our histories and defects without focusing on debilitating guilt, shame, or anger. These limiting reactions are not positive teaching tools, and none of them serve to resolve situations in a healthy way. Instead, they tend to lead one to be defensive or to submerge the pain as a self-protection strategy.

It is also important to realize that working through white privilege is a process, not an event. I cannot say that I have fully come to grips with my white privilege. Sometimes I am blind and insensitive to others in ways that I see only upon reflection. Sometimes I am overly critical of myself and attribute insensitivity where none existed. Part of my struggle is to find balance, and tolerance—that is, tolerance for others, and for myself, as well.

DISCUSSION QUESTIONS

1. What options can you think of for handing the stories discussed in this chapter?
2. What other options did the author have for resolving his conflicts?
3. What would you have done differently in the last story? Why?
4. What have been some of the benefits of white privilege to you or people you know?
5. What are some of the emotional consequences of white privilege for you and those you know?
6. Have you recognized your own privilege, whatever area it is in? If so, what is it?
7. What was the most important lesson you learned from the narrative?

REFERENCES

McIntosh, P. (2000). White privilege and male privilege: A personal account of coming to see correspondences through work in women's studies. In A. Minas (ed.), *Gender basics: Feminist perspectives on women and men.* Belmont, CA: Wadsworth/Thomson Learning.

5

*

Understanding and Experiencing Class Privilege

COLLEEN LOOMIS

The social construction of social class in the United States is controversial (Fussell, 1992; Storck, 2002). Many people would agree that there is a middle class and an upper class (for example, Kennedy and Rockefeller families), but there is not a consensus about the class or classes beneath the middle class. In this arena, perhaps most well known is the "working class" made popular by essays written from adult children in academia who were raised in working-class families (see Dews & Lee, 1995; Tokarczyk & Fay, 1993) and by popular media (for example, Hollywood films such as *Goodwill Hunting*). One challenge I face in writing this chapter is how to categorize my childhood social class. I began with the label "lower class" and migrated to "working class" or "working poor." My life experiences are dissimilar from the Hollywood and academic versions of working class as well as those of a few friends and colleagues who self-identify as having "working-class roots" or having been raised as "poor White trash." My social, economic, and cultural context differed. In this chapter, rather than address my understanding of various classifications of social class, I focus on ways that these aspects of my life circumstances influence my understanding of class privilege through experience.

GROWING UP WITH MORE THAN A FEW
AND LESS THAN MOST

My three brothers and I grew up in low-income circumstances in the United States. Shelter, clothing, and food were sometimes scarce during our early

39

childhood. For example, our mother speaks about my not having shoes during a New York winter. Moving often to where my father had work or where extended family would help us, we lived in a variety of housing situations (a few without conventional plumbing). When I was seven years old, we settled for the next six years into a two-bedroom, 60-foot trailer—one of a few in the neighborhood—located on a dirt road in a relatively rural area. I have fond memories of this neighborhood, such as swimming in a nearby lake and riding the bus to school because it was too far to walk. Social welfare assisted with the support of our family by providing food stamps, and a few kind neighbors supported us with offers of food, shoes, and hand-me-down clothes before and after my father left. My memory of going with my mother to buy groceries and hearing derogatory remarks about us while we made our purchase with food stamps seems to mark the beginning of my awareness of social class differences at the individual level. (For the group level, see Storck, 2002.)

The infiltration of middle-class families into our neighborhood brought with it more experiences with classism. A few years after we had settled in, wealthy individuals and property-development companies purchased land in our neighborhood and built homes for middle-class and upper-middle-class families. As more and more families moved into our neighborhood, the local swimming hole gave way to privately owned and commercially developed waterfront properties, and resource-rich public schools were built within walking distance.

By the time I went to high school, the neighborhood transformation was nearly complete, although a few homes with families living in poverty remained (protected by a "grandfather clause"). I attended high school with students whose families had much more material and educational wealth than I had ever seen. My mother and father had eleventh-grade and sixth-grade educations, respectively. Our family did not have opportunities to socialize across class boundaries, and we did not always have a working television, so my exposure to working- and middle-class culture was limited. However, economic class distinctions in the high school were apparent daily. The stigmatization began on Monday morning when I, along with about seven other students of 500, had to stand in line to receive my free-lunch ticket for the week. During the week, peers excluded me from their friendship circles, and teachers excluded me from certain preparations for higher education. Speaking generally from my experience, middle-class families socialized their children to spend time with similar others, and teachers tended to help those students whose families were preparing them for college. The way I talked (for example, "We was goin' to the store and . . .") and where I lived (in a trailer on a dirt road) excluded me from many social and college-preparation activities. Parents, teachers, and guidance counselors did not advise me to take college-prep courses or to pursue other resources that would prepare me for higher education, although I was an honor student from primary through secondary school. Instead, they (my parents, teachers, and guidance counselors) focused on what they viewed as my basic needs, such as food, safety, and completing high school (they knew that my two older brothers had dropped out and were, as we say, "in trouble with the law"). During that time, researchers reported a strong direct effect of social class on university access, regardless of race and gender (Lang, 1985; Thomas, Alexander, & Eckland, 1977).

I graduated from high school after completing my third year of studies. At 17 and not "culturally" prepared for college (for example, I had not taken the SAT, and I did not understand the process of seeking college admission), I enrolled in basic courses at a community college. To support myself, I worked full time operating a check-sorting machine at a bank from midnight to 8:00 A.M.

Through meeting other employees who had been called in to fix problems, I learned about and was interested in becoming a computer programmer. My interest was mostly in the money and the hours—programmers were well paid, worked "eight to five," and were on call occasionally. But the only viable option to career development while supporting myself was to join the military, or so it seemed at the time. I reasoned that in the U.S. military service, food and shelter would be provided, I would have work and income, physical exercise (i.e., I would not have to pay member fees to go to a gym); and I could get a college education (at the time, TV advertisements often highlighted that joining the military was a way to get a college degree as well as to "see the world"). After visiting a recruiter and scoring well on exams, I was selected and encouraged to choose between the Navy and the Air Force. I wrote my employment letter of resignation and met with my supervisor.

After discussing with my supervisor my reasons for wanting to quit and join the military service, he suggested he tear up my resignation letter and create a position for me as a computer-programmer trainee. I agreed. I continued to work at the same place, transferred to the day shift, and sporadically attended community colleges part time. One year later, I moved to a city two hours away to live with a partner and obtained a computer-programmer job at another bank. I enrolled in a two-year college and completed an associate's degree in liberal arts six years after graduating from high school.

FORAY INTO MIDDLE CLASS

Several relocations and relationships later, I was living in a different state working as a computer programmer for a computer hardware manufacturer. I applied for positions as a programmer in the oil and gas industry but was not hired because I did not have a four-year university degree. My partner at the time respected my intellect in spite of my not having a degree, and encouraged me to become my own boss. He taught me the basics of starting a business. With only $500 capital, which I used to incorporate, I founded a computer consulting company and subcontracted myself to a major oil company. In this case, as a business owner, I did not need a pedigree. After a few months, when I was no longer living paycheck-to-paycheck but was one paycheck ahead of my bills, I used my income to hire another employee. Repeating this method of building the business, within five years my company had 12 employees.

During the first three years of being the janitor, bookkeeper, employee working on client sites, and president of my company, I focused on garnering material symbols of middle-class culture, such as driving nice cars, wearing a designer wardrobe, dining out, buying music, and traveling. But I did not simultaneously pursue further education.

Although I had obtained, but not secured, many middle-class markings, I felt a deep emptiness inside whenever someone asked me what university I attended. When I told them I did not have a degree, my coworkers at client sites and my employees paid me (seeming) compliments such as "Wow! You started and run your own business without having a degree?" It was expected that my not being university educated meant that I was somehow less capable. In a more prestigious social circle, I dined with other entrepreneurs and adults who had trust funds and raised money for worthy causes. I had never heard of a trust fund before moving in the oil and gas social circle. I dated within this group of friends and at least twice men broke off their relationships with me very soon after they learned that I was not "born with a silver spoon in my mouth." A kind friend explained this point to me because it was the first time I remember hearing that expression, and I did not know what it meant. Other men were wiser, so to speak, and flirted, learned my background, and did not pursue me further. One potential suitor told his sister that it was okay for me to be a friend of the family and perhaps even charitable of them to be kind to me, but that he would never "date" me, given my family background. I began to realize how my past socio-economic standing limited my intimate life as well as my educational, professional, and social life. Again, I felt a need to hide my background to be included or to participate more fully in my current seeming peer groups, which I've since learned is common among us folks with a history of lesser economic means (Granfield, 1991). Consequently, I simultaneously enjoyed the status of being a successful entrepreneur without a four-year degree and suffered the stigma of not being formally educated nor having a middle-class or better family background.

I wanted a degree to remove stigma, but I also wanted it so I could participate in conversations about university life and for its intrinsic qualities. I longed for a traditional university experience (for example, living on campus, attending classes, reading, spending endless hours in the library, and, importantly, not having to work), which I had heard in retrospective accounts within my social circle of the time. I realized that a traditional experience was not possible given my accidents of life history—in this case, age and circumstances—(for more information on how contexts shape choices, see Sloan, 1996), so I continued working full time and enrolled in a four-year university to complete a bachelor's degree. Sixteen years after graduating from high school, I graduated with a four-year university degree with a major in psychology and a minor in computer science, having decided that a computer-related degree would not change my income potential as a business owner. It was during those final two years of undergraduate work that I learned enough about the system of higher education (for example, student loans, mentoring, and letters of recommendation) to dream and to pursue the dream of living a scholar's life.

SIMULTANEOUSLY OPPRESSED AND OPPRESSOR

Backing up a bit, beginning in high school, I became aware of class markers and began hiding my inherited class and pursuing middle-class symbols such as speaking Standard English (see also Dews & Law, 1995), wearing classic clothes, and obtaining a formal education (Granfield, 1991). I operated mostly under the model of assimilation (Berry, Poortinga, Segall, & Dasen, 1992)—that is, the more one looks and acts like a person from the middle class, the more access one gains to the middle class.

Occasionally, throughout the years, folks questioned me in ways that seemed like tests of my authenticity as a "middle-class" person. However, the question that most frightened me was the one listed on several graduate-school applications: Please describe your background and discuss any adversity you have had to overcome. I panicked, but was cognizant enough to seek advice from an uncommon mentor, Tod S. Sloan, who helped me to see the connection between my personal experiences of oppression and my professional interest in using psychology for liberation. He also provided some of the socialization for higher education (for example, criteria for selecting graduate programs, strengthening an application) and helped me to tell my personal story in a way that would be acceptable to the academic audience. In graduate school applications, I made what I recall as my first, nonapologetic public disclosure of the circumstances of my childhood. I explained how those experiences contributed to the development of my sensitivity to the issues reflected in my interest in community psychology, a discipline dedicated to "liberating oppressed peoples."

Later, through graduate study and my postdoctoral fellowship, mentors gave me varying and sometimes conflicting advice on this issue of class disclosure. I wondered to myself whether they would give the same advice to my colleagues about race, ethnicity, or sexual orientation. I began to realize that my questions about if, when, how, to whom, and why to disclose my class background would continually surface, and that the consequences of that disclosure would often be unclear. I also noted that my middle-class peers do not carry this burden. A few scenarios illustrate this point.

During my third year of graduate studies, I worked on a research project, conducting a process evaluation of a local, community-based career and learning resource center. One objective of the center was to facilitate women's work and movement from unemployment and underemployment to living-wage jobs (Loomis et al., 2003). My childhood experiences, my passionate concern and respect for the hardships of poverty, my care surrounding issues of women's poverty, and an opportunity to grow professionally all had attracted me to the research project.

Our research team leader built a diverse team of women who differed by ethnicity, race, age, religious background, educational background, sexual orientation, and years of study. Obviously, not all these categories are visible, so information about members' identification with one or more groups was not necessarily common knowledge. One afternoon, the team leader talked about her recent recruitment of another research team member, noting how this new member was similar to an existing member because both had attended prestigious, private high schools that developed intellectual prowess. My jealousy of those who enjoyed the benefits of parochial education and the subsequent favoritism that often followed them into higher education surfaced. In spite of, or perhaps because of, previously being oppressed by the act of "classism favoritism" based on educational privileges, I oppressed another woman on the team on similar grounds by criticizing her writing abilities and implying that she had not overcome her "working-class language skills." Retrospectively, I see how my access to at least some language instruction on Standard English, as well as my independent study of "middle-classness," provided me a level of privilege. Naively, I simultaneously was the oppressed and the privileged oppressor.

On another occasion, while we were discussing research-interview transcripts, one team member made a pejorative, stereotypical remark something like "that's the way poor people think." I was incensed although unaware of the depth of my anger until I analyzed my desire to get back at her because she was one of "them"—the middle- or upper-middle-class oppressors. First, I felt personally affronted, because in my mind I often identify with being a poor person—or, more accurately, one who lives in poor circumstances. Second, I thought I was the "classism police" and that a comment like that was cause for citation. I was determined to raise class consciousness among my colleagues at all costs, even at the cost of outing myself as a product of poverty. I said something like "Oh really?" and asked further questions, in an effort to reveal others' underlying assumptions (for example, "Poor women have children as a way of generating income," and "Poor women are not smart enough to know . . ."). From this exchange and other similar ones, I was dubbed the "class expert" in particular and the "diversity expert" in general. I proudly wore the badge and enjoyed respect from team members for what seemed like the first time. I felt as though I was finally the one with the privileged knowledge. It is only in retrospect that I see the conundrum of my being "the class expert." My placement in a position as expert on classism was an act of classism. That is, team members tended to defer to me because of my class background. My voice became privileged. This dynamic is a problem because the diversity and voices of "outgroups" is lost when one person appoints another as "the voice" of those who are Black, gay or lesbian, women, or poor.

To further complicate the class issues on the research team, each of us wrote a brief biography that provided our individual and collective standpoint as researchers. Through personal reflection and graduate education, I came to value the subjective aspects of the research process that included self-disclosure of researchers' standpoints (Reay, 1996). In my personal experience of this process, however, I became aware that asking someone for her or his standpoint might sometimes be a classist act. The form of the request (for example, orally, in writing, confidence, or anonymously) for this type of information is another way that standpoint determination is classist. Thus, the thought of submitting my biography to all of my colleagues—particularly those who marginalized me because of my class—was not a welcome thought. Even though they had some idea of my roots, I did not want to explicitly describe my background in this particular context with all the individuals on the team. Not without self-incrimination, I spoke up and asked that one person collect our biographies and write the method section describing the researchers in a way that our identities would remain somewhat anonymous, at least to our reading audience.

CONCLUSIONS AND LESSONS LEARNED

This narrative highlights some of the unintentional consequences of classism and provides insight into professional and personal struggles and triumphs I encountered from such experiences. The early acts of oppression related to my socioeconomic circumstances were often subtle and largely unnoticed by me. As I progressed from childhood to adulthood, these indicators became more obvious and hurtful. By adulthood, I had learned to hide some of my class markers to avoid being a subject of oppression (similar to Carolyn Leste Law, in Dews & Law, 1995). Instances of class oppression often go unnoticed by me until someone else points out these transgressions. My own lack of awareness of personal acts of classism is in part a residual effect, or artifact, of class socialization within the poverty class. We are socialized to believe that we are not oppressed by others. It also reflects my present position as more a part of the middle-class culture.

Biases in my thinking contribute to professional and personal behaviors that perpetuate classism. Working through the process of developing personal and professional identities that acknowledge the issues associated with my past and present access to resources is a continuous exercise. A central issue in this process is asking and answering the question "What are the consequences of showing my class?" This question is multifaceted in that it brings to the surface other questions, such as, "Should I, a seemingly middle-class professional with roots in poverty, disclose my socioeconomic background?" and "If so, to whom, when, how, and under what circumstances do I disclose?"

Like a few others fortunate to experience some degree of social mobility, I face both oppression and privilege. Oppression, in its most obvious form, most often occurred at times when I did not hide or could not hide my class background. Alternatively, privileges came most often when others perceived me as a middle-class person, perhaps because I consciously, or unconsciously, presented myself as middle class, or the interactions provided incomplete class clues. There were times when I received the unearned privileges associated with being, or presenting, middle class, and times when I was oppressed because of acts of classism when I was designated or self-ordained as the oracle of a particular socioeconomic class. Privilege and oppression coexist.

Recently, I decided that one of my biggest professional challenges is the personal struggle of constantly evaluating and reevaluating the circumstances under which to include or exclude my class experiences—including contributing to this book. Paradoxically, I believe that my greatest triumph is that I continue to struggle with these issues. In conclusion, I suggest that professionals carefully consider the context and the consequences of disclosing, or asking another to disclose, one's class background (see also Hoyt, 1999). It is often difficult to assess the effects of disclosure. But simultaneously, we have a responsibility to challenge and confront classism by having or not having information about an individual's socioeconomic class status and by using or not using that information to appropriately circumvent its perpetuation.

DISCUSSION QUESTIONS

1. In what ways are your childhood circumstances similar to and different from the author's?

2. Contrast the author's report of material and educational resources to your own understanding of "working-class" resources.

3. To broaden the classism framework, consider ways social categories interact. For example, reflect on what you learned about the author. What is her ethnicity? What is her sexual orientation? Is she faced with disabilities? Which if any of these characteristics did you assume? Were you right?

4. Thinking specifically about the lack of preparation for higher education, how might the author's experiences have differed if she were Asian?

5. The author writes that she often identifies as a person living in poor circumstances, even though she no longer does. How does identifying with "the poor" affect professional interactions?

6. How did the author approach consciousness-raising about social class? How do you do it? What are some other strategies that might be helpful?

7. Consider the roles of oppressed and oppressor. The author tells us about being oppressed in her personal life, particularly as a child and young woman, and being both oppressed and the oppressor in her professional life. How might she avoid oppressing others (for example, should she not disclose personal experiences)?

REFERENCES

Berry, J. W., Poortinga, Y. H., Segall, M. H., & Dasen, P. R. (1992). *Cross-cultural psychology: Research and applications*. Cambridge: Cambridge University Press.

Dews, C. L. B. & Law, C. L. (Eds.). (1995). *This fine place so far away from home: Voices of academics from the working class*. Philadelphia: Temple University Press.

Fussell, P. (1992). *Class: A guide through the American status system*. New York: Simon & Schuster.

Granfield, R. (1991). Making it by faking it: Working-class students in an elite academic environment, *Journal of Contemporary Ethnography Special Issue: Stigma and Social Interaction*, *20*(3), 331–351.

Hoyt, S. K. (1999). Mentoring with class: Connections between social class and developmental relationships in the academy. In A. J. Murrell and F. J. Crosby, (Eds). *Mentoring dilemmas: Developmental relationships within multicultural organizations* (pp. 189–210). Mahwah, NJ: Lawrence Erlbaum Associates, Publishers.

Lang, D. (1985). Stratification and professional education within the academic hierarchy, *Journal of Research & Development in Education, 19*(1), 10–20.

Loomis, C., Brodsky, A. E., Arteaga, S., Benhorin, R., Rogers-Senuta, K., Marx, C., & McLaughlin, P. (2003). What works in adult educational and employment training? Case study of a community-based program for women, *Journal of Community Practice, 11,* 27–45.

Reay, D. (1996). Dealing with difficult differences: Reflexivity and social class in feminist research, *Feminism & Psychology, 6*(3), 443–456.

Sloan, T. S. (1996). *Life Choices: Understanding Dilemmas and Decisions.* Boulder, CO, Westview Press.

Storck (2002). 'Reality' or 'illusion'?: Five things of interest about social class as a large group, *Group Analysis, 35*(3), 351–366.

Thomas, G. E., Alexander, K. L. & Eckland, B. K. (1977). *Access to higher education: How important are race, sex, social class and academic credentials for college access?* Baltimore, Maryland: Johns Hopkins University Center for Social Organization of Schools.

Tokarczyk, M. M. & Fay, E. A. (Eds.). (1993). *Working-class women in the academy: Laborers in the knowledge factory.* Amherst, MA: University of Massachusetts Press.

AUTHOR'S NOTE

I thank my family for the wealth of experiences that enriched my life, in spite of (and because of) our circumstances. I acknowledge that my debt to Tod S. Sloan for his ongoing contribution to our dialogue on oppression cannot be repaid, but I am grateful. Also, I thank Keith Humphreys and Tod Sloan for their feedback on early drafts of this chapter. Support for preparation comes from the Department of Veterans Affairs Office of Academic Affairs and Health Services Research and Development Service.

6

✷

Seeing Through Another Lens

KAYING LO

I am a Hmong woman born in Thailand and raised in the United States. My family came to America as refugees when I was three years old. I am bilingual in Hmong and English. I have a master's degree in marriage and family therapy and practice in a nonprofit mental health organization. It is my hope to continue my education after a few more years of doing therapy. Ultimately, I would like to open a private practice and teach. As a woman of color and the daughter of refugee Hmong parents, I am continuously balancing the demands of my culture with mainstream expectations.

UNDERSTANDING AND EXPERIENCING
PRIVILEGE: CRITICAL INCIDENTS

I was invited to a birthday party for a close acquaintance of a friend, Susan. (Pseudonyms have been used to protect the privacy of all individuals involved.) When I agreed to attend, my assumption was that this would be a typical college party with loud music, drinking, smoking, and socializing. However, when I arrived with my partner, I was shocked to find that almost everyone had a disability and was in a wheelchair. The only people without physical disabilities at this party were Susan, my partner, and I. Due to my limited experiences with people with disabilities, it had never occurred to me that they could hold the same type of parties as everyone else.

When my partner and I first entered the party, I felt awkward in trying to maneuver through all the people in wheelchairs to find a place to sit. As Susan introduced us to everyone, I became consciously aware that I had inappropriate ideas about what was acceptable behavior for interacting with people who have disabilities. I kept reminding myself not to stare or say anything that might be perceived as

49

offensive regarding individuals with disabilities and noticeable physical differences. My fixation with acting appropriately may have come across as rude because I did not make much eye contact with the people to whom I was being introduced.

Tim, a man who was a quadriplegic, was sitting next to me. He called a friend over to help him light a cigarette and hold it in his mouth. Their interaction was natural, but I found I felt protective of Tim. Inside, I ignorantly thought *your body is under physical strain already, and smoking will only make it harder.* This was the same thought I had when everyone started drinking.

It was difficult for me to view the people at the party as physically capable or healthy because of their disabilities. I became aware that I felt overly protective of them. For example, when Tammy wanted to go to the bathroom and had to manipulate her wheelchair down a small, cluttered hallway, I was worried that she might have a hard time. I had a compelling desire to get up and help her. When I saw that she creatively maneuvered her way to the bathroom, I felt foolish for not having enough faith in her capabilities to deal with such a minuscule task, a task that she undoubtedly dealt with daily.

During the course of the evening, everyone had consumed a large quantity of alcohol, and Tom wanted to impress all of us. He gracefully leaped out of his wheelchair to the center of the room, where he did a handstand. His performance was astonishing, and it shocked me. Despite his flawless efforts, I kept thinking that maybe someone should have assisted him in case he could not do it. I am ashamed to say this thought stemmed from my foolish assumption that a person with disabilities is completely dependent and helpless without his or her wheelchair.

Strauss and Quinn as cited in Pengra (2000) stated that some specific schemas (for example, how women should act, how people with mental retardation should be treated, what behavior is appropriate in the workplace) affect our perceptions and subsequent behaviors in terms of what to notice and how to act. These schemata provide the broad themes around which a person's own actions are organized and the actions of others are judged (Strauss & Quinn as cited in Pengra, 2000). Seeing others through these schemata then guides the analyses of and responses to situations and other people. For example, a schema about certain physical characteristics identifies some people as less valued. Therefore, it is probable that those characteristics will be noticed. In my ignorance, I failed to recognize at the party that the wheelchair is only a tool, and it does not define the person who uses it. Just like everyone else, people with disabilities are whole individuals, with or without their wheelchairs.

At one point during the evening of the party, I had a conversation with Tara, who informed me of her personal struggles with being labeled "disabled." She stated that many people do not treat her as a valued individual, instead seeming to focus only on her disability. In Tara's process of coming to understand her position as a woman with a disability, she told me that she has acknowledged and coped with stereotypes by not allowing society's misconceptions to affect her self-esteem and personal worth. One of Tara's fears was being a burden to others simply because she uses a wheelchair. Like most people, she also expressed wanting to be loved, accepted, and valued.

After my conversation with Tara, I gained a new understanding of how issues of privilege and oppression are comparable for people with disabilities and people of color. Yet, I also understand how these issues are not the same, and how they should not be compared. I also gained an understanding of how my dominant culture status (able-bodied) automatically puts me in the category of privileged. In my role as a member of the privileged group, I inadvertently participated in stereotypical thinking and behavior. My experience at this party shows me that although I might be sensitive to discriminatory or oppressive issues that affect me as a woman of color, I am often unaware of similar issues that plague others.

In another situation in which I recognized my privilege, I was invited to a holiday dinner with many of the same individuals who attended the aforementioned party. When we arrived at the restaurant, Todd, the coordinator of the event, went to inform the host about the number of people in our party. The host was conversing with Todd about accommodations when I walked over to inquire about the waiting time. Immediately after I walked over, the host shifted his attention and questions from Todd, who was in a wheelchair, to me. The host attempted to set up arrangements with me, overlooking Todd, even though he was in front of me and had been dealing with the situation. Shortly after I noticed this, I indicated that I was only a guest and that Todd could answer his questions more accurately.

In my life, I have experienced both privilege and oppression. The holiday dinner scenario put me in a position of privilege in relation to Todd. The host presumed that I had knowledge and authority over our dinner plans because I did not have a visible disability. I did not earn the position of privilege; rather, it was offered to me regardless of its validity. In my interactions involving people with disabilities, I have experienced unearned power and advantage, and I have seen what being in a privileged position is like. I did not have to demand or work for respect; rather, it was simply given to me because I did not have a physical disability.

In contrasting situations, my partner and I have gone to restaurants, and he was given respect and authority because he is a Caucasian male and I am a woman of color. These discriminatory acts, whether conscious or unconscious, send messages of incompetence, dishonor, and irresponsibility regardless of merit and provoke in me feelings of anger and discouragement. I imagine that Todd, Tara, and others experience similar emotions when they are overlooked, disregarded, or patronized.

CONCLUSIONS AND LESSONS LEARNED

To understand the consequences of labeling, in comparing interracial relationships to those between able-bodied and people with disabilities, Liachowitz (1988) discussed Gordon Allport's classic study of prejudice. Several writers have used the concept of "stigma" to explain responses, both to racial and physical differences. There are clear similarities between biased responses to people with disabilities and to people of color. First, most people who diverge from either racial or physical norms share the problem of evoking unpredictable, but unusually negative, responses from the majority populations. Second, whether based on biological ascription or social attribution, minority groups often face a common personal and political dilemma. Third, members of both groups are often forced to meet their need for belonging, and their need for personal and political recognition, by establishing or joining groups composed "of their own kind." Many nonmainstream members simply want the same opportunities afforded those ascribed to their mainstream counterparts.

Upon reflection, I realize that the party scenario helped me to begin my process of examining how I stereotype others because I associate myself with being able-bodied. The restaurant scenario increased my sensitivity in recognizing my own privilege. My recognition of how Todd was treated by the restaurant host was largely the result of my own experiences of being treated in a similar manner.

Although I am somewhat embarrassed and angered by these experiences, I am also very grateful for them. These experiences gave me the opportunity to gain insight into myself and refute my assumptions about the potential of people with disabilities. However, I did come to realize that one of my initial assumptions was true: It was indeed a typical college party, complete with loud music, drinking, smoking, and socializing.

DISCUSSION QUESTIONS

1. What physical characteristics and/or social conditions influence the distribution of privilege in America?

2. How is individual privilege defined? What does it mean to have privilege?

3. Can someone gain or lose privilege in our society?

4. Can you list at least one situation in which you were automatically given privilege over someone else? Were you aware of your privileged status? If so, did you address the situation?

5. What can one do to become more aware or sensitive to the experiences of how privilege affects different groups of people?

6. You are at the grocery checkout lane and you witness a situation in which a non-English-speaking person is struggling to find the appropriate amount for payment. The cashier repeats this person's total a few times as the person continues to count out dollar bills. The line is moderately busy, and you are next. You are unable to speak the same language as the non-English-speaking person. Would you interfere with this situation? If so, what would you say? What issues of privilege are happening here?

REFERENCES

Liachowitz, C. (1998). *Disability as a social construct.* Philadelphia: University of Pennsylvania Press.

Pengra, L.M. (2000). *Your values, my values.* Baltimore, MD: Paul H. Brooks Publishing Co., Inc.

7

❋

Dirty Secrets and Unholy Unions

Disability-Based
Oppression and Privilege

PAUL E. PRIESTER

UNDERSTANDING AND EXPERIENCING
PRIVILEGE

I am a 40-year-old, European American, non-physically-disabled, heterosexual male. My awareness of privilege associated with being nondisabled developed through a friendship with Eric. I met Eric, a fellow counselor, when I was working at a community-based substance-abuse treatment center. Eric has a spinal cord injury as a result of a tractor accident when he was a child. Due to his spinal cord injury, Eric uses a wheelchair for transportation. I had, up to the point at which I met Eric, viewed such individuals as "wheelchair-bound;" however, Eric educated me that this view itself is offensive and pejorative. He views his wheelchair as a source of freedom and mobility, not as a deficit. For example, he says that most people are highly dependent on their automobiles for transportation, yet we do not refer to them as "automobile-bound."

Before my discussions with Eric, I had never really analyzed the language our society uses to describe individuals with disabilities. Eric offered me some of his favorite examples—the terms *invalid* or *cripple*—to demonstrate the negative connotations imbedded in our language. These phrases suggest that an individual who uses a wheelchair for transportation purposes is somehow an invalid person, or deformed (as *cripple* would suggest). Later in my rehabilitation counseling education, I would learn that these are excellent examples of the ways in which our society participates in the process of the "deification of normality" (DeLoach & Greer, 1981). That is, a standard is established, based on nondisabled norms, and then any individual who does not "rise" to that standard is seen as deficient, incapable, pathetic, and in need of assistance.

INCREASED AWARENESS OF PRIVILEGE

As I became closer friends with Eric, we began to socialize together outside of work. As a former restaurant worker, I have strong preferences about my choice of restaurants, which resulted in a pattern in our dining. Typically, I would suggest a restaurant, and then Eric would ask, "Is it accessible?" I would ponder the question for awhile and then say, "Yes." When we arrived at the restaurant, we would find obstacles, such as three steps leading to the front door. While there were only three steps, these steps rendered the establishment off limits to a person in a wheelchair. At first, I did not understand Eric's anger and refusal to eat at any of these businesses—until he expressed the sentiment that, in his view, having those three steps was equivalent to having a sign hanging outside that said, "African Americans are not allowed to eat here." Eric felt that he was being excluded in a similar way.

Accessibility issues also affected Eric in his role as a talented billiards player, successful in professional tournaments. Eric often participated in tournaments that were not wheelchair accessible. The accommodation for accessibility that these businesses offered was having two or three bulky bouncers lift and carry Eric up the stairs. Eric found this "accommodation" to be offensive in that it maintains the myth of helplessness and perpetuates dependence on others for participation in daily activities. By spending time with Eric, I have become more aware of how I benefit from the privilege bestowed upon me as a man without a physical disability.

One way in which I personally struggle with my awareness of privilege is that I accept the benefits without questioning the need for change. Each time I enter a restaurant with three stairs before the front door, I am made aware that I am entering a space that is explicitly excluding my friend Eric. This is an uncomfortable awareness, yet I do nothing to challenge the restaurant owner to make changes. The analogy that comes closest to portraying the way I feel is when someone tells me a very salacious and inappropriately intimate piece of information about a third person. Afterward, each time I am in the presence of that third person, I am keenly aware of the information and highly uncomfortable that it was disclosed to me—it is the "dirty secret." My privileged access to a location actively denied to individuals with disabilities is my "dirty secret."

I will admit that, at this point, I do not have the energy or enough of a compelling sense of social justice to demand change in the physical environment to make it accessible to individuals with disabilities. I am presently at a stage at which I continue to learn to challenge my own internal attitudinal barriers. For example, I realize that it is OK for me to feel grateful for my own physical health, but not to do so by thinking, "It could be worse, I could be in a wheelchair." To do this is to prop up my sense of self-worth by standing on the backs of individuals with disabilities. For an empirical example of this same process, see Fein and Spencer (1997). I sometimes feel overwhelmed with knowing that I am at a stage at which my energies are spent changing just my own privileged mindset when there is often a greater need for intervention in the surrounding physical world.

Another incident that brought my relative privilege to awareness was when Eric and his fiancee, who were childhood sweethearts, decided to get married. They were both Roman Catholics and and began the process of arranging for a wedding within the Church. The priest who was guiding them through this process inquired of Eric specifics relating to his spinal cord injury (i.e., at what vertebrae level the trauma had occurred). Later, when they met to complete paperwork, the priest informed them that he was not going to allow the marriage process to proceed within the Church. He went on to explain that the sole purpose of marriage was for procreation, and that he had contacted medical professionals and determined that whether Eric would be able to sire offspring was uncertain, given his spinal-cord injury. This pronouncement caused a fury of outrage from Eric, his fiancée, and their families, but the priest refused to reconsider. They were forced to marry "outside of the Church," which is highly stigmatizing to traditional Catholics.

I had spent considerable time pondering the heterosexual privilege that I have to marry the person of my choice. I think often about how it would be to be gay or lesbian and have this right denied by our society. But I had never thought that this privilege to marry the person of my choice was also potentially denied to Catholic individuals with disabilities. Many heterosexual and nondisabled individuals take this privilege for granted. Indeed, one of the notions that we hold sacrosanct is that we are free to choose whom we will marry. This incident brought to my attention the injustice that exists in our society regarding this privilege.

CONCLUSIONS AND LESSONS UNLEARNED

Much noise has been made by counseling educators to include issues of disability in multicultural counseling training. A recent content analysis estimated that only 28 percent of multicultural counseling course syllabi explicitly address disability as a content area (Priester, 2001). If this consciousness raising is not occurring in the majority of formal multicultural classes, the counseling trainee is compelled to explore these issues independently.

So how can individuals learn about these issues on their own? My suggestion is to explore and challenge your internalized negative stereotypes and then intentionally cultivate personal relationships with individuals with disabilities. It is my opinion that only in the context of an ongoing personal relationship can we learn about how the world is for other people. Similarly, it has been only through my personal, intimate relationships with people of color that I have also come to an awareness of the extent and pervasiveness of racism in our society. Through my relationship with Eric, my eyes were opened to the reality that our society is set up to specifically exclude and devalue individuals with disabilities. The flipside of this awareness is that the world in which I live has specifically been arranged so that I, as a nondisabled individual, am included, invited, and valued at the expense of individuals who are different from me.

I have learned this reality in professional areas of my life, as well. When I first discovered that I was going to be working as a therapist for adolescent sex offenders with developmental disabilities, I had considerable trepidation. The "sex offender" label is not what concerned me because I had been working with similar adolescent clients. Rather, the "developmental disability" label is what caused me to question the job assignment. I thought that it would be terribly boring to do clinical work with individuals with mild mental retardation. My assumption was that a high level of intellect in my clients was required to do effective psychotherapy, and that such a process with adolescents with mild retardation would be tedious and unrewarding. In this situation, I was basing the value that I held of an individual upon his or her relative intelligence.

Our society makes this same value judgment in many subtle and explicit ways. An example of an explicit devaluing of an individual is the use of in vitro amniocentesis tests. Amniocentesis is a procedure in which embryonic fluid is assessed for evidence of chromosomal disorders. The results of this test can suggest whether or not a fetus is likely to have Down's syndrome. When my wife was pregnant with our first child, her physician offered this test to us. The physician's suggestion was that if the fetus has Down's syndrome, we may want to reconsider having the baby and chose to abort the pregnancy. Hypothetically, for each one of us, the fact that in the absence of results suggesting the presence of Down's syndrome, the decision was made that fetal development was allowed to proceed and we were allowed to grow and live is a concrete, explicit example of nondisability privilege.

I was not even aware that I harbored a similar, albeit subtler, form of the same oppressive attitudes related to relative worth based on intellectual ability until after I developed relationships with these aforementioned clients with mild mental retardation. These individuals soon became my favorite group with which to work. I got past my personal barriers and realized these were loving, wonderful kids who deserved respect, and who had much to offer in a relationship. In that clinical situation, I believe that I changed more than my clients as I "unlearned" the lessons I had been taught in our society about individuals with developmental disabilities. For me, this process of "unlearning" starts with my identification of, and then challenging, the negative stereotypes that I hold of individuals with disabilities. If I am lucky, the unlearning process can continue in a personal relationship with an individual who happens to have a disability.

The unlearning process will continue indefinitely as I come to awareness of new ways in which I benefit from unearned privilege. My journey started with awareness of White privilege. Then, I discovered the privilege to which I benefit from not having a physical disability. I have also learned about the subtle ways in which I oppress individuals with developmental disabilities by devaluing them based on their intellectual abilities. And then when I had children, I discovered subtle ways in which I benefit from gender-based privilege (i.e., not "hearing" the baby crying because I know my wife will take care of the problem, or similarly not "smelling" the dirty diaper). Where will my unlearning process take me next? I am starting to explore ways in which I depersonalize individuals based on their social class. For example, when a busboy clears my table at a restaurant, am I appreciating this individual as a complete human being with a family and dreams? Or am I viewing him in a role as a servant?

I experienced this class-based invisibility once in my life. During graduate school, I worked as a waiter to support my family and my studies. At one point, I was working at an upscale, private dining club. One night while working at a private reception at the dining club, I was walking through a room when a wealthy, middle-aged woman in full gown started gesturing at me. As I approached her, she pointed to dirty cocktail glasses on a nearby table and loudly over-enunciated, "*Por favor*" (indicating that she would like me to clear the glasses). I should note that at this dining club I was the only White (Irish and German) waiter. My colleagues were all Latino or Pilipino. In this situation, I was invisible to her. She did not see me as an individual, but in a role, as a servant. Because she was used to interacting with Latino servants, she responded in her stereotypic manner similarly to how I often fail to see the woman checking out my groceries or the janitor in my building. An important component of class-based privilege is having the power to decide who is visible and who is playing a depersonalized role. For my unlearning process to continue, I need to be open to the process, challenge myself, and seek out relationships with individuals who differ from me.

DISCUSSION QUESTIONS

1. You or your partner is pregnant. The doctor tells you the results of your amniocentesis test. Your baby will have Down's syndrome. Do you choose to terminate the pregnancy? Explain? What does this option say about the relative value that is placed on infants based on their intelligence potential? Is this an example of the consequences of deifying normalcy?

2. You are entering a nightclub and see a sign posted that says, "No African Americans Allowed in This Establishment." What do you do?

3. You are entering a nightclub with three high steps outside the door. What do you do? Discuss the similarities and differences in your response to questions 2 and 3.

4. How would you feel if your faith community did not allow you to get married to the person that you love? How does this impact your thoughts on faith communities or states that deny individuals the ability to marry the person that they love based on sexual orientation, intellectual capacity (i.e., mental retardation), or inheritable conditions?

5. Identify a situation in which you benefitted while someone around you was oppressed?

REFERENCES

DeLoach, C., & Greer, B. G. (1981). *Adjustment to severe physical disability*. New York: McGraw-Hill.

Fein, S., & Spencer, S.J. (1997). Prejudice as self-image maintenance: Affirming the self through derogating others, *Journal of Personality and Social Psychology*, *73*, 31–44.

Priester, P. E. (2001, August). An overview of current cross-cultural counseling training practices. In P. E. Priester (Chair), Current practices and innovative approaches to multicultural counseling training. *Symposium conducted at American Psychological Association*, San Francisco, CA.

8

Increasing Awareness of Heterosexism and Homophobia

A Personal and Professional Exploration

ALLISON L. CASHWELL

CRITICAL INCIDENTS THAT INCREASED AWARENESS OF PRIVILEGE

With the exception of my gender, I typify the dominant culture of the United States. I am an English, Irish, Scottish American female, pale White with freckles and red hair. Additionally, I am (relatively) young, Christian, able-bodied, of middle-class socioeconomic status (or at least I was before I went to graduate school!), and, most importantly in this context, heterosexual.

While attending graduate school, I became friends with Linda, a European American, lesbian classmate, my first such close relationship with a woman with a different sexual orientation from my own. As our relationship progressed, I also came to know her partner, Polly, and their young son.

In November, 1998, the city in which we lived would vote on Human Rights Ordinance Number 22, which if passed, would legally prohibit discrimination against citizens based on their sexual orientation. While the original Human Rights Ordinance, including sexual orientation as a basis for discrimination, had been unanimously approved by the City Council on March 3, 1998, constituents of our city successfully petitioned to separate sexual orientation from other forms of discrimination (for example, race, color, creed, gender). Thus, failure to pass Ordinance 22 would make it possible for citizens to continue to legally discriminate against citizens on the basis of their sexual orientation. Hoping to educate others about this important vote, Polly and I decided we would distribute literature door-to-door, encouraging the citizens of our city to vote to approve Human Rights Ordinance Number 22.

It was during this time that Matthew Shepard, a gay, European American male, was brutally beaten and murdered in Wyoming by two males because of his sexual orientation. He died on October 12, 1998. While attending a memorial ceremony that night, surrounded by my friends, allies, and members of the gay, lesbian, bisexual, and transgendered (GLBT) community, I heard sadness, outrage, disbelief, and fear expressed at the fact that something this horrible could happen in the late twentieth century. I will never forget that night, listening to the speeches of faculty, staff, and students, marching *en masse* through town following the memorial service. I was crying, and for the first time in my life, feeling afraid for the lives my friends, Linda and Polly, and for the lives of GLBT Americans everywhere.

After this experience, Polly and I were strengthened in our resolve to convince voters to pass Ordinance 22. We spoke to many, left literature for others, made phone calls, and knocked on many doors. Sadly, despite the public awareness of homophobia and the highly publicized murder of Matthew Shepard, Ordinance 22 did not pass. Linda and Polly told me they feared for their safety now more than ever before and intended to move away from our city when Linda completed her studies. And that is just what they did.

HOMOPHOBIA

Merriam Webster's Collegiate Dictionary defines *homophobia* as an "irrational fear of, aversion to, or discrimination against homosexuality or homosexuals" (p. 556). Because GLBT individuals face discrimination in the United States, many are forced to decide whether they will "come out" or not "pass" as heterosexual. Fonken (1996) states that "the process of coming out [is] rarely a one-time event" (p. 19). Deciding whether to not "pass" as heterosexual or to "come out" could be viewed as the primary issue members of the GLBT co-culture face. Decisions about who to come out to and on what occasions was a constant topic with my lesbian friends and their gay male friends. Linda was out to her peers at school; however, Polly, although she desperately wanted to, had not come out at work, for fear that she would (and could, legally) be fired if she revealed her sexual orientation.

HETEROSEXISM

Neisen (1990) defines heterosexism as "the continued promotion by the major institutions of society of a heterosexual lifestyle while simultaneously subordinating any other lifestyle" (p. 25). This idea of heterosexual privilege is subtle, and less evident than overt homophobia, to many heterosexuals. Before befriending

Linda and Polly, I myself was unaware of the privileges afforded me in this society because I am "straight." When I questioned them about how to increase awareness of heterosexism in our culture, Linda and Polly (and other members of the GLBT community) suggested two cognitive-behavioral changes: 1) use inclusive language—for example, *partner* in lieu of *wife/husband* or *boyfriend/girlfriend*, and 2) do not assume that all new people are straight. I took these suggestions to heart and began to use them, personally as well as professionally.

PROFESSIONAL CONTEXT

I am a Licensed Professional Counselor, a Certified Addictions Counselor, and an Approved Domestic Violence Offender Treatment Provider for the state of Colorado. Since 1998, I have worked predominantly with nonvoluntary clientele, people who are adjudicated through some form of public institution (for example, university disciplinary boards, city and county courts, drugs courts, social services) and are subsequently mandated to attend various types of counseling for educational purposes. The majority of my clients view these requirements not as education but rather as punishment.

Homophobia and heterosexism are two issues I am required by law to address in my work with male, court-ordered, domestic-violence offenders. In working with mostly White, able-bodied, heterosexual offenders, I am met with constant resistance when I present these issues in counseling. To decrease my frustration and increase empathy for my clients, it is helpful for me to recall my own journey toward awareness of heterosexism. Additionally, I use the Key model, created by Scott and Robinson (2001). Based on Helms' (1990) White Racial Identity Development model, the Key model describes five types of males who typify the dominant culture. Type I, Noncontact type, operates on a "fairness principle," which implies that White men want to continue the status quo and are not aware of the need for legal steps to correct discrimination in its myriad forms. Type II, Claustrophobic type, tends to blame members of nondominant cultures (for example, women, people of color, homosexuals) for preventing them from realizing "the American dream." Type III, Conscious Identity type, experiences dissonance between existing belief systems and reality. The Empirical type, Type IV, "recognizes that his privileged existence—earned through no effort of his own—is at the expense of" others who do not belong to the dominant culture (p. 420). Type V, the Optimal type, functions with an awareness of privilege and discrimination, and understands "that survival is assured not by oppressing others but by living peacefully and harmoniously with self and others" (p. 420).

Most of my clients fit squarely into Types I and II of this model. To encourage them to move toward the Conscious Identity type (and beyond) regarding the issues of homophobia and heterosexism, I am reminded of my friends' suggestions for increasing awareness around these issues. I am vigilant in my use of the words "partner" and "significant other" in describing relationships with intimates, and I tell all my court ordered clientele the story of my journey to increased awareness of heterosexism and homophobia vis-à-vis Linda, Polly, and Matthew Shepard.

CONCLUSION

It is my hope that readers of this chapter will come to appreciate personal and professional opportunities and challenges to increasing awareness of heterosexism and homophobia in our society. Using tools such as inclusive language, self-disclosure of personal experiences, identity development models, unconditional positive regard, education around preconceptions and stereotypes, and, most importantly, client empathy, those of us in the helping professions can influence the lives of many who might otherwise never have the opportunity to expand their understanding and acceptance of members of the GLBT community and other nondominant cultures of the United States of America.

DISCUSSION QUESTIONS

1. How do your personal experiences of privilege influence your work in the helping professions?
2. If you typify the dominant culture, discuss which Type within the Key model best suits your awareness at this time. If you are a member of a nondominant co-culture, describe your experience of coexisting with the dominant culture of the United States.
3. How does your personal philosophy or theoretical orientation affect your clients' intercultural communication, understanding, and acceptance?
4. Make a list of tools you can use to increase your clients' awareness of heterosexism and homophobia.
5. Identify any critical incidents in your life that led to the increased awareness of privilege in your culture.
6. Discuss how privilege oftentimes unintentionally excludes members of non-dominant cultures, and describe techniques those in the helping professions can utilize in increasing awareness of privilege in clients and co-workers.
7. How does the use of inclusive language (for example, "partner" instead of "spouse" or "boyfriend/girlfriend") affect your communication in the helping professions? Do you strive to use such language?

CASE SCENARIO

You are a counselor performing group therapy with heterosexual male, court-ordered, domestic-violence offenders. A client reveals to you during his initial interview that, although he offended against a female, he has recently discovered that he is gay. You explain to him that groups are gender and sexual-orientation specific, and that you must refer him to another agency because your agency does not have any gay male groups going at this time. Your client insists that he be allowed to attend the straight male group. Do you allow him to join the group? Why or why not?

REFERENCES

Fonken, L. E. (1996). *A phenomenological study of lesbian faculty experience in institutions of higher education*. Unpublished doctoral dissertation, Colorado State University, Fort Collins, CO.

Helms, J. E. (1990). *Black and white racial identity theory*. Westport, CT: Praeger Press.

Neisen, J. H. (1990). Heterosexism: Redefining homophobia for the 1990's, *Journal of Gay and Lesbian Psychotherapy*, *1*(3), 21–25.

Scott, D. A. & Robinson, T. L. (2001). White male identity development: The key model, *Journal of Counseling and Development*, *79*(3), 415–421.

9

Reflections on Heterosexual Privilege

S. CHERICE SOMMER,
SUZANNE M. WEATHERMAN,
AND DEBORAH L. COX

Heterosexual privilege is accompanied by an assumption of normalcy such that individuals do not realize they have it unless they give it up, either because they can no longer live the lie that they are heterosexual when they are not, or that they decide to become an advocate against heterosexism. People with heterosexual privilege are not presumed to have a sexual identity; they are simply considered normal. People without heterosexual privilege are reduced to only their sexual orientation and all the false stereotypes that go with it (Allen, 1995).

This discussion highlights the personal experiences of two White, lesbian counselors in training and their contemplations of heterosexism and privilege as graduate students in a counselor education program. They reflect upon themselves as both privileged and silenced in relation to their student peers and their community at large. The discussion also incorporates the thoughts of one counselor educator who tells about her own relationship to the issue of heterosexism.

CHERICE: FIRST AUTHOR

I am a European American woman, living in a conservative, Christian, predominantly White, Midwestern environment as a lesbian, and as a partner to an African American woman. When we are together we often experience heterosexist prejudice, while my partner also experiences racism. Separately, we more often experience prejudice through others' unknowing comments and behaviors associated with the assumption of heterosexuality. Assumptions enforce oppression.

CHERICE: "COUNSELOR IN TRAINING"

In one of my classes, a professor related a story of a female client who came to him seeking help. Included in the story was her sexual orientation as a lesbian. She warned the professor throughout the course of therapy never to try to change her in this regard—she was happy with this part of herself, and it was none of his business. Some years later, the client sent a letter to the professor, thanking him for his help. As a final statement, the professor laughed and told the class that the client ended up marrying a man and having children, despite her many warnings to him to steer clear of her sexuality. The class laughed along with him.

After I presented a paper, for different class, on counseling with gay, lesbian, bisexual, and transgender clients, the professor acknowledged the information as both correct and valuable for other students to know. His final statement to the class was that he had never counseled anyone in a situation in which sexual orientation or gender identification was the main issue—and that although it was good to keep these issues in mind, he warned us against putting too much emphasis on the subjects once we were practicing in the field.

After "coming out" in one other class, I was taken aside by a woman who told me she was also a lesbian, but she felt it more appropriate to assess a situation more carefully and consider whether to come out was really important or necessary. She remained silent on the subject throughout the semester and never addressed me on a personal level again.

I was fortunate in yet another class of seven students to be one of two "out" lesbians. On numerous occasions, discussions would turn to our experiences, thoughts, and feelings as lesbian women on various subjects. Once the conversation became "too gay," discomfort and disconnection showed on the faces of other students. A silence would come over the group, and eventually someone would change the subject. I always felt as if we were pushing the envelope of acceptance or overstepping our boundaries when this happened.

CHERICE: REFLECTIONS

As I contemplate the profound issue of heterosexism, my mind wanders to the numerous moments as a graduate student when I have felt my emotions range from uncomfortable to angry. I knew I would face challenges, but I never realized they would be ones of such a personal nature. I have felt the very essence of who

I am becoming, both drawn under a magnifying glass and shoved under the bed. . . . people quietly resisting my experience, my reality; people silently wishing I were not quite so honest about myself. Although I am given verbal permission to express myself and to feel accepted by my classmates and professors, I rarely feel comfortable. I am being encouraged on one hand to speak and reveal myself, and then silenced and pushed back into the sameness of the crowd on the other hand. I am acknowledged, but not visible. I am tolerated and accepted, but not nurtured and encouraged.

Alone, each of these experiences seems small and meaningless. No one has realized the impact of her or his statements. The threads of heterosexism seemed almost invisible at the time. And yet I vividly recall each incident, and more . . . far too many stories to tell.

Many times, I question my experiences. Is that how it really happened?
A constant questioning, evaluating, and sifting of my life story.
The push to identify and fit in with my dominant culture counterparts—
subtle yet overwhelming.

My words represent many other stories, stories that will never be heard, or possibly never even expressed. In this respect, I am validated in my frustration and know that to share such pain is meaningful. If I am not the only one, my voice surely does count. But what if I were the only one? Would it still count? As counselors, doesn't each story we hear become a vehicle by which to connect to individual experiences?

SUZANNE: "I AM"

Because it was expected, I grew up heterosexual in a heterosexual world. I had boyfriends at the expense of my relationship with my girlfriends. I had boyfriends at the expense of my relationship with my sister and my parents. I had boyfriends at the expense of my relationship with my community. I had boyfriends at the expense of my relationship with myself. I was thankful that I was pretty enough to be attractive to the boys because having a boyfriend added interest and value to my identity and allowed me to be accepted as a proper young girl in the 1950s and 1960s.

It is well established that in this country, as we grow up, the idea of heterosexual, romantic love is promoted and advocated through most experience: fairy tales, religious myths, books, television, movies, advertising, news broadcasts, magazines, music, and theatre. Most of us learn from our families, our churches, our schools, our legal systems, our government, and our peers the unpleasant and sometimes intolerable consequences of being different from the heterosexual ideal.

As a young girl, I learned that if I didn't get married and have children, I would not be fulfilled as a woman. I was taught the conflicted message that I must be sexy but also virginal to "catch" a man. My parents stressed the importance of getting an education and even a profession, but their implication was to do these things before I ultimately settled down, got married, and had children.

SUZANNE: "COUNSELOR IN TRAINING"

Toward the end of my master's degree program in counseling, I read Adrienne Rich's (1982) *Compulsory Heterosexuality and Lesbian Experience*. I became interested in Rich's theory that the social requirement to be heterosexual keeps all women dependent on men by denying them the choice to explore and determine the meaning and place of sexuality in their lives. This theory informed my own research on a relatively new construct called heterosexism. After getting my degree, I wondered why I had not heard of heterosexism until I was 48 years old—a full 18 years after I identified as lesbian.

SUZANNE: NAMING THE PRACTICE

"Until we name the practice, give conceptual definition and form to it, illustrate its life over time and in space, those who are its most obvious victims will also not be able to name it or define their experience" (Barry, 1979, p. 100). Heterosexism is usually defined in ways that imply only lesbian, gay, bisexual, transgender, and queer (LGBTQ) individuals experience its negative effects (Fassinger, 1991; MacGillivray, 2000; Neisen, 1990; and Stewart, 1999). My experience of heterosexism compels me to use a much broader and far more inclusive definition: the ideological system that denies, denigrates, and stigmatizes any nonheterosexual form of behavior, identity, relationship, or community (Herek, 1990).

As a result of heterosexism (using this broader definition of it), all relationships except those based on sex between a man and woman, not just LGBTQ relationships, are valued less and often stigmatized by society. Such stigmatization undermines an individual's relationship with anyone and anything other than a romantically based relationship with a person of the other gender. This denigration includes our relationships with friends and acquaintances, with our parents and siblings, with our children, with our higher power(s) of choice, with the earth, and with ourselves.

SUZANNE: REVISITED

I now consider my role models brilliant radical feminists such as Adrienne Rich, bell hooks, Mary Daly, Carter Heyward, and Sarah Lucia Hoagland. These women profoundly suggest that the heterosexual worldview be set aside and that time be taken to consider a view that is not based on limiting, dualistic, hierarchical tenets that oppress women and force both genders to carry out that oppression to their detriment. Such role models entreat us to consider the idea that heterosexual norms are not necessarily normal and inevitable but perhaps unnatural and fraught with emotional and social problems.

What these radical feminists suggest is risky and takes courage. The risk is that of losing privilege. The more "out" I become, the more "vocal feminist advocate" I become, the more prejudice I experience. But even with the stigma of being a feminist lesbian, I'm still pretty high on the social, hierarchal ladder . . . a White, able-bodied American who is well educated and financially secure, and who enjoys family acceptance. Admitting that I use these privileges as convenient excuses to escape and deny what is going on around me is the very thing that humbles me and allows me to see others' oppressions and, maybe more importantly, allows me to put my own oppression in perspective.

If you are a heterosexual or pass as heterosexual, the privilege you enjoy will be hard to surrender. I know this because even though I am a lesbian, when I teach and counsel, I remind myself constantly not to act according to the heterosexual norms that are a part of me: to limit my advice, narrow my vision, and take the accepted path. I push myself to challenge my students' and clients' thoughts about heterosexuality because, until we all do this, no individual or group can truly be free.

DEBORAH, "THE INSTRUCTOR": REFLECTIONS

As a White, heterosexual, middle-class woman, I enjoy many privileges that accompany my statuses in society. I live in two different worlds—the world of dominance, definition, and access that is mine whether I endorse it or not, and the world of ever-increasing discomfort about the roles I'm asked to invalidate or define as "other" by my participation in a patriarchal culture.

In my work as Counseling Psychologist and Counselor Educator, I serve a primarily White/European and Christian graduate student body, one that tends to resist contact with "the other," particularly when that other is thought to represent ideas that conflict with dominant religious values. I teach a course on diversity issues, giving a great deal of attention to the topics of gender and sexual orientation.

I believe it's important for me to help dominant-culture students learn about their heterosexual identities (Worthington, Savoy, Dillon, & Vernaglia, 2002), and grapple with the biases they've learned so that they can meet their clients with respect and nurturance. However, I often hear the question, "Why must we spend so much time [typically three weeks of a semester] dealing with gay issues?" Recently, a student wrote in a reflection paper that she was offended and outraged that I would ask the class to attend a youth meeting at our local GLBTQ community center. Remarks such as "I think we need to focus more on ethnic groups than on gays and lesbians," or "Being gay is a choice, not something a person is born with—so it's not a real culture," toughen my resolve to keep heterosexism in the forefront despite the often angry reactions I encounter among students.

My feelings and responsibilities regarding heterosexism come also from my history. I grew up in a small southern town very rooted in fundamentalist Christian traditions. There were no openly gay or lesbian couples in our community, but we did have a disproportionate number of suicides—many of which I later came to realize were related to the pervasive heterosexism and impossibility of being for individuals who found themselves attracted to people of the same sex. For these people, the life choices were slim: Either live a lie, reject an enormous part of who you are, or accept the surety of denunciation from family, loved ones, church, and in this context, God.

As a young woman witnessing these people's deaths, I had the privilege of considering them "other," "troubled," or "unfortunate," even though I did not know the details of their emotional lives. Now I understand that their despair was in a way connected with my own developmental crises because we all faced the imperative to marry and fit into those narrow roles accepted by our community. In this social sphere, the possibilities for self-expression and fulfillment were constricted for everyone, including me, because the marriage imperative formed the center of our relational world. Every rule and norm related in some way to the urgency for marriage. Roles for women and men were clearly marked out; for those unlucky souls who happened to appear too feminine to be real boys/ men or too masculine to be proper girls/women, blatant social and emotional costs included social ostracism and religious condemnation.

As an illustration, I think of voices. People's voices were expected to fall within a limited range of volume and pitch, given their gender. In particular, women whose voices sounded deeper or whose speech sounded blunter, less apologetic, tended to be viewed with suspicion, labeled "mannish," or simply left out of mainstream social life. Whether or not a person was primarily heterosexual, to have a nonnormative style, sound, or personality rendered her or him an icon for that which had been defined undesirable by the dominant, naming class.

Not until much later, when I was in graduate school and building friendships with people who were openly gay, lesbian, bisexual, and transgendered, did I become aware of my sexual privilege and embark on the discovery of a positive, integrated heterosexual identity. My first encounters with people who were openly gay or lesbian made me squirm with anxiety and disapproval. Talking openly about these feelings with my mentors and new friends gave me the opportunity to become familiar with myself as oppressor—and to begin incorporating a new worldview that could accommodate sexual diversity and, in fact, come to celebrate it.

Sometimes I reflect upon the angst I now experience as students criticize my emphasis on heterosexism, and I ruminate over their concerns and begin to question my motivations for teaching the way I do. Then I realize that the same uncomfortable resistance I'm getting, can be magnified hundreds of times to approximate a sense of what GLBT individuals face in communities like these every day.

For counselor trainees to sharpen their empathic skills, I think they must learn to celebrate the sexual/relational differences among individuals. To do this, they probably need to first deal honestly with sexual privilege. If they are heterosexual, they must come to see themselves as oppressors because of their participation in defining what will be included in—and what will be excluded from—the circle of acceptability.

So for me to teach about heterosexism requires that I not only encourage dialogue between my students and those who differ from them in sexual orientation, but that I also relinquish certain of my privileges as a member of a dominant, defining class. By questioning the marriage imperative and asking others to do the same, I open myself to their criticism and their pain, the pain of letting go of ingrained notions about what is and what should be. By making my classroom language more inclusive (for example, "relationship status"), I shed the protective cloak that endorses heterosexual privilege by defining the norm. By expanding our class discussions of sexuality to include a broader, more complex, and more fluid view of people's relational patterns over a lifetime, I invite people to wonder whether I am ever or was ever attracted to women. What do I give up in this process? Perhaps the false respect of heterosexual people that often comes from assuming we're all insiders, members of a system that calls us superior.

CONCLUSION

Instructors and students are challenged to hear the voices being educated, particularly when those voices represent "the other," and to resist heterosexism in their classrooms and mentoring relationships by promoting honest dialogue. To prepare for this kind of activism, educators may benefit from taking inventory of their unearned sexual privileges and considering which of these they might be willing to forfeit to help their students and communities grow. As examples, instructors can: 1) evaluate the ways in which they present themselves to their students (for example, as "married" versus "partnered"); 2) assess the case examples they use for elements of heterosexism and make changes where needed; and 3) suggest and include texts written by and about GLBT individuals. Activities such as these, although they may appear to be simple, can have a profound and lasting effect on the way a course is received both by GLBT and heterosexual students, through challenging common notions of what is normal and providing new frameworks for understanding sexual difference.

The real acceptance of unique experience, as a valuable and necessary part of student education, informs our training and contextualizes the world in which we work. The visible nurturance of diversity within any program shows its trainees how to accept the worldviews of others, even when those views are very different from the trainees' own.

DISCUSSION QUESTIONS

1. What are the threads of heterosexism in this counselor training program? In other types of programs?
2. What impact does heterosexism have in the lives of heterosexual students? What impact do assumptions of heterosexuality have on GLBTQ students?

3. What social, emotional, and/or professional impact results from relinquishing heterosexual privilege for students? For educators?

4. In what ways could you give up heterosexual privilege? What kind of impact could that have on your teaching, counseling, learning, or social advocacy?

5. Carter Heyward (1989) suggests, "Our sexuality is our desire to participate in making love, making justice in the world; our drive toward one another; our movement in love; our expression of our sense of being bonded together in life and death" (p. 295). If sexuality is more than romantic bonding but encompasses nonsexual relationships with friends, family, community, and world, how can we best encourage our clients and students to seek the more complex meanings of their own sexuality?

6. Try constructing scenarios of interactions between friends of different sexualities and genders. How does heterosexism change the nature of the friendships? How does a nongay male and gay male show affection to each other in a friendship? A lesbian and a nongay male? Two lesbians? Does the intimacy level change? What are the expectations between two nongay women friends versus a nongay woman and man friendship? What about other relationships?

REFERENCES

Allen, K. R. (1995). Opening the classroom closet: Sexual orientation and self-disclosure, *Family Relations*, *44*(2), 136–141.

Barry, K. (1979). *Female sexual slavery*. Englewood Cliffs, NJ: Prentice-Hall, Inc., 100.

Fassinger, R. E. (1991). The hidden minority: Issues and challenges in working with lesbian women and gay men, *Counseling Psychologist*, *19*, 157–176.

Herek, G. M. (1990). The context of anti-gay violence: Notes on cultural and psychological heterosexism, *Journal of Interpersonal Violence*, *5*, 316–333.

Heyward, C. (1989). Sexuality, love, and justice. In J. Plaskow, & C. Christ (Eds.). *Weaving the Visions* (pp. 293–301). San Francisco, CA: Harper.

MacGillivray, I. K. (2000). Education equity for gay, lesbian, bisexual, transgendered, and queer/questioning students, *Education and Urban Society*, *32*(3), 303–324.

Neisen, J. (1990). Heterosexism or homophobia? *Out/Look*, *3*(2), 36.

Rich, A. (1982). *Compulsory heterosexuality and lesbian existence*. Denver, CO: Antelope Press.

Stewart, C. (1999). *Sexually stigmatized communities*. Thousand Oaks, CA: Sage Productions, 221.

Worthington, R. L., Savoy, H. B., Dillon, F. R., & Vernaglia, E. R. (2002). Heterosexual identity development: A multidimensional model of individual and social identity, *The Counseling Psychologist*, *30*(4), 496–531.

10

✳

How I Became a Counseling Professional Lesbian

Privilege and Challenges

JOY S. WHITMAN

INTRODUCTION TO MY PRIVILEGE

I am a lesbian who is educated, middle-class, White, Jewish, and in midlife. I have a doctorate degree in Counseling Psychology, a status respected by my religion and my cultures. It is this privileged identity, being a Counseling Psychologist, I am most aware of as I write this chapter and that has helped me understand my other identities. My journey to understanding each of these identities is layered and though I value each of them, I do so differently. I have listed my identities in order of salience to me around issues of privilege and oppression. They have each allowed me to experience acceptance and rejection in different measure.

My parents were born into working-class families who emigrated from Eastern European countries either as a result of the pogroms in Russia or the threat of annihilation during the Holocaust. It was their heritage to feel persecuted and their goal to ensure their children did not. At the age of 18, I came out to my parents as a lesbian. Unfortunately, their efforts to protect me from the realities of oppression as a Jew would not and did not protect me from the realities of homoprejudice (Logan, 1996) and heterosexism (Morin, 1997).

We lived comfortably in a predominantly Jewish, middle-class neighborhood in New York until I was 12 years old when my father relocated our family of six to Mexico to pursue his dream of becoming a doctor. It was in Mexico that I learned what it meant to have privilege in regard to education, race, and socioeconomic status. The privileges I benefited from while living in New York as an educated, middle-class, White Jew did not protect me from the experiences of being different and seen as suspect in Mexico. I paid attention to how I was watched, followed, and talked about in stores because of my "gringa" status. Patrons assumed I did not speak Spanish and therefore talked about me, in front of me. Our socioeconomic position changed because we became less financially stable while in Mexico and consequently, we returned to the United States. At almost 16 and back in the United States, I learned quickly how to use food stamps and how to navigate the looks from others who eyed my shopping cart at checkout. Trying to fit back into "American" culture seemed to require many possessions that I could not purchase.

Prior to leaving New York and moving to Mexico, I was unaware of the unearned privileges my White skin and middle-class status afforded me. It was clear to me that I had taken my various privileges for granted. I never had to wonder about myself other than to know being Jewish was not the norm in the United States and that the history of persecution my family experienced was part of me. I took for granted my family's financial position, the quality of my education, and the opportunities I had because of it. Living in another country and returning to the United States in a different economic class awakened me to how I had benefited from my identities and at what cost to others. These were strong lessons at a young age and I believe I needed to have that level of intensity to get me out of my middle-class, White comfort zone.

OH, AND LESBIAN TOO

These experiences also prepared me to enter into my next position of oppression. During my senior year of high school, the awareness of being "different" continued to present itself to me. I wrote off the crushes I had on my female best friends as my need to find others with whom I could fit in, but I knew that my attraction to them was more than theirs for me and that my disinterest in boys meant something. It will be forever memorable to me the morning I woke up and told myself, "I am lesbian." I was relieved to finally have the words to describe my feelings. Even though I was aware that this was not a good thing to be in 1979, I was not ashamed. Because of my parents' liberal political and social positions and the education I had been privileged to have, I knew the identity itself was not wrong but that the societal view of it was. Declassification of homosexuality as a mental illness from the *Diagnostic and Statistical Manual* (DSM) had only occurred six years prior to my coming out and it was not until 1987 that it was removed from the DSM as ego-dystonic.

My father, who specialized in psychiatry, also knew that homosexuality had been classified as a mental disorder and acted both as a disappointed parent and an unenlightened psychiatrist when I came out to him. He requested I see a psychiatrist to be sure of my proclaimed sexual identity, and though I agreed, I did so primarily to discuss how to manage the homophobia of my father and that of others. I was aware at age 18 that the reaction of others would not always be favorable and that I would need to educate others to make my life safe. Again, I returned to the security of my privileged educated status to help me navigate the oppression I was experiencing.

COUNSELING PROFESSIONAL LESBIAN

I embarked in college on a trajectory that made being lesbian a profession for me; one I continue today in my clinical work and position as a Counselor Educator. I was the poster child for coming out, moving from Cass's (1979) stage of identity confusion right to identity pride. I found an outlet for my need to educate through the human sexuality courses offered on campus and volunteered to tell my coming out story to hundreds of students whenever I could. I did not want anyone else to be asked to see a psychiatrist or to be rejected because of his or her sexual identity. I experienced this type of rejection from a high school friend after my first semester in college, and though I still was not ashamed of being lesbian, the pain of the rejection fueled my need to educate others. I wanted everyone to know I was lesbian as a way for them to face their own homoprejudice and heterosexism and to explore their reactions based on fear and misinformation.

After my college years, as I integrated this identity into my other identities, I moved in and out of the closet by choosing when and where to come out. I had no outlets to educate others until I entered my master's counseling program. I learned from another student that one of the professors believed the topic of homosexuality (the terminology was still being used then) was "overdone" and therefore would not be addressed in his course on multicultural counseling. When I heard that, I knew I had work to do. I ensured I came out to him and used class assignments to write about issues pertinent to counseling lesbian and gay clients. I thought I would educate this professor and others who read my work. This particular professor was a White Jewish male in a Catholic university, and I used my privileged statuses as an educated White Jewish female to educate him.

My professional lesbian identity was solidified during my doctoral program. I sought out a practicum site where I knew I would be supervised by a psychologist experienced in providing affirmative counseling to lesbian, gay, and bisexual (LGB) clients. I continued to write and study about counseling LGB clients and I chose my dissertation topic to be centered on lesbian identity development. During my last year of education prior to my clinical internship, the Director of the Counseling Psychology program offered me an opportunity that concretized my professional lesbian identity. He asked me to create a master's level counseling course and gave me free reign to create one focused on counseling gay and lesbian clients. He didn't know this, but he helped to heal the wound created in my master's program by the professor who did not acknowledge his own homoprejudice and heterosexism. I began to believe that other counseling professionals were aware of the need to educate counseling students and practitioners about providing affirmative treatment to LGB clients. I was encouraged as well by my dissertation advisor to write an article about the class I created and have it published in a counselor education journal.

I felt validated as a Counseling Psychology professional lesbian and made a career of being one. All of these mentors, the Director of the Counseling Psychology program and my dissertation advisor, were heterosexual allies, and through them, I learned about the privilege of education and the protection the academy could afford me when addressing clinical issues for LGB clients and individuals. I was also aware of the opportunities granted to me because I was lesbian and the elevated status I held as lesbian in a Counseling Psychology program and then in my internship. This previously classified mental disorder had become not only a key to opportunities that fostered my professional career as a Counseling Psychologist but also an asset to others who wanted representation in their clinical sites. *Only a Jew would ask, "Who knew?"*

HOMOPREJUDICE AND HETEROSEXISM
REVISITED

As a Counselor Educator, I continue to write and educate others about providing affirmative treatment to LGB clients. I have had little to deter me from continuing my career as a counseling professional lesbian though I have had some moments of concern. One moment of doubt about the wisdom of making my professional mark in this area of scholarship and practice occurred during my first academic position while attending an American Counseling Association conference when I met with the former professor from my master's program. He wanted to mentor me, one Jew to another, and asked me to reconsider my research as "I did not want to sacrifice my professional advancement or ability to publish by narrowing my focus so early in my career." His homoprejudice and heterosexism were clear to me once again because he had narrowly focused his scholarship and was still respected in the profession. Yet his advice made me pause as he was a seasoned professional who could be in a position to review my work. *Did I need to worry about professionals' homoprejudice?* I had not given this serious consideration until he questioned me. I hesitated in my zeal for just a moment.

My first position as a Counselor Educator at a small regional campus in the Midwest also made me concerned about coming out in classes as lesbian and Jewish. Wondering whether I would get favorable evaluations, a crucial component toward obtaining promotion and tenure, I decided not come out as lesbian until the end of my first semester course on multicultural counseling when it seemed appropriate to do so. Teaching the course was personally challenging for many reasons, but predominantly when I read papers by students expressing their negative beliefs about same-sex attractions prior to my coming out to them. Grading them fairly created an internal battle. I wanted them to freely express themselves to learn, and yet they were talking about me.

When I did come out in class, students commented that they thought I was lesbian because of the considerable amount of work I required and their belief that I had no social life and therefore, time to grade papers. Others thought so because of my shoes! Apparently big black chunky shoes equals lesbian. I wanted to fail them, as it appeared they learned nothing from the course. And yet I knew that we all come to awareness in our own time and that if nothing else, they could no longer say they did not know a lesbian.

At this same university, I had a colleague who thought it endearing to call me his "favorite lesbian." I believe I was the only lesbian he knew and therefore of course was his favorite, but the ease with which he said it in front of others and with the privilege that came with being a heterosexual White male, always made me uncomfortable. He was also tenured and I was not, and I did not feel safe to tell him how offensive his endearing term was to me. I knew he wanted me to see him as "cool" and open to my sexual identity, but he never asked my permission to out me in front of others or to reduce my identity to this one qualifier. Only I had the right to name myself.

I want to offer one last incident which reinforces how far we still need to go in academia around issues of sexual identity. In my next academic position at another university, the marketing department was updating its information about our school of education and soliciting feedback from faculty about the content. I reviewed the material and found no mention of sexual orientation included in the print material list of diverse identities served by our unit. Soon enough, I was called to the Dean's office to meet with someone from public relations to discuss my belief that sexual identity be included. I was told we could not add these words to the list because the sentence contained the word "children" and we were at a Catholic university. Huh? How did any of this justify the omission of sexual identity? I was aware of how the null environment (Fassinger, 1991) impacts invisible identities and thought it my obligation in an institution of higher education to ensure that this invisible identity be made visible. At first I was speechless and unsure how to respond without jeopardizing my tenure prospects or communicating my intolerance for the homoprejudice I was experiencing. At the time, I was president of the LGB counseling division in the American Counseling Association and could not violate my sense of integrity to this organization by backing down. It was not until the person from public relations communicated to the Dean how we did not want to turn potential students away from our unit by omitting these words from our print material that the Dean acquiesced; not because it was the right thing to do, but because it was the lucrative thing to do. I felt assaulted and demoralized having my sexual identity reduced to a financial decision and seeing the Dean's lack of awareness of her heterosexual privilege which permitted her to say "no" to me. This experience was gravely disheartening. The battle was won, but I was scarred.

In spite and because of these experiences, I made a career by being a counseling professional lesbian. In my first academic position I created a mentoring program for LGBT faculty and students on the campus and was even able to teach the course I created on counseling LGB clients. I became nationally involved in the counseling profession's division for LGBT counseling issues and wrote and presented on the subject. Though I am acutely aware of the privilege academia and my education provided me to do so, I am also aware my heterosexual colleagues were not questioned about their narrowly focused scholarship, concerned their high expectations for their students would be attributed to their sexual identity and ostensible abundance of time this identity provided, nor called pet names ascribed to their sexual identity. Heterosexism is a privilege I will never experience.

CONCLUSION AND LESSONS LEARNED

I hope you as readers will take away from this chapter two key issues. First, privilege is elusive and context dependent. All of the identities I spoke of changed when I moved among environments. For example, inside of academia and in my profession of Counseling and Counseling Psychology, my identity as a lesbian now has cache. It opens doors for me professionally such as getting to write this chapter. Yet outside of higher education and the world of counseling, legislation continues to be passed or not regarding my ability to marry, to foster children, to have legal rights with a partner, to be protected from employment discrimination, etc. My educated White middle-class identities do not offer me protection from oppression when it comes to the most intimate aspects of my relational life. I am acutely aware of this and therefore use my status of lesbian in academia to educate others who, hopefully, will change the world outside.

Second, navigating a stigmatized identity can be psychologically taxing. The literature on minority stress for lesbian, gay, and bisexual individuals bears this to be true (Meyer, 2003), yet the transformation of the oppressed identity into a source of strength and personal power is also possible. A recent study by Riddle, Whitman, Rostosky, Olson, and Strong (2008) discussed the positive aspects of being lesbian and gay and found that participants "appreciated that their gay and lesbian identities provided them with insight and awareness, and key tools for making meaning out of one's life and circumstances" (p. 214). I learned this lesson at 18 when I began to transform the rejection I experienced into a source of pride and power through education.

Coming out never ends. Every time I teach beginning counseling students, we participate in an exercise that asks participants to stand if they have ever been a target of or agent contributing to a continuum of experiences. I always stand when I read aloud the statement, "Stand if you have ever been discriminated against because of your sexual orientation." Sometimes I stand alone and sometimes students stand with me. But I always stand and always feel vulnerable when I do. I am aware that the very identity, which opened up doors for me to stand in front of them, also opens up the possibility that I will be discriminated against by one of them. I have received evaluations, though not many, that I talk too much about LGBT people. What those students are not aware of yet is their heterosexual privilege to make this statement; just as it was my Dean's heterosexual privilege to question the inclusion of sexual orientation in publication material representing our school. If more people stood with me, then coming out would be less of an event and less of an opportunity for others to be ignorant of their homoprejudice and heterosexism. For now, however, I am very aware that coming out and labeling myself as lesbian gives me power, pride, and relief from the oppression I feel in many aspects of my life. It also makes my life safer through educating others. Education continues to be my best ally.

DISCUSSION QUESTIONS

1. How do your identities and resulting statuses change depending on the context? How does it affect your belief in yourself and your professional career?

2. How do your various privileged identities intersect and inform one another? How do they conflict?

3. How are you aware of the impact of your own homoprejudice and heterosexism on others? What might be the significant implications and consequences for colleagues and clients?

4. In what way(s) are you privileged by your sexual identity? In what ways are you oppressed? Discuss whether or not a nondominant status can also be a privileged status.

5. How have others tried to "name" you in terms of one of your identities? What was that experience like for you? What did you say or do when this happened?

6. What stereotypes do you hold about people who identify as lesbian, gay, bisexual, or queer? How have you attempted to combat those stereotypes?

REFERENCES

Cass, V. (1979). Homosexual identity formation: A theoretical model. *Journal of Homosexuality*, *4*, 219–235.

Fassinger, R. E. (1991). The hidden minority: Issues and challenges in working with lesbian women and gay men. *Counseling Psychologist*, *19*, 157–176.

Logan, C. (1996). Homophobia? No, homoprejudice. *Journal of Homosexuality*, *31*(3), 31–53.

Meyer, I. H. (2003). Prejudice, social stress, and mental health in lesbian, gay, and bisexual populations: Conceptual issues and research evidence. *Psychological Bulletin*, *129*, 674–697.

Morin, S. E. (1997). Heterosexual bias in psychological research on lesbianism and male homosexuality. *American Psychologist*, *39*, 247–251.

Riggle, E. D. B., Whitman, J. S., Olson, A., Rostosky, S. S., & Strong, S. (2008). The positive aspects of being a lesbian or gay man. *Professional Psychology: Research and Practice*, *39*(2), 210–217.

11

*

"Head Ladies Center for Teacup Chain"

Exploring Cisgender Privilege in a (Predominantly) Gay Male Context

N. EUGENE WALLS AND
KELLY COSTELLO

Marginalized communities and social movements are not without their internal struggles around issues of power, oppression, and privilege (Goodman, 2001; Kendall, 2006). Both the women's (Butler, 2004; Calhoun, 2003) and the LGBTQ (lesbian, gay, bisexual, transgender, and queer) movements, for example, have been critiqued for their privileging of whiteness, middle- and upper-class values, and cisgender (nontransgender) identities (Duggan, 2003; Ferguson, 2006).

In this chapter, we explore our experiences of cisgender privilege within the context of an organization that primarily serves a marginalized community—a gay and lesbian square dance club to which both authors belong. Briefly, cisgender privilege is defined as the unearned advantages that individuals who identify as the gender they were assigned at birth accrue solely due to their cisgender identity. Because one author identifies as transgender and the other as cisgender, we use our differing social locations to interrogate our experiences of the traditionally gendered space of square dancing to illustrate how privilege functions to maintain oppression of trans-identified individuals, while reinforcing cisgender supremacy. While the scholarship on issues of privilege has been expanding (Manglitz, 2003) and has included examinations of different types of privilege (see, for example, Blumenfeld, 2006; Farough, 2003; Pewewardy, 2007); as well as different aspects of teaching about privilege (Anderson & Middleton, 2005; Curry-Stevens, 2007; Walls et al., 2009), the academic literature on cisgender privilege across all of these different arenas is almost nonexistent (Nickels & Seelman, 2009). What does exist has been written primarily by trans-identified activists and published in nonacademic publications (Koyama, 2002; T-Vox, 2009).

We begin the chapter by defining terms as well as providing a brief discussion of square dancing to acquaint the reader with the context about which we write, and follow this discussion by sharing our individual social locations. Next we examine our experiences to illustrate how cisgender privilege functions and end with a discussion of what we have learned and the questions we are still exploring.

AN ACKNOWLEDGMENT

While there is much overlap in the constellation of our identities (male, White, queer/gay—identified), the reality that one of us identifies as transgender and the other as cisgender shaped this interaction from the onset and our different identities are important to acknowledge and interrogate. The social and political risks for writing about cisgender privilege and transgender oppression are different for each of us. Individuals from privileged groups can write about, advocate for, and challenge systems of oppression from which they benefit without being seen as self-serving or biased, while individuals who are oppressed in relation to that same system can be demonized for reporting the same information (Goodman, 2001). In addition, acknowledging a cisgender identity carries minimal risks because publicly being cisgender-identified is not stigmatized; however, making a transgender identity public is a much riskier endeavor (Grossman & D'Augelli, 2006, 2007). Finally, writing about an oppression that one experiences has potential emotional costs as one is once again exposed to the social, political, and emotional violence of that oppression. Prior to the process of writing this manuscript, we discussed and acknowledged these differences, and revisited this discussion numerous times during the development of the chapter.

VERNACULAR AND CONTEXT DEFINITIONS

It is only within the last couple of decades that transgender issues and concerns have gained any traction in the academic literature, and what has traditionally existed has focused on medical and psychological treatment of trans-identified individuals (Factor & Rothblum, 2007).

Trans-identified individuals have, however, been contributing to the knowledge-base regarding gender through writing narratives, zines, blogs, and theorizing about their lived experiences for significantly longer (Buchanan, 2009; Shortandqueer, 2008). Because of this invisibility and marginalization of transgender voices in academic writing, many readers may find themselves unfamiliar with a number of terms we use in this chapter.

We use the term *transgender* within this chapter to refer to individuals whose gender identity differs in some way from the one they were assigned at birth. They may identify and feel internally as the "opposite"[1] sex or identify as another gender altogether, and/or they may feel the gender they were assigned at birth is a misleading, incorrect, or incomplete description of themselves (CAVP, 2007). Some of these individuals may choose hormones, surgery, and/or legal name changes to allow them greater ability to externally express their gender identity. Access to hormones and surgery is, however, class-based and rarely covered by insurance, thus only those with wealth privilege are able to access many such options, should they choose.

By *cisgender*, we mean individuals whose experience of gender is such that their internal sense of their gender matches the one they were assigned at birth (for example, a female-identified individual who was designated as a female at birth). Cisgender individuals' identities, behaviors, and roles are considered "appropriate" for their sex within the society in which they live (Crethar & Vargas, 2007).

As defined above, *cisgender privilege* is the set of unearned advantages that individuals who identify as the gender they were assigned at birth accrue solely due to having a cisgender identity. This set of advantages includes material, political, and social advantages. Some material examples include not having to worry about being fired based on hostile reactions to one's gender identity, and feeling certain that medical insurance will cover most any medical needs. In the political realm, mainstream gay and lesbian organizations are more likely to advocate and prioritize what they deem as civil rights focused on sexual orientation,[2] and one can expect government-issued documents to accurately represent who one is. In the social arena of privileges, cisgender individuals don't live with the fear of being targeted for violence, humiliation, and exclusion based on gender identity, nor do they face interrogation about what their bodies look like. (For a more complete list of cisgender privileges, see T-Vox, 2009.)

THE SQUARE DANCING CONTEXT

By *square dancing* we mean modern Western square dancing (dosado.com, n.d.), something many readers who were raised in the context of United States public schools may remember from middle school physical education classes. Most urban areas in the United States have square dance groups, including at least one LGBTQ club. LGBTQ square dance clubs emerged in the 1970s and now exist in approximately 80 cities (IAGSDC, 2009).

Calls in square dancing are grouped in a series of increasingly difficult and complex sets (mainstream, plus, advanced, and challenge), and were standardized in the 1970s by the International Association of Square Dance Callers (Callerlab, 2008). Part of the title of this chapter, *head ladies center for a teacup chain*, for example, is a 32-beat plus-level call.

Square dance is a highly gendered activity where gender is reinforced by assigning certain roles to specific genders. For example, in most nongay square dancing clubs, men typically lead and women typically follow. Some of the square dance calls are such that "men's" parts are not interchangeable with "women's" parts. In other words, one may very well know how to *weave the ring* as a "man," but not be able to dance the same call as a "woman." In LGBTQ clubs, individuals often do not follow the gender norms when choosing to lead or follow.

This gender-reinforcing pattern in square dancing can be so institutionalized that callers have noted some heterosexual square dance clubs find all-position dancing—an approach that does not follow the strictures of gender-based calling—"undanceable" (Hurst, 2005). The difficulty in dancing all-position style is partly due to differences in executing the call, as mentioned previously, and is further reinforced by both the gendered language of some calls (for example, *ladies center, men sashay*) and the square dance norms that use gendered notation when directing the dancers to execute a certain call (for example, *ladies touch a quarter* when *centers touch a quarter* would result in the same movement). All-position dance calling is much more common in LGBTQ square dance clubs.

SOCIAL LOCATION AND PERSONAL CONTEXTS

Kelly

I am a 28-year-old, White, queer, trans person on the FTM spectrum. I was born and raised in Philadelphia, the only child of divorced parents. I came out as queer during my freshman year of college, but struggled with finding identity labels that fit comfortably. It took several years for me to find the term "queer," a word that gave me flexibility and movement in both my sexuality and gender expression. I graduated from American University with a degree in elementary education and a minor in mathematics.

At the age of 23, I came out as transgender, openly identifying as male to my friends, family, and co-workers. At 24, I began taking testosterone and my physical characteristics began to change such that I am most often now perceived as male.

Since 2004, I have been self-publishing a 'zine series that often focuses on my experiences regarding sexuality and gender identity. I have rarely found media that reflects my experience as a trans person, so it has been important for me to publicly create a counter narrative that disrupts the binaristic gender narrative as well as creates new transnarratives. In line with that, I co-founded the Tranny Roadshow in 2005, a multi-media performance art tour with an all self-identified transgender cast.

I am currently the Director of Advocacy at the Colorado Anti-Violence Program, a statewide organization that works to eliminate violence within and against LGBTQ communities. I have been a member of the Denver-based

LGBTQ square dance club since September of 2008, and currently dance at the plus-level of square dancing.

Eugene

I am a 47-year-old White, gay man who was born in Conway, Arkansas, and assigned a male gender. I was raised in Arkansas in a working class, conservative, Southern Baptist family, attended public schools, and came out as a gay man when I was a senior in high school. I graduated with an undergraduate degree in sociology from the University of Arkansas at Little Rock, a master's degree in Social Work from the University of Texas at Austin, and a master's and doctoral degree in sociology from the University of Notre Dame.

I practiced as a community-based social worker for approximately eight years after my MSW and prior to returning to school for my doctorate. During that time I worked with people with disabilities; homeless men, women, and children; ran a therapeutic foster care agency; and worked part-time as a therapist with a mostly LGBTQ clientele.

I am currently an Assistant Professor at the Graduate School of Social Work at the University of Denver where I teach research methods, multicultural social work practice, and, a course on privilege. My research is focused on three primary areas: risks and resiliency among queer youth and young adults, modern forms of prejudice, and multicultural education. Like Kelly, I am also a plus-level dancer. I have been square dancing since September of 2007.

CISGENDER PRIVILEGE FROM THE INSIDE

Kelly

In 2008, I was invited to attend the open house of the LGBTQ square dance club. I attended with a friend, not really sure what to expect. Within minutes of dancing, I was having a blast. Thoughts of middle school square dancing, where I think I was the only one who enjoyed myself, came flooding back. This time though, I was surrounded by lots of people with smiles on their faces and the excitement was contagious. Before the night ended, I decided that I wanted to begin taking the mainstream class. I had previously wanted to find more settings where I could meet new people and learn new skills. In many ways, at first glance, this seemed like a perfect opportunity.

I showed up, enthusiastic for class every week, but also with some amount of reservation. This was the first time I experienced being surrounded primarily by older, gay, White men.[3] As a transman, when participating in gay spaces, I am very aware of my history of female socialization and am still learning the cultural norms that are assumed and expected in those spaces—some norms which are similar to heterosexual male norms, but others which are unique to gay male culture.

Now that I am primarily perceived as male, when entering new social spaces I am conscious of the fact that many people no longer read me as female, genderqueer, or transgender. I generally surround myself with queer community that celebrates fluidity in gender and sexuality. My experience in gay and lesbian spaces (as opposed to queer spaces) has been much more rigid and I've often encountered ignorance of transgender issues or explicit transphobia. For instance, there have been several occasions where, after telling gay men that I am transgender, they respond, "I don't know what that means" indicating ignorance, or, in an explicit transphobic manner, people *intentionally* using the wrong pronouns.

In most of my life, I am out as transgender because it is personally important to me to stay visible as a transgender person. This isn't to say that I come out to every stranger I meet in passing. On the whole, though, I am consistently out and open about talking about this aspect of my identity. It took me by surprise when I realized that I was making a conscious decision to not out myself in the context of square dancing.

I left square dancing each week, energized about using my body and meeting new people, but struggling with feeling like I had to check my transgender identity at the door. Most of this fear of losing access to this space was self-imposed as I have had past experiences of dynamics shifting once I came out as transgender. I wasn't prepared to lose what I viewed as an exciting new activity and an expanded community, and therefore policed my own behavior and identity disclosure (Foucault, 1975). Still, I found myself wondering when I should come out, in what context, or if it were even relevant. I wasn't particularly avoiding the issue, it just never came up. I know that many people feel entitled to this information and are often upset when they find out after knowing me for a while.

I'm not exactly sure how I was eventually outed, but at some point, I was aware that many people knew I was transgender without my ever telling them. On one hand, it was positive reinforcement that there was no discernible shift in relationships based on this knowledge. On the other hand, a few of the people I know and trust let me know that people were approaching them with inappropriate personal questions about my identity and my body.

Square dancing is a physical activity that includes holding hands and holding one's partner. While I haven't had experience in heterosexual square dancing clubs, I am aware that there is more physical contact in the LGBTQ clubs which have different norms around personal space and physicality (IAGSDC, 2009). Many transgender people have different boundaries around physical contact as our bodies are often sites of victimization and violation. I am constantly aware of the way my body is being perceived, most often visually, but sometimes through physical contact. There have been many times when I wondered if my dance partners perceived any incongruence with what they expected. Only one time have I been asked a direct question about my body after physical contact with a dance partner.

There are times when I'm aware of inconsistencies for what I'm "allowed" to do or how I'm "allowed" to behave with the club. For the most part, the policing that occurs is not brought directly to my attention, but instead I find out about it later. Much of this is rooted in standards of masculinity that are different for me than for cisgender men with whom I dance—even cisgender gay men. Eugene writes below about his own process around my choice to dance in the follow position, which, as mentioned above, is typically the "woman's" role. When we were initially choosing positions to learn, we were told that if we like to twirl, we should be follows. That was all of the information I needed. I did not realize that in my choice of dance part, my performance of masculinity would be up for questioning—even by colleagues who I consider to be allies.

Another clear inconsistency occurred at the graduation for my square dance class. I had sewn a dress from scratch and accessorized with a blue wig, blue eyelashes, petticoat, and stockings. I shaved my beard and knew that many people would not recognize me at first glance. As someone who enjoys drag and costumes in general, I was excited to bring this part of myself into this space. I was even more excited to see, for the first time, the presence of the drag contingent of the club. While I wasn't wearing the club's official drag outfit, I felt more comfortable having other folks join me in drag in the space. After the graduation, one friend in the club let me know that people who know that I'm transgender had a "hard time" with my outfit. Why would I want to be feminine if I wanted everyone to perceive me as male? Interestingly, this was not a question posed for any of the cisgender males wearing dresses.

There has been only one major incident with explicit transphobia where one club member began a conversation by policing the validity of another transgender person's identity.[4] This conversation, while frustrating at the time, escalated further in follow-up conversations. What I found when engaging in a process of accountability, both for this specific member and the club in general, is that there is a general desire to be inclusive, but a lack of knowledge about the best way to move forward. The lack of knowledge exists not only about trans oppression and the lived experience of trans people, but also about how gay and lesbian people embody cisgender privilege and play a role in the marginalization of trans-identified people. This marginalization is further complicated in a recreational setting such as a square dancing club, where one wonders if issues of oppression and privilege should be addressed and how one educates others in an effective way. Like many social settings in my life, being a member of the club presents me with complicated relationships where I am constantly aware of my transgender identity, how my gender influences my interactions, and the ways I call on the allies around me for support.

CISGENDER PRIVILEGE FROM THE OUTSIDE

Eugene

The first incident where I found myself consciously face-to-face with cisgender privilege was not something "out there" in the square dance club, but was rather something inside myself. Such was the case when I found myself surprised that Kelly, upon joining the club, had decided to learn the follow dance position. It took two weeks of me processing my confusion over his decision to follow before it dawned on me that I was clearly speaking from my cisgender privilege. To make it more explicit, let me outline the string of thoughts that led me to this place of confusion. First, I clearly knew from my friendship and conversations with Kelly that he was assigned a female gender at birth, but now identified as male. Second, although our particular square dance club does not solely rely on gender-based teaching of square dance calls, I was clearly conscious that traditionally the lead role is thought of as the "man's" part, and the follow role as the "woman's" part. I then reasoned that Kelly would want to learn the "man's" part so that he could *more convincingly perform the masculinity that was associated with his identity as a male.*

Now this string of thoughts may seem very logical and, of course, at some level it is.[5] However, what makes this line of reasoning problematic is that in the context of LGBTQ square dancing clubs, it is not unusual at all for men to dance the follow part, or for women to dance the lead part. In fact, I myself, dance the follow part. When other *cisgender* men in our club make that choice, I do not question why they would want to learn the follow part. However, in Kelly's case, I did. Cisgender men doing so creates no cognitive or emotional dissonance for me, but when a transman made that same choice, I found myself suddenly having a reaction. Why was it that I—a cisgender man—could learn to follow without my maleness being suspect, but for my friend Kelly this was different? Why did I expect and need him to perform more stringently masculine behaviors? Does his maleness as a transman become somehow suspect?

In this excavation (Kendall, 2001) of my cisgender privilege, there was the expectation that Kelly had to go above and beyond what I expected of cisgender gay men in order to be able to fully claim his maleness. When I first recognized the entitlement that I was carrying about how loose my performance of masculinity could be without my maleness being questioned, I was sickened.

The second incident, or really a string of incidents over a fairly short period of time, came from well-meaning members of the square dance club. The similarity in the incidents is that they are all based on the notion that cisgender people have the right to ask very personal questions about trans folks' identities and bodies. The fact that I was a friend of Kelly and another transman who joined the club and members were asking me questions about the two of them should have been a clue to the members themselves that their questions were problematic. Among other things, I was asked, (a) whether Kelly (who is most often read as male rather than as a transman) is transgender; (b) if Kelly was on hormones or had had "the surgery;"[6] and (c) at what point Kelly—since he identifies as a gay man[7]—tells potential sexual partners about his anatomy. On repeated occasions I had to correct pronouns, even after the member I was correcting had already been repeatedly corrected. Finally, in a social setting at a local bar, I experienced a member sharing information in a very blasé manner about a surgical procedure that one of the transmen had undergone.

A third incident occurred when the square dance club officers were confronted with the transphobic event that Kelly mentions above in his narrative. In the follow-up discussions that ensued, I had to intervene to explain that expecting the transgender members of our club to educate and train our club members on transphobia and cisgender privilege was not appropriate, and is a form of cisgender privilege, in and of itself. This dynamic of privileged people expecting marginalized people to be responsible for educating them on power, oppression, and privilege is, of course, all too common (Goodman, 2001; Kendall, 2006).

While I am fairly knowledgeable about transgender issues from both the standpoint as an academic who is fairly well read and teaches in the area, and as a supporter to the local transgender community, I have no illusions that my work on understanding my own embodiment of cisgender privilege is anywhere near complete. No doubt, I probably fail to recognize and acknowledge my cisgender privilege more often than I actually see it.

CONCLUSIONS AND LESSONS LEARNED

While it is often mistakenly believed that marginalized communities somehow automatically understand oppressions they do not experience because of an empathy that reaches across experiences of marginalization, this is not the case in our lived experiences of our participation in a LGBTQ square dance club. In no way do we believe that this organization is more problematic than most organizations or groups in the LGBTQ community, or, for that matter, most organizations or groups in most marginalized communities. In fact, the groups' explicitly stated commitment to inclusivity across axes of difference situates the group further along the progressive continuum than many other groups who have yet to publicly communicate such a commitment to inclusivity. However, intention to be inclusive is not enough.

Our experiences in the group—of which we are still active and supportive members—demonstrates that the vast majority of problematic interactions are not at the end of the continuum that we would classify as overtly transphobic (although one incident clearly was), but rather fall along the part of the continuum that we would classify as cisgender privilege. These behaviors, regardless of the well-meaning intent of the members who engaged in them, illustrate how members of the LGBQ community often take part in policing gender. By doing so, the system of gender stratification that is oppressive to trans-identified individuals, and ultimately damaging to cisgender people as well gets reinforced (Kendall, 2006).

Within marginalized communities, certain identities continue to be privileged over others, both mirroring and maintaining the hierarchical paradigm that exists outside in the dominant culture. This within-group ranking based on within-group differences illustrates the importance of intersectionality not only in understanding complex social locations, but also in illustrating the role that marginalized others play in reinforcing the stratifying ideologies of the dominant culture.

Of course it is not only the identities of the individuals that are important in the interaction, but also how those identities get read by others. In one incident, Kelly was being misread as a gay man while he identifies as a queer male. Those identity differences are significant and shape experience in fairly significant ways. Likewise, the question arises as to the authenticity of how people are reading Kelly's maleness. Using male pronouns while still viewing him as female or as an "inauthentic" male is still problematic as it privileges one's own view of Kelly's gender over his ability to self-define. The arrogance of privileging one's own definition of marginalized others (persons or communities), rather than trusting that others have more knowledge about their own experience than we do, is of course another hallmark of privilege.

The privileges that we have uncovered are similar to dynamics of privilege as it exists in other communities. They include the sense of entitlement that privileged people often have with regard to very personal knowledge about marginalized others, having higher expectations regarding standards of behavior for marginalized others than for people in the privileged group, and judging behaviors very differently depending on the privileged or marginalized status of the person engaging in the behavior. We also raise the issue of how our different social locations as coauthors potentially have very different consequences. Co-creating across difference can be a powerful way to explore, deconstruct, and challenge issues of privilege, but failure to attend to the potentially differential consequences in that process can just as easily reinforce the power dynamics the co-creators are trying to explore. The relationship between co-authors, the level of trust, and the writing process must attend to differences in power or be suspect.

Throughout the writing of this chapter, we have continually asked ourselves how the process of our joint exploration of our different experiences of oppression and privilege has impacted our friendship. Has it lead us to a deeper and more authentic understanding of one another or has it created distrust and fear as Kelly has been exposed to Eugene's disclosure of his own struggles with cisgender privilege? Was it even appropriate for this interaction to occur across this axis of difference? How is Eugene's vulnerability about his own struggles different from Kelly's vulnerability at being exposed to a broader understanding of the cisgender privilege that is part of the square dance club—a group that is very important to both of us? On an even larger scale, how does reporting our experiences with the square dance club shape our relationships with the club, both from our own internal perceptions and narratives about our participation in the group as well as the groups' reactions to hearing about our experiences?

In relationships across cultural differences, these questions are likely to emerge. What we do with them—whether we ignore them or grapple with them in an honest, vulnerable way—no doubt depends upon the context and history of the relationship. In some situations opening them up may be destructive, while in others the same thing has the potential to lead to deeper and more authentic connections. Regardless of the context and history, however, those questions are still there.

DISCUSSION QUESTIONS

1. What are the myriad ways that cisgender people benefit from cisgender privilege, and how are those benefits related to the costs paid by transgender people?

2. How does one bring up issues of power, oppression, and privilege in the context of social and recreational groups whose primary aims are not "political" or "educational"?

3. How often does the issue of privilege get raised in communities in which you participate that are organized around some aspect of your identity that is

marginalized, both privilege that corresponds to the marginalization the group experiences as well as privilege that some (many?) in your marginalized community might embody?

4. On what cultural axes of differences do people in your marginalized community get unjustly ranked? How do you make those within-group differences and their connected consequences visible?

5. How do you talk about differences with your friends and colleagues who do not share your marginalized or privileged identity? When is it appropriate? When is it not?

ENDNOTES

1. We place opposite in quotes to indicate the problematic nature of viewing gender as an either/or construct.

2. We want to acknowledge that it is not only the rights and needs of transgender folks that get de-prioritized by the mainstream organizations, but also the rights and needs of LGBTQ people of color, LGBTQ people with disabilities, and low-income and working class LGBTQ people, among others.

3. While the Denver-based square dance club includes members of all genders, ages, and sexual orientations, the majority of regularly participating dancers are white gay-identified men from their mid-30s into their 50s.

4. The policing of gender was not in relation to anyone in the square dance club, but rather of a transman who was in the news when he and his partner decided to have children, and they made the decision for him to become pregnant and bear the child.

5. While logical in the academic sense of the word, we want to insure that readers do not confuse this statement with supporting, or condoning cisgender privilege. Many logical inferences—when divorced from issues of power and contexts of social justice values—are highly problematic, even as they are logical.

6. Not an infrequent assumption, this statement is problematic because (a) there are multiple types of surgeries and medical procedures that are options and those options differ for transmen and transwomen; (b) some trans-identified individuals choose not to alter any part of their body; and (c) some individuals choose different combinations of surgical and medical procedures.

7. This question not only misreads Kelly's sexual orientation (queer), but also fails to recognize the same dynamic emerging regardless of the gender/sex of Kelly's potential sexual partners.

REFERENCES

Anderson, S. K., & Middleton, V. A. (Eds.) (2005). *Explorations in privilege, oppression, and diversity*. Belmont, CA: Brooks Cole.

Blumenfeld, W. J. (2006). Christian privilege and the promotion of "secular" and Not-so "secular" mainline Christianity in public schooling and in the larger society. *Equity & Excellence in Education, 39*, 195–210.

Buchanan, R. (2009). Zine Narratives: Subjectivities and Stories of Five Influential Zine Creators. PhD dissertation, Temple University.

Butler, J. (2004). *Undoing gender*. New York: Routledge.

Calhoun, C. (2003). *Feminism, the family, and the politics of the closet: lesbian and gay displacement*. New York: Oxford University Press.

Callerlab. (2008). The history of callerlab. Topeka, KS: International Association of Square Dance Callers. Retrieved June 2, 2009 from http://www.callerlab.org/Aboutcallerlab/Callerlabshistory/tabid/75/default.aspx

Colorado Anti-Violence Program. (2007). *Sex, Gender, and Orientation: Terms and Definitions*. Denver, CO: Colorado Anti-Violence Program.

Crethar, H. C., & Vargas, L. A. (2007). Multicultural intricacies in professional counseling. In J. Gregoire & C. Junger (eds.). *The counselor's companion: What every beginning counselor needs to know*. Mahwah, NJ: Lawrence Erlbaum.

Curry-Stevens, A. (2007). New forms of transformative education: Pedagogy for the privileged. *Journal of Transformative Education, 5*, 33–58.

Dosado.com. (n.d.) *Square dancing history in the U.S.* Retrieved June 5, 2009 from http://www.dosado.com/articles/hist-maca.html

Duggan, L. (2003). *The twilight of equality? Neoliberalism, cultural politics, and the attack on democracy*. Boston, MA: Beacon Press.

Factor, R. J., & Rothblum, E. D. (2007). A study of transgender adults and their non-transgender siblings on demographic characteristics, social support, and experiences of violence. *Journal of LGBT Health Research, 3*, 11–30.

Farough, S. D. (2003). Structural aporias and white masculinities: White men confront the white male privilege critique. *Race, Gender, & Class, 10*, 38–53.

Ferguson, R. A. (2006). Race-ing homonormativity: Citizenship, sociology, and gay identity. In E. P. Johnson & M. G. Henderson (eds.), *Black queer studies* (pp. 52–67). Durham, NC: Duke University Press.

Foucault, Michel (1975). *Discipline and punish: The birth of the prison*, New York: Random House.

Goodman, D. J. (2001). *Promoting diversity and social justice: Educating people from privileged groups*. Thousand Oaks, CA: Sage.

Grossman, A. H., & D'Augelli, A. (2006). Transgender youth: Invisible and vulnerable. *Journal of Homosexuality, 51*, 111–128.

Grossman, A. H. & D'Augelli, A. R. (2007). Transgender youth and life-threatening behaviors. *Suicide and Life Threatening Behavior, 37*, 527–537.

Hurst, A. (2005). My first Callerlab. *The Call Sheet*. Retrieved May 31, 2009 from http://www.Danceinfo.org/articles/firstcl.html

International Association of Gay Square Dance Clubs. (April 9, 2009). *Minutes of the meeting of the 2009 IAGSDC Executive Board*. Washington, DC: IAGSDC.

Kendall, F. E. (2006). *Understanding white privilege: Creating pathways to authentic relationships across race*. New York: Routledge.

Kivel, P. (2004). *You call this a democracy? Who benefits, who pays, and who really decides?* New York: The Apex Press.

Koyama, E. (2002). *Cisexual/ cisgender: Decentralizing the dominant group*. Retrieved June 10, 2009 from http://eminism.org/interchange/2002/20020607-wmstl.html

Manglitz, E. (2003). Challenging white privilege in adult education: A critical review of the literature. *Adult Education Quarterly*, *53*, 119–134.

Nickels, S., & Seelman, K. (2009). Exploring cisgender privilege in social work education: A qualitative approach. Unpublished manuscript.

Pewewardy, N. (2007). *Challenging white privilege: Critical discourse for social work education.* Washington, D.C.: Council on Social Work Education.

Shortandqueer, K. (2008). *Trans(in)formation*, 2nd edition. Available from http://www. shortandqueer.com

T-Vox. (2009). *Cisgender privilege.* Retrieved June 5, 2009 from http://t-vox.org/index. php?Title=Cisgender_Privilege

Walls, N. E., Griffin, R. A., Arnold-Renicker, H., Burson, M., Johnston, L., Moorman, N., Nelsen, J., & Schutte, E. C. (2009). Graduate social work students' learning journey about heterosexual privilege. *Journal of Social Work Education*, *44*, 289–307.

12

✳

Fierce Dyke Caught Doing Husband's Laundry

Marriage—The New Frontier

JESSICA PETTITT

I am a die hard, activist dyke. My former students even went so far as to call me a "Fierce Dyke," a title that I wore with boastful pride in the streets of New York City. It was when I worked professionally as "gay for pay" on a college campus as the point LGBT person for faculty, staff, students, and the surrounding community that I really understood who I am in regards to my sexuality, gender expression, and passion for social justice. Now I bring my "Fierce Dyke" crown to the stage while doing trainings and speaking engagements focusing on LGBT Advocacy and Inclusion. Who knew that from my office swivel chair, I would meet my *husband*? (Boylan, 2009).

I was born and raised in Texas and got out as soon as I could. I didn't understand sex or gender or identity let alone the social construction of these concepts and how they in themselves uphold heterosexism, sexism, and heterophobia. I did know that gays (now I would say Lesbian and Gay men) weren't treated equally and became a loud (and I mean a loud!) ally in middle school and high school. "Why does anyone care what anyone else does romantically or sexually? If consent is given, then it shouldn't be anyone's business," I argued. I continued to question authority on my college campus, an elite private liberal arts school in Arkansas.

"I DO"

While attending graduate school in South Carolina, I researched Ally Identity Development (Wall & Evans, 1991, 2000). I came out as a lesbian in my late twenties; no one was shocked except me. I continued doing LGBT service work which led to a number of typical and atypical lesbian relationships. Like most advocates, I began focusing on the "L" and the "G" of the "LGBT" acronym, but it was lessons from my students that really got me advocating for the bisexual and trans populations. Fluidity of sex and gender made so much sense to me once I understood the terms and applied them to my own life, relationships and identities. The more I understood about gender and sexuality the more freedom I had to express myself. I realized I am attracted to what I like to call "checked masculinity" and he/she/sie are usually wearing a hoodie, carrying a book, wearing glasses, and walking around lost but enjoying the view. My attraction has nothing to do with hormones experienced at puberty or later in life or genitalia. So, one fateful day, before packing up the office and going home to the stereotypical U-Haul girlfriend at home, my appointment walked into my office and changed everything—including my views on marriage forever.

Loren told me that he had started transitioning and had been on hormones for a month or so. He was doing fine, and wanted suggestions on how to edit his name and gender marker on his faculty and student records. Reading him as male, I assumed he was transitioning from male to female; I am sure he was flattered at this gender validation on my part. The direction of Loren's transition is female to male. He is a transman. Motorcycles, Peace Corps stories, home cooked meals, and long dog walks, later, I can confidently say that I married the man of my dreams; dreams I didn't know I had or even wanted to have for that matter.

We got married, legally, in Las Vegas as the true romantics tend to do. Nevada only requires two legal documents of those of the "opposite" sex when applying for a marriage license. He and I plopped our Arizona issued driver's licenses on the counter of the court house, paid our money, and without hesitation, reserve, or even a second glance, we got our marriage license. Somewhere between the woman behind the bulletproof glass at the courthouse and Elvis's stand-in at the Chapel (Elvis had the day off), we marched down a white gauzed aisle and unexpectedly grabbed heterosexual privilege with such gusto that watching the wedding video somewhat saddens me. Neither of us wore political t-shirts or interrupted the service demanding equity for all. I just smiled and cried; I said "I do" and we kissed. I instantly became a certificate carrying member of an institution that is historically based on ownership, sexism, capitalism, dowries, property, enslavement, and other evils that I have spent most of a lifetime fighting against.

IS LANGUAGE AT MY DISPOSAL OR YOURS?

I am troubled now with using the word "partner." Some LGBT folks feel that when an Ally uses the word "partner," they may be forgetting their heterosexual privilege or by saying "husband" or "wife," they are being insensitive and showcasing a socially constructed norm. I find I'm stuck in a contradiction too. What term should I use? I am more comfortable using the word "partner," but I don't want to out my husband for my own identity's benefit. I am growing accustomed to, if not proud of, the fact that I am his wife. I even like that strangers validate my relationship by making comments about my wedding ring. There seems to be a weight given to my relationship that seems to mean that I am a success as a woman in my 30's. One issue with my validation theory is that I also get asked about the inclusion of children. This is a topic that I didn't get asked when open about my committed relationships with women. When I choose to say that Loren and I aren't going to have children, I feel my success as a woman begin to recede a little in others' eyes.

I find that I am comfortable with the word "husband" since I am more comfortable with that gender role in the context of lesbian relationships. Like a discount bra, "wife" doesn't seem to fit (yet). I associate the word "wife" with my Texas upbringing and the expectations placed on a "good woman" that I rejected long before coming out as a lesbian. I remember quietly asking my dyke friends, the ones I could really trust, if it was bad that I liked to do laundry, keep a clean house, cook meals, and pack a healthy lunch. They would be surprised at my domestication, but then that seemed to be ok with both of us—because I certainly was still a dyke. I realized that I could still be accepted as a dyke to my close friends because they didn't see my husband as a straight man.

We don't identify as heterosexual, but *heteroqueer*. Depending on whom I am talking with and the context, I am fluid with my personal identities, respectful of my partner's preferences, and vary the language used to describe the multiple areas of "outness."[1] Because of my attachment to the lesbian and queer community, I find that I am literally heterophobic and have had to really work on the fact that I will be perceived as straight by others. When visiting regular dyke bars, we have been questioned if not warned prior to entry and welcomed in straight venues in a "look how progressive we are at this place" over the top lesbian inclusive language. Neither context feels welcoming to both of us. Transmen and women are stuck between full disclosure and guarded privacy, as are their family members, partners, etc., It seems that when my identity is validated, Loren's isn't. This works both ways.

TRANSITIONING AND TRANSITIONS

Upon the announcement of our marriage or maybe the 48 hour engagement, people were shocked to say the least. I really thought folks were surprised that we would do something so quickly and spontaneously, but it turns out that their reactions were more about sex and gender politics. Where his friends and family,

---

1. I believe this statement to be more true for me than for Loren. He is male, a man, and occasionally may identify as a transman to bring visibility to that community. I am much more fluid in identifying myself, my partner, and/or labeling my relationship with language based on the context of the conversation.

and to a large degree he himself, are dealing with gender validation both legally and socially, I am seen as no longer a part of the lesbian community. Loyalties, respect, friendship, and camaraderie within my lesbian community seem to slip through the hands that at one point were locked with mine in a movement toward equity for all. Luckily, I have my partner's hand as we support each other in our ongoing fight for equity.

Transitioning, much like being lesbian, gay, bisexual, or queer isn't something someone would ordinarily choose in our society. Due to transphobia, homophobia, fear, hate, bias, and other elements instilled in western culture, coming out as well as transitioning is arduous and painstakingly difficult. For some transmen who were once labeled "lesbian" becoming a man is seen as being a traitor; as being disloyal to his feminist roots. I hear people talk about "when butch isn't enough" or even that a transman is "just butch who use couldn't cut it." There was an article recently about butch lesbians transitioning and its impact on the lesbian community (Vitello, 2006). Judith Halberstam's *Female Masculinity* (1998) in her chapter *Transgender Butch: Butch/FTM Border Wars and the Masculine Continuum* adds to the conversation as well.

Just as transmen are sometimes thought of as traitors to lesbianism or womanhood, so too is the "traitor" description leveled at a Fierce Dyke who legally marries a man. I am still the Fierce Dyke that marched in New York. I would think it might even be easy for some to justify my legally marrying a transman as a form of activism being that our union must be recognized in all states, or better yet, as a political loop hole to show how stupid marriage laws are in the first place (Cannon, 2010). However, I am not getting this reaction from others. There is a similar conversation internally too. I find myself financially dependent on a man, compromising, taking his direction, and at times following his lead. This is hard to grapple with personally and even harder when I wouldn't want to be anywhere else.

DISCUSSION QUESTIONS

1. Marriage laws currently address a union between a man and a woman. How is a "man" or a "woman" defined? Who else is limited by these definitions outside of the trans community?

2. Each state has its own process (or lack thereof) for transmen and women to change their names and gender markers on social security cards, state-issued identification cards, birth certificates, and passports. Who develops these processes and systems? Who has access to these systematic changes and who doesn't?

3. What degree of responsibility do either person in this relationship have to fully disclose their identity and that of their partner to their family practitioner, real estate agent, neighbors, co-workers, new friends, etc?

REFERENCES

Boylan, J. F. (2009. March 11). Is my marriage gay? *New York Times*. Retrieved July 27, 2009, http://www.nytimes.com/2009/05/12/opinion/12boylan.html?_r=1

Cannon, L. (2010). Trans-marriage and the unacceptability of same-sex marriage restrictions. In J. Rowan (Ed.). *Social Philosophy Today* (Vol. *25*), Charlottesville, VA: Philosophy Documentation Center.

Halberstam, J. (1998). *Female Masculinity*. Durham and London: Duke University Press.

Vitello, P. (2006. August 20). The trouble when Jane becomes Jack. *New York Times*. Retrieved July 27, 2009, http://www.nytimes.com/2006/08/20/fashion/20gender.html?_r=1

Wall, V. A. & Evans, N. J. (1991). Beyond tolerance: Gays, lesbians and bisexuals on campus. American College Personnel Association, University Press.

Wall, V. A. & Evans, N. J. (2000). Towards acceptance: Sexual orientation issues on campus, American College Personnel Association, University Press.

13

✹

"Men Can't Be Raped"

The Challenge of Sexism in Counseling

HEATHER TREPAL

DESCRIPTION OF CRITICAL INCIDENT

On the college campus where I work, we have an annual rape-prevention program for all first-year students. A peer theatre troupe performs skits related to different rape scenarios (for example, date rape, drug-facilitated rape, female victim-male perpetrator, male victim-female perpetrator), which are followed by a question-and-answer session with the students. During one of these sessions, several of the students, both male and female, strongly argued that a scene in which a male was the victim and a female was the perpetrator was unrealistic. When asked to defend their positions, one student replied, "Everyone knows that men can't be raped."

It has been suggested that gender is a social construction (Mintz & O'Neil, 1990; Thompson, 1995). How we come to view men and women, and how we participate in dialogues about those views, is how others come to construct their ideas of gender. It has also been suggested that gender socialization and sex-role rules have an impact on the issue of rape for both men and women (Pino & Meier, 1999). Statements such as "Men can't be raped" are formed by a social construction of gender that includes specific and limiting sex-role expectations for both men and women. Statements such as "Men can't be raped" are also part of a social construction of gender that has an impact on male survivors' experiences of rape and the meaning that is made from those experiences. Different aspects of gender socialization may impact a person's experience and personal interpretation of rape and healing. For example:

As a woman, I am generally accepted if ...

- I express my anger, fear, or hurt (to a friend or a counselor). In both the college counseling center where I now work and in the rape crisis center, we see far more female clients than male clients, particularly clients with issues involving rape and sexual assault.

- I hear stories about rape that have happened to members of my own sex, in which women are the victims and men are the perpetrators (Groth & Burgess, 1980). For example, television movies about rape frequently involve some variation of the female/victim–male/perpetrator situation.

- I comment on the attractiveness of a member of my own sex and show affection for her without being tormented (Pollack, 1998). Men are often criticized for showing affection for a same-sex friend while women are socially conditioned to show affection to their female friends.

- I enjoy both the physical and emotional components of sex. Haines (1999) states that although many messages about sex are incongruent, women— particularly women survivors—are encouraged to break the myths and restrictions about sexuality,

As a man, I am generally accepted if. ...

- I do not express a variety of emotions, seek help, or tell others (such as a friend or counselor) when I am hurting (Lew, 1988; Pollack, 1998; Thompson, 1995). As a colleague of mine said, "Anger is the default emotion for men—the only emotion they are socially allowed to convey." Another colleague also told me that once, when he was doing a presentation on counseling services, men in the group told him that "counseling was for the weak," and that they were afraid that someone might find out if they went to the campus counseling center. For a man to seek help can take a lot of courage.

- I do not hear stories about rape in which members of my own sex are the victim and not the perpetrator (Groth & Burgess, 1980). For example, sexual-assault presenters inform audiences typically that, although men are also victims/survivors, they will use the pronoun "she" for the sake of ease. By doing so, presenters not only reinforce masculine-sexist stereotypes (for example, men as perpetrators) but also disqualify the experiences of the male survivors in the audience.

- I avoid things that could be associated with femininity. Pollack (1998) has stated that a code that exists for boys, part of which dictates that expressing feelings or emotions and behaviors that could be associated with femininity is "taboo" (p. 24). This situation connects with the point above: Expressing emotions (for example, sadness) and the behaviors associated with these emotions (for example, crying) is socially acceptable for women and not for men.

- I have "fear or hatred" toward nonheterosexuals. Pollack (1998) states that this attitude comes from a combination of gender socialization and misunderstanding about sexuality in general. Many male survivors question the effect of rape on their sexuality (Lew, 1988).

- I enjoy nonrelational sex. Lew (1988) alluded to the fact that men are expected to enjoy sex without the constraints of emotional involvement and to be the aggressors in sexual situations. Sexual healing can be a component of healing from rape. Ideas about sexuality can hinder or help that process.

Many of the issues for male survivors of rape are invisible. Society suggests to men that they (a) be reluctant to seek help, (b) restrict their emotions, (c) engage in competition and aggressive behavior, among other things, and (d) accept gender-specific roles (Thompson, 1995).

REFLECTIONS

Although this is difficult to admit, in the past, I inwardly and unconsciously believed that "men can't be raped." Whenever I worked with a male survivor as a client, I looked for a sign to show that he somehow wanted the sexual activity and that he was not raped. I had unwittingly become part of the problem by somehow convincing myself that men always wanted sex, no matter the circumstances of the encounter. If a male client didn't show any emotion or or didn't cry when discussing his sexual assault, I had to fight off the thought that he must have enjoyed the sex! Given a display of rage, I might have assumed that somehow the male was less responsible for the assault. By believing that my male clients were any more responsible for their rapes and sexual assaults than my female clients, I was truly practicing sexism.

MAKING CHANGES

To overcome my struggles with sexism, I decided to start with self-monitoring. I realized that I did not know a lot about men's issues, so I studied the literature on men and sexual assault. I learned that men do not report rape for many different reasons. Some buy into myths such as (a) all men who get raped are gay, (b) men don't get raped—they are the strong ones, and (c) women cannot rape men—rape is a sexually motivated crime (Lew, 1988). In addition to buying into the myths, men are taught by society that they will be made fun of if they report rape (for example, teasing by male peers, "Hey, *I'd* like to get *raped* by a woman").

Pino and Meier (1999) state that men are far less likely to report a rape or sexual assault when it calls into question their male identity. This has implications for both heterosexual and homosexual men. For example, both heterosexual and homosexual men might begin to question their sexual orientation. While heterosexual men might wonder why they didn't fight back, homosexual men might wonder whether they were being punished for their sexual orientation.

Sue and Sue (1999) have stated that the culturally skilled counselor be (a) aware of his or her own cultural heritage; (b) aware of value differences; (c) aware of biases and values, and the effects they might have on others of a different culture; (d) comfortable with differences; (e) sensitive to circumstances and able to refer clients to counselors of their choice; (f) aware of and acknowledge beliefs, attitudes and feelings that are prejudiced (for example, sexist, racist, anti-Semitic, homophobic, ageist); and (g) engaged in the ongoing process of change. Counselors have a tendency to define gender roles narrowly (for example, crying as weakness for males, anger as pathology for females). By first addressing oneself and examining one's own beliefs, values, assumptions, and biases, and then addressing differences in these perspectives between oneself and one's client in therapy sessions, a counselor is able to work effectively within the *constraints* of a gendered socialization.

In addition, as counselors, by addressing our own beliefs as well as those of our clients, we hope to create space for our clients, both male and female, to develop broader conceptions of masculinity. We, as counselors, can challenge socially and historically constructed views of masculinity and teach our clients to do the same.

CONCLUSION

My male clients have also taught me a lot. For instance, working in a "feminist" organization, I felt free to decorate my office as I chose—with pictures, quotes, and items representing all things feminine and empowering to women. Quite a few men clients informed me that this was not only unsettling to them, but also irresponsible. By decorating with feminine gender objects, I was possibly negating their experiences and not providing empowering models for my male clients. They also suggested incorporating male-centered contexts into our program literature (for example, brochures, advertising) and using nonsexist language.

By examining my attitudes and beliefs about men, and by working with men, I was able to begin to have a dialogue with myself about my work. I concluded that I needed to actively seek out training on men and their issues including men with disabilities, men who are transidentified, gay, or bisexual, and men of various racial, ethnic, and religious backgrounds. In addition to training, I needed to take it upon myself to read about men's issues, talk about men's issues, and write about my work so that I could share ideas and educate others.

DISCUSSION QUESTIONS

I had the privilege of attending a conference presentation about working with male survivors. I am borrowing the following activity, "Attitudes toward working with men" from the presenter, Thomas Neill, MSW, LISW (2001) of the Cleveland Rape Crisis Center.

Close your eyes and think of the following questions:

1. How do you feel about talking to men about their history of sexual assault? Comfortable? Uncomfortable? Indifferent? Really uncomfortable?

2. How comfortable are you discussing sexuality issues with men? Are you comfortable asking men about their sex lives, sexual orientation, and sexual and reproductive health, including use of correct or slang terminology based on the language they use?

3. What comes up for you when a male client expresses strong emotion (for example, anger, rage, sadness)? Do you feel you are less likely to challenge a male client, or possibly likely to try to pacify him, to keep him from "going there"?

4. Does talking to male survivors ever make you revert to thinking about the men in your own life—your father, brothers, partners, friends? Do such discussions make you fear for the safety of other men you know?

5. Are you afraid that seeing men vulnerable and fragile will shatter some of your own societal myths that you uphold for certain men in your life? ("My husband is the rock of the family and I can't imagine him dealing with anything like that.")

6. Do you ever think it must be more difficult physiologically, or physically, for men to be raped than it is for women? Does it seem impossible for men to be raped by women? Does any part of you think that it is easier for a guy if a woman rapes him than if a man does?

7. Why does the notion of a 30-year-old man having sex with a 15-year-old girl nauseate people, while the idea of a 15-year-old boy having sex with a 30-year-old woman is easier to tolerate? Are you one of those people? Do you honestly feel that a 15-year-old girl's experience is more traumatic?

8. When do men push your emotional buttons—both in real life and in direct service work?

9. Do you feel that you are competent to work with male survivors because you are skilled working with female survivors? Do you feel as though gender makes no difference—a survivor is a survivor?

10. What does your staff look like? Are there any men on your staff? Do you actively recruit men as you would any other demographic to ensure a diverse team and promote choice among whom clients can work with?

11. Do you feel that men are equally capable of working with female clients? With female survivors?

12. Do you "own" your biases, assumptions, values, and beliefs around men and discuss them with your supervisor so those biases do not interfere with your work?

Carefully think about and reflect on your answers to the preceding questions. Pay attention to which ones struck a chord with you. Where are your growing edges? Where is the work that you need to do to keep your gender lens from interfering with your valuable clinical work?

REFERENCES

David, D. & Brannon, R. (Eds.). (1976). *The forty-nine percent majority: The male sex role.* Reading, MA: Addison-Wesley.

Erikson, B. M. (1996). Ethical considerations when feminist family therapists treat men. *Journal of Family Psychotherapy,* 7(2), 1–19.

Groth, N. A. & Burgess, A. W. (1980). Male rape: Offenders and victims. *American Journal of Psychiatry,* 137, 806–810.

Haines, S. (1999). *The survivor's guide to sex: How to have an empowered sex life after child sexual abuse.* San Francisco, CA: Cleis Press Inc.

Lew, M. (1988). *Victims no longer.* New York, NY: Harper-Collins Publishers Inc.

Mintz, L. B. & O'Neil, J. M. (1990). Gender roles, sex, and the process of psychotherapy: Many questions and few answers. *Journal of Counseling and Development,* 68, 381–387.

Neill, Thomas (2001, October). Treating male survivors of sexual assault. Paper presented at the meeting of the Ohio Coalition on Sexual Assault, Columbus, Ohio.

Pino, N. W. & Meier, R. F. (1999). Gender differences in rape reporting. *Sex Roles,* 40(11/12), 979–990.

Pollack, W. (1998). *Real boys: Rescuing our sons from the myths of boyhood.* New York, NY: Henry Holt and Company, Inc.

Stevenson, M. R. & Medler, B. R. (1995). Is homophobia a weapon of sexism? *The Journal of Men's Studies,* 4(1), 1–8.

Sue, D. W. & Sue, D. (1999). *Counseling the culturally different: Theory and practice* (3rd ed.). New York, NY: John Wiley & Sons.

Thompson, N. (1995). Men and anti-sexism. *British Journal of Social Work,* 25, 459–475.

14

✳

Exploring Male Privilege

Journey of Two White Middle-Class Men

DAVID H. WHITCOMB AND
JAMES A. CUMMINGS

INTRODUCTION

The highly educated, White, middle-class male of the 21st century is in a lofty but precarious position in our society. Wealth, power, and privilege have accrued to men of European ancestry ever since our "Founding Fathers" established the principles of a new form of government that was to be more egalitarian than any other in Western civilization. Until 2009, all of the United States presidents have been White men, and all of the massive American fortunes until very recently have been acquired by White business men, who have generally benefited greatly from the labors of women, children, and people of color. Some of these men have risen through the ranks without the benefit of formal education or an economically stable family. But the more typical pattern is for power and prestige to be passed down from father to son in our patriarchal society, with formal education serving as a rite of passage for maintaining a family's economic security. In the late 20th century, however, societal forces such as the women's movement and affirmative action started to shift power, in some instances, away from White middle-class men. For example, in the case of gender, fewer women stayed at home to raise the children, and some even started to break through the "glass ceiling" by becoming corporate executives. With a divorce rate of nearly 50 percent in the United States, many men who are awarded limited or no custody of their children lash out at the legal system and scapegoat women for being required to pay child support but having limited access to their children. With regard to race, many

White men have witnessed an increasing proportion of persons of color in occupations that historically were occupied nearly exclusively by White men. They have blamed reverse discrimination for rates of unemployment among White men that are higher than at any time since the Great Depression. On two fronts, gender and race, many White men feel threatened and react with anger in a backlash against feminism and affirmative action.

Perhaps not surprisingly, the reaction of many White men to perceived loss of power may be disproportionate to actual losses of privilege. In fact, it is very common for White men not to recognize their own privilege until either it is pointed out to them, by women or persons of color, or it is eroded by the empowerment of these traditionally oppressed groups. Although the loss of power may be felt most strongly in the working class (Weis, 1993), it is also experienced by White men in the middle and upper-middle classes. In this chapter, two White middle-class men with advanced degrees will look at the changing face of male privilege, using experiences from their own lives, including a particular graduate-level course. They will also refer to feminist perspectives (Gergen, 2001; Miller, 1986; Pipher, 1994) and insights from the newer field of the psychology of men and masculinity (Levant, 1995; Pollack, 2000; Pollack & Levant, 1998).

PROFESSIONAL AND PERSONAL CONTEXTS
OF UNDERSTANDING PRIVILEGE

We first explored gender issues together when the first author, David, was co-teaching a gender course in which the second author, Jim, was a student. We are both White middle-class men who grew up in privileged surroundings, but differences in our professional and personal backgrounds influence our experiences with and outlook on male privilege. We discuss these similarities and differences throughout the chapter as we present our experiences with male privilege and reflect on research and theory that speak to our experience.

David's background

I am a 42-year-old man who was raised in a small, upper-middle-class commuter town with other White Anglo-Saxon Protestants (WASPs). Since age 17, I have worked in human services. My earlier career positions included work with clients who had developmental disabilities, work that focuses on welfare-to-work concerns, and work with youth residing in shelters and/or hospitalized in psychiatric settings. My post-master's experience includes work in university and substance-abuse counseling centers, a cancer institute, and a hospital emergency room. I am currently in my sixth year as a tenure-track assistant professor and director of a master's degree program in counseling. My clinical focus includes preventing HIV, counseling persons living with

HIV/AIDS, and addressing coming out/adjustment issues with gay, lesbian, and bisexual persons.

At 18, I came out to my family as bisexual and settled into a gay identity upon entering my first long-term relationship a few years later. I am currently single and live in a rural region where GLBT people often find it difficult both to build a community and to be accepted by others who are not gay.

Jim's background

I am a 32-year-old White, heterosexual male of German and Northern Irish decent. I was born and raised in a rural Minnesota community and had a Roman Catholic, middle-class upbringing. I come from a heterosexual two-parent household and am the youngest of six children.

My higher educational training has been in the area of education. In 1993, I completed my undergraduate work with degrees in history and secondary education. After graduation I substitute taught, hoping to find a full-time teaching job. Between substitute-teaching assignments, I worked as a nurse's assistant at my father's care center for people with developmental disabilities. In 1995, I left teaching to pursue full-time work in sales until deciding in 2000 to resume my education by pursuing a graduate degree in school counseling, I combined my full-time studies with work as an adult-education instructor and a high-school tutor. I graduated in 2003, and I am currently employed as a school counselor in a rural school district.

I am married and have three preschool-aged children, including a newborn. One or two days per week I stay home with the children while my wife goes to work as a store-side manager for a major discount retailer. My wife began working for her current employer around the same time I decided to pursue my graduate degree. Prior to that, she was a stay-at-home mom.

We arrived at our current division of labor through a process that started a few years ago when I was selling insurance. Because we had only enough income for the basics, my wife decided to take a few evening shifts at the discount retailer. Soon after, she was recruited for a management mentorship program. She asked me whether I would be all right with staying home with the kids so that I could quit my job, which I hated. In other words, she would become the breadwinner of the family. Because this arrangement was a way out of the job, I said, "That sounds perfect." But I soon discovered that it didn't sound so perfect to some of my male relatives. The looks on their faces when I told them spoke volumes and seemed to suggest, "You're going to be the housewife?" My wife's family, in contrast, accepted the changes well.

After a couple months, I started to have second thoughts related to my feelings about gender roles. I felt that I should be the one out there "bringing home the bacon" and my wife should be at home with the kids. We were new to the area and with no local friends, I started to get depressed and wanted to move back home. Spending your days with the kids isn't supposed to be depressing, but sometimes for me it was. My wife and I started talking about my going back to school. I did, and there was more balance in my life.

I feel fortunate that my wife is so open to nontraditional gender roles in the family. The flexibility offers us more freedom than the traditional system of male dominance and privilege.

SEEING WHITE MALE PRIVILEGE FROM THE OUTSIDE

Sometimes we cannot recognize our own privilege (McIntosh, 1992) until we see it through a shared experience with another who does not share in that privilege. In the following stories we each describe a significant life event. These critical events increased our awareness of male privilege in our lives.

David's story

One evening my perception of privilege changed forever, despite the fact that the precipitating event seemed so minor at the time. That evening I was with a friend I will call Rebecca, whom I met as a child at summer camp. Although we had lost touch for many years, a camp reunion a few years earlier had renewed our childhood friendship. Rebecca is from a prosperous Jewish family, grew up in a nearby suburb, and started a successful career after completing an MBA. During one of my brief visits in her home city, we went to a stylish midtown restaurant for dinner. It was crowded, but a young, attractive hostess quickly found a table for us. I thought nothing of it. So I was surprised when, soon after we were seated, Rebecca commented that she would not have been offered a table as quickly had she not been with a "blond man."

My initial reaction to Rebecca's comment was disbelief. My experience of being seated quickly at a fashionable restaurant was one I had come to expect, and I had never thought that any other well-dressed person elsewhere in the United States in the 1990s would be treated any differently. My immediate thoughts were that my interaction with the hostess, which lasted only a few seconds, was civilized, sophisticated, and entirely normal; it was unsettling for a trusted friend to view it any other way. I suppressed these thoughts and feelings, however, by politely validating Rebecca's experience of being commonly overlooked by hostesses due to her gender and ethnicity, and by quickly changing the topic to more familiar ground not related to perceptions of privilege and oppression. Only later, and gradually, did I start to deconstruct the experience and enrich my understanding of White male privilege.

I had known since childhood that, as an able-bodied, upper-middle-class WASP, I was a member of the dominant cultural group. I had been told repeatedly by my parents and others how "lucky" I was, but I had never before considered how the many interactions that make up my ordinary day could so often be facilitated by being, and perhaps more importantly, looking like, an upper-middle-class male WASP. There was no way to prove that we were seated at the restaurant more quickly because of the hostess' perception of my physical characteristics. I had to trust Rebecca's perception that the treatment she often receives as a woman who appears Jewish is of lower quality than that I am accustomed to receiving. My interactions with Rebecca over the years consistently demonstrated her pride in her cultural heritage and the accomplishments of her family. Her disclosure that she believes she is often marginalized by others' reaction to her gender and religion changed my perception of her self-concept and how she regards my cultural and gender status. In turn, my new perspective on our differences created an opportunity for me to explore my own privileged status.

Although this experience with Rebecca opened my eyes to my privilege as a White male, it was not the first or last such experience. And this experience is not unique to me. Other White males also experience privilege. McIntosh (1992) was one of the first feminist writers to discuss extensively the intersection of White privilege and male privilege. She lists dozens of examples of ways in which individuals benefit, often unknowingly, from their privilege. Similarly, Goodman (2001) describes many aspects of privilege that those who possess the privilege take for granted. Although sometimes we discover our own privilege from chance experiences such as the one I have described, we can help our students and others we work with in this learning process.

Jim's story

From 1996 to 1999, I worked as a salesman for an automobile dealership in central Minnesota. Three women were employed at the dealership—a secretary, a bookkeeper, and a part-time finance and insurance consultant. The rest of us—salesmen, managers, service representatives, mechanics, and car washers—were all White men.

As a member of the sales team, I witnessed sexism and sexual harassment on a number of fronts, but mainly in the accounting office and on the sales floor. For example, in the office where our bookkeeper and secretary worked, sexual banter was exchanged freely on a daily basis. The comments revolved around sexual acts, male and female genitalia, or the recent sexual conquests of certain male staff members. I remember a lot of nervous laughter, and the general feeling among most of us was "If the wrong person heard what we were talking about, we'd be sued!" Though the women in the accounting office seemed surprised and shocked by some of the statements, they contributed to these conversations at times. They would make vulgar comments too, in the spirit of the moment by talking crudely about sex, for example. I don't think they felt good about it, but we didn't talk about that. There seemed to be pressure for them to be OK with the comments, to give the guys a break just for acting like guys.

The women, as far I know, were never pressured into "hooking up" with the male employees who engaged in this type of behavior, but the atmosphere nevertheless remained uncomfortable for me and some of the women. An older secretary, for example, would sit with her head down, shaking it in disgust when such talk occurred. Another woman in the financial area would sometimes walk away when the talk started. They didn't know how I felt about it because I bluffed pretty well about being just like the other guys.

At the time, what was happening seemed like fun and games. After all, the women did not vocally object to any of the comments or gestures made by the men. I can see why they didn't object. In fact, I now believe that their participation in the sexual talk represented self-protection. After all, my boss always liked to have nice-looking women working in the office and felt that they could be replaced at a minute's notice. Deep down, I knew these women were being harassed, but I thought my job would have been in jeopardy had I reported it. In the car business, for the most part, if someone has bad chemistry with the group, he becomes subtly ostracized and made to feel so uncomfortable that he doesn't want to work there anymore. As a man, I had the privilege of not being the target of the harassment, and with my educational background, I had the privilege of entering another field in which harassment would be less likely to occur.

The first class I enrolled in as a master's degree student was Psychology of Women, Gender, and Development. At the same time, I saw myself as an open-minded person when it came to human relations. During my undergraduate experience, I had worked and studied with people from diverse cultural backgrounds who possessed far differing beliefs and values from my own. Looking back, I learned much by having some of these students as my friends. On the other hand, I felt a lot of fear and apprehension when I thought about attending and participating in this course. Because of my religious and politically conservative upbringing, I was worried that my sense of masculinity and my belief system about men and women would be challenged by my instructors and classmates. That made me uncomfortable, because I wanted to stay true to myself. Many thoughts entered my mind: "Am I going to say something that's going to offend somebody or get me kicked out?" "What are my brothers going to say if I tell them that I'm taking this course?" "Am I going to become a feminist or a liberal?" (This was the scariest thought of all.)

I decided to go into the class with an open mind, prepared to explore a variety of ideas. As a result, I enjoyed a surprise and had my eyes opened! The surprise was that many of my beliefs and attitudes toward women, men, and gender roles (such as the value of boys and men being able to express their emotions, and that of criticizing the media for exploitation of women's physical appearance) concurred with the beliefs of many of those in the feminist movement! My eyes were opened to the cultural contexts and conversations that are toxic to women and girls (Pipher, 1994). The readings and class discussions also helped me to realize that the women I worked with at the car dealership participated in the sexual banter as a means of protecting their jobs and perhaps their "friendships" in a toxic environment. I started to understand my position of power and privilege as a male, and the responsibility I hold to address conversations and contexts that demean and objectify women. The two books that made the biggest impression on me were *Masculinity Reconstructed* by Ronald Levant (1995), and *Reviving Ophelia* by Mary Pipher (1994). As I absorbed the messages offered by the authors, the worries I had going into the course dissipated. The course helped me, coming from a background of privilege, understand the struggle of those trying to gain a voice in a White, male-dominated society.

Despite my great relief at learning so much about gender roles and male privilege in a course I entered with so much apprehension, I continued to struggle with some of the content presented. For example, when reading and discussing *Silencing the Self: Women and Depression* (Jack, 1991), the focus on the women's relationships with men was solely on the negative actions by the men and negative reactions of the women. No one else seemed to be questioning, as I was, what responsibility women should take in bad relationships. Similarly, when we discussed the news story of a woman who killed all of her children during an episode of psychotic post-partum depression, I sat there seething, but I stifled my reactions when classmates assigned the responsibility to the husband rather than the wife who committed the crimes. I silenced myself rather than go out on a limb and risk being attacked. On another occasion, however, I did assert my opinions supporting the value of certain actions considered chivalric (such as saving the women and children first on the *Titanic*). I disagreed with a classmate concerning his views that gender stereotypical compliments made to parents of a baby girl were inappropriate. In these instances, I found more allies among classmates than I had expected, yet at other times I felt certain that my conservative views would not be well received. I was relieved not to have the opportunity to defend my position on abortion because the topic was never discussed.

CONTINUED AWARENESS OF MALE PRIVILEGE

David's challenge

Recently, in co-teaching a gender course with a senior female colleague, the intersection of privilege and minority status challenged me. A few years earlier, this colleague had experienced a life-threatening illness that resulted in disability and a reduction in her teaching load. I felt honored to be invited to co-teach a course she had taught for years, and I was excited about the perspectives I could offer as a gay man who had studied gender issues. At the same time, I was aware of my authoritative tendencies and the fact that, since the onset of her disability, I talk more than she does. I wanted to fit into *her* course and gently mold it into *our* course. In a gender course, I believed that for me, an outspoken man, to upset the harmony of a traditionally woman-led curriculum would be disastrous role modeling. I shared my concerns with my colleague as we prepared for the class, and I mentioned them during our second class meeting. I hoped my self-disclosure in class demonstrated cross-gender sensitivity and teamwork. I felt the constant challenge of when to speak up and when to hold back. Marks (1995), another male professor who teaches a course on gender, shares his struggles of trying to teach on the topic without overpowering the female voices present.

Overall, I was pleased with our collaboration, though at times I wondered whether I was starting to pontificate on issues when my colleague and students became silent. Whenever I became aware of this dynamic, I would quickly conclude with what I was saying, though I now wish I had asked for feedback on my use of power during mini-lectures. Students seemed to accept my self-disclosure about not wanting to overpower the female voices, but it is difficult to know for sure.

Jim's challenge

As I prepared to write this chapter, I read an article that examined issues of gender and social class among the Good Old Boys (Farr, 1988) and reflected on how this concept relates to my own experience. I've heard the phrases such as "Good Old Boys" and "Old Boys' Club" several times in my life. The first time was when I was a paraprofessional in an educational setting. A middle-aged, divorced, White female staff member used the term to identify a group of older men who all worked for the school system. She described this "club" as "a bunch of old guys that get together to play basketball and then go out for drinks." According to her, what made it a Good Old Boys Club was that they, or the "club," had a long history of subtly but systematically excluding outsiders, especially women. Beneath this seemingly harmless surface, however, were harmful dynamics recognized by some of the women employees. Because some of the group members held positions of power, some women felt that the male employees (some of whom were club members) were held to lower standards of performance in the school system.

My second exposure to the phrase happened when I was a counseling trainee; it came up again in reference to the district leadership. Two of the female school counselors oftentimes spoke bitterly about the men who were in charge of district policy. One of the counselors claimed that her ideas were ignored at a recent district-wide meeting. When I asked her why she thought she wasn't being heard, she replied, "That's easy—he's a man!"

My most recent experience with this phrase relates to my wife. As a store-side executive for a large discount-retail chain, she and her female team members often discuss the negative presence of what they call "The Boys' Club." This group consists of the male store manager and several male executives at the same rank as my wife. These men share a camaraderie like the group mentioned previously, meeting outside the work setting for sports activities, dinner, and drinks. Occasionally, the female executives are asked to join in these activities, but they are usually excluded. The male executives are viewed by the female employees as "butt kissers" who are held to a lower standard of performance, are often praised for deeds done by others, and often receive opportunities for recognition and advancement not offered to the women executives. Although I had heard all of these stories before I read Farr's article on male-dominance bonding, they didn't come together in my mind as living examples of male privilege in my community until I read her critique of the Good Old Boys' Club. In sum, the article enlightened me to the fact that the "good ol' boys" phenomenon is something that is actually being studied as a destructive component of male privilege. At the time, I thought the female educators were male bashing. After hearing about my wife's experiences at her job and reading the Farr (1988) article, I began to understand where these women were coming from. If their experience was similar to my wife's at her job, I can understand why they would feel a sense of injustice at being excluded by the privileged men's group. I wouldn't go so far as to say they were oppressed, but I know I shouldn't have judged them so harshly at the time.

REFLECTIONS

Jim reflects

Despite my preconceptions that I would be inducted into radically different political thinking, the Psychology of Women, Gender, and Development course was the perfect springboard for me as I entered my master's program; it inspired me to learn more. As far as where I sit on the political spectrum is concerned, the course did not affect me that much. I've always considered myself a fiscal conservative and a social moderate. One thing the course taught me was that women should have the same opportunities as men when it comes to exploring, discovering, and developing interests and talents. It also made me realize just how much privilege I had as a boy growing up in my house, and how much of that privilege I took for granted. By taking the course, I feel better prepared to work with young people who are trying to cope with the damaging effects of our girl-hurting culture.

As a school counselor, I feel I now have some of the necessary tools for helping girls rediscover and nurture their authentic selves. I also want the boys I work with to understand that being a real man means treating people with respect and appreciating their differences. I also think the course has given me the needed skills for working with the parents and teachers of these children. When the emotional well-being of girls and boys is under attack, parents and teachers must learn how to recognize that truth. When I first wrote about my experience taking this course, I concluded that I would encourage teachers and parents to read books such as *Reviving Ophelia* and *Real Boys' Voices*. In my first two months on the job, I already have done so. I see that the boys I work with are suffering from the gender straitjacket Pollack (1998) describes, and I have recommended his book to them. In response to my recommendation to read Pipher's (1994) book, one mother told me: "This book is helping me see things that I didn't notice before about our society—a lot of this stuff is really scary!" It seems the book had a great impact on both her and her daughter. I recall feeling the same way when I read *Reviving Ophelia*.

In learning about male privilege, I offer the following advice for students taking a course focusing on the issue:

> It's important to be flexible, to consider and respect other viewpoints; but you don't have to abandon everything you believe in. If you have a rigid attitude, you won't learn anything about male privilege or gender roles. I also think it's important not to judge people unless you really

know what their experience has been—to walk a mile in their moccasins, as Native American wisdom teaches us. I recommend that you look at a class like this as an opportunity for self-growth, and an opportunity to learn more about yourself, your family, and the people you live, work, and study with.

When I went home, I tried to inform others a little bit about what I learned in class. Doing so didn't get me anywhere with my family of origin. I tried to tell them that their old ways aren't working in today's society. I imagine I sounded too uppity or preachy in my approach. So I think we need to be careful how we tell people what we've learned and how we think we've grown as a result of what we've learned, because it's tough to change people. Some people are more resistant to new ideas than others, and some will be turned off with what you have to say. This happens with men and women alike. Of course, many men don't want to change, but I have found that some women, even in my own family, also like gender roles just the way they are. If men end up having an advantage in society, that's all right with them as long as they are being comfortably provided for. If their husband happens to control family decisions and the family's money, that's fine with them. It's not that way in the family I'm raising now, however, and learning about male privilege and alternatives to traditional gender roles has helped me come to new understandings with my wife and has influenced my early work as a school counselor.

David observes

During the process of writing this chapter, I became more aware of how male privilege shaped my upbringing and continues to affect my daily experience. I understand better how heterosexual privilege diminishes, but does not eliminate, my experience of male privilege. Having reflected upon these issues and delved into the literature more, I feel better prepared in my clinical practice and all of my teaching, but particularly in courses focusing on diversity issues, to self-disclose about my experiences with male privilege, and to encourage others to take risks to discover issues of privilege in their own lives. In particular, I now appreciate that openness and readiness to change are key aspects in coming to terms with one's own privilege. Whereas sometimes individuals have a sudden transformative experience leading to a cognitive paradigm shift, change is more often gradual and incremental. Forcing concepts foreign to one's worldview is likely to alienate a student and possibly encourage a retreat into a developmentally earlier, more traditional, construction of power dynamics.

I now recognize that part of my privilege is having a career that allows time to study these issues. My understanding of male privilege is enriched by my relationships with women who point out my blind spots and inspire me to study gender issues in greater depth. Similarly, my experience as a gay man gives me enough of an outsider's perspective to enhance my understanding of male privilege; I draw upon that experience to guide my academic inquiry into the intersections of different kinds of privilege, and I attempt to pass along my insights. As an educator and therapist, I must be patient with those who have not been given the opportunity for such study. Typically, their beliefs will not suddenly transform, but I can help to open new horizons by challenging my students and clients at a level that allows them to feel somewhat grounded in a familiar worldview. I must also accept that the degree to which they come to understand male privilege as a powerful societal force will vary greatly from person to person. Some will start to conceptualize gender in ways that are new to them, whereas others will represent the feminist backlash (Faludi, 1991), viewing the idea of male privilege as a myth created by a feminist fringe movement.

My co-author Jim's learning experience implies a constant challenge that what is learned in class may be easily unlearned because students have important connections with others outside of class who hold steadfastly to traditional views. I also note that learning about male privilege does not stop even when one has started to teach about it—in fact, many new aspects come to light, as noted throughout this paper and summarized below.

In teaching about male privilege, I recommend that the instructor initially step back from advanced theoretical considerations of gender and try to understand the life experience of students who may be quite content with a patriarchal society they have not questioned to any extent. How could you help these students understand the privileged status of males in our society without eliciting defensive reactions that would last throughout the semester? What would be a good first step for your students to take to increase their awareness of gender inequality? What readings would you select to meet them at their level of understanding and advance that understanding at an appropriate pace?

Considering my experience as a junior faculty who was asked to co-teach a course by the senior faculty who had developed the course years earlier, I suggest that teachers consider the following questions when preparing to discuss male privilege in a classroom in which diversity in gender, race/ethnicity, sexual orientation, and ability/disability are represented:

1. In preparing for and co-teaching this course, to what extent would you blend or distinguish various "-isms" that could arise in this situation, such as sexism, racism, heterosexism, and ableism?

2. How would you deal with male privilege in your interactions with your co-teacher and students, both in the classroom and in meetings and correspondence outside the classroom?

3. In trying to help students understand issues of male privilege in their future work as counselors, how would you decide what to self-disclose about your past experience and your experience teaching this class?

In working with male privilege with our clients, we believe it is important to understand who is benefiting and who is suffering from gender inequalities in their family, work, and social settings. For example, if your male client is directly benefiting from male privilege at work, and he entered a marriage assuming that male privilege may continue to be the norm, he may not understand his wife's increasing resistance to his dominance as her own feminist identity expands.

Helping your client understand how he ultimately suffers from a gender hierarchy that initially benefited him may help him explore avenues for valuing his wife in new ways, thereby enhancing his marriage. In working with children, it may be helpful to ask what boys and men do well, ask the same about girls and women, and challenge any perceptions of gender inequality that arise. Any hints that the children believe that opportunities are not available to them because of their gender should be addressed with the children, their teachers, and their parents, even if some or all of these groups do not seem receptive to the issue. Classroom instruction can be modified and extracurricular activities offered so that male privilege does not restrict opportunities for girls and boys.

CONCLUSION

In summary, these are some insights we have gained about male privilege: Often, male privilege is invisible to men but very visible to women; sexual harassment in the workplace is perpetuated when men who may not participate in it don't take a stand against it; and an outside perspective, specifically from women, was needed for us to recognize aspects of privilege we had taken for granted. Male privilege shares much in common with white privilege and heterosexual privilege, so much can be gained by discussing these issues in tandem.

Introducing the concept of male privilege to a man can engender denial even when suggested by a trusted friend, and defensiveness when presented by authors who sharply challenge mainstream views. Accepting one's privilege as a White man in today's society forces one to face the possibility of giving up unearned status that one has nevertheless felt entitled to by birthright. Such a possibility is often seen as threatening, so it must be handled carefully, acknowledging the important role that men and boys will still have in a more gender-equitable society.

DISCUSSION QUESTIONS

1. How do you open people up to the idea of male privilege without turning them off?
2. What thoughts are running through your mind as you prepare to enter this possible "unknown" of male privilege?
3. How would you describe female roles?
4. How would you describe male roles?
5. If someone brings up the topic of male privilege and wants to know what you think, what would you say?

Consistent with the discussion above, we recommend that practitioners consider the following questions when preparing to work with their clients regarding male privilege:

1. How aware is your client of how male privilege is affecting him or her in various life roles?
2. How receptive is your client likely to be to a challenge of his or her beliefs about gender?
3. How will you deal with client resistance to changing his or her perceptions about male privilege?
4. What readings or exercises could you introduce that would meet your client's readiness for exploration and change?

REFERENCES

Anderson, K. J., & Accomando, C. (2002). 'Real' boys? Manufacturing and erasing privilege in popular books on raising boys. *Feminism & Psychology (12)*, 491–516.

Badgett, M. V. L. (1995). The wage effects of sexual orientation discrimination. *Industrial and Labor Relations Review, 48*, 726–739.

Badgett, M. V. L. (1998). *Income inflation: The myth of affluence among gay, lesbian, and bisexual Americans.* New York: Author and the Policy Institute of the National Gay and Lesbian Task Force (NGLTF).

Carlton Parsons E. (2001). Using power and caring to mediate White male privilege, equality, and equity in an urban elementary classroom: Implications for teacher preparation. *The Urban Review, 33*, 321–338.

Faludi, S. (1991). Backlash: The undeclared war against American women. New York: Doubleday.

Farr, K. A. (1988). Dominance bonding through the Good Old Boys Sociability group. *Sex Roles (18)*, 259–277.

Gergen, M. (2001). *Feminist reconstructions in psychology: Narrative, gender, and performance.* Thousand Oaks, CA: Sage.

Goodman, D. J. (2001). *Promoting diversity and social justice: Educating people from privileged groups.* Thousand Oaks, CA: Sage Publications.

Jack, D. C. (1991). *Silencing the self: Women and depression.* Cambridge, MA: Harvard University Press.

Levant, R. F. (with Kopecky, G.) (1995). *Masculinity reconstructed: Changing the rules of manhood.* New York: Dutton/Plume.

Marks, S. R. (1995). The art of professing and holding back in a course on gender. *Family Relations (44)*, 142–148.

McIntosh, P. (1992). White privilege and male privilege: A personal account of coming to see correspondences through work in women's studies. In M. L. Anderson & P. H. Collins (Eds.), *Race, class, and gender: An anthology* (pp. 70–81). Belmont, CA: Wadsworth.

Miller, J. B. (1986). *Toward a new psychology of women* (2nd ed.) Boston: Beacon Press.

Mooney, T. F. (1998). Cognitive behavior therapy for men. In W. S. Pollack & R. F. Levant (Eds.). *New psychotherapy for men* (pp. 57–82). New York: Wiley.

Pilkington, N. W., & Cantor, J. M. (1996). Perceptions of heterosexual bias in professional psychology programs: A survey of graduate students. *Professional Psychology: Research and Practice, 27,* 604–612.

Pipher, M. (1994). *Reviving Ophelia.* New York: Ballantine Books.

Pollack, W. S. (1998). *Real boys: Rescuing our sons from the myths of boyhood.* New York: Henry Holt and Company.

Pollack, W. S. (2000). *Real boys' voices.* New York: Random House.

Pollack, W. S., & Levant, R. F. (Eds.). (1998). *New psychotherapy for men.* New York: Wiley.

Sherrill, K. (1996). The political power of lesbians, gays, and bisexuals. *PS: Political Science and Politics, 29,* 469–473.

Sherrill, K. (1991, August). Half empty: Gay power and gay powerlessness in American politics. Paper presented at the annual meeting of the American Political Science Association, Washington, DC.

Vaid, U. (1995). *Virtual equality: The mainstreaming of gay & lesbian liberation.* New York: Anchor Books.

Weis, L. (1993). White male working-class youth: An exploration of relative privilege and loss. In L. Weis & M. Fine (Eds.) *Beyond silenced voices: Class, race, and gender in United States schools* (pp. 237–258). Albany, NY: State University of New York Press.

15

✳

How I Got My Wings

CAROL L. LANGER

GROWING UP FEMALE IN THE 1950S:
CAROL'S STORY

I was born and raised on a farm. At age 5, I had the task of gathering eggs; my brother, at 13 years old, was already driving a tractor, helping in the fields, and doing chores such as milking the cows, feeding the pigs, and taking care of the horses. At age 7, I was allowed to cook for the wheat harvest and hay crews. I cooked the one meal I knew how to cook: pork and beans with ground beef in them, canned peas, bread and butter, and a "scratch" German chocolate cake. My other chores included cleaning house, doing the laundry, helping with meal preparations, and babysitting for three neighbor children who were only slightly younger than I. I recall wishing that I could drive a tractor, milk the cows, and take care of the horses, because I'd much rather have been outside than inside. However, my father refused to teach me how to drive a tractor, saying, "That's man's work."

In 1967, when I graduated from high school, my career options were secretary, nurse, or teacher. I wanted to go to college and eventually become a doctor, but my mother threw me out of the house when I refused to go to secretarial school. I turned to some distant relatives who had set aside $500 for my college education, but they limited my options by refusing to allow me access to the money without their approval of my major. Becoming a doctor was not one of the options. Five hundred dollars would have paid for a year of my college in 1967. In fact, I graduated in 1971 with a four-year degree and owed only $900 in student loans. My father persuaded my mother to allow me to return home, so by default, I chose teaching as my occupation. He didn't agree with my mother's actions, but he did agree with and reinforce my career options. His reasoning was that "if the children become sick, you can be with them; and you'll have all summer to spend with them."

I think my father was the kindest, most compassionate person I've ever met. He was a sensitive male who was attempting to live up to the standards of Jessie Bernard's (1981) "The Good Provider." I believe he measured his self-worth by his ability to house, feed, and clothe his family. He was a tenant farmer and the day came when the crops failed. My mother had to get a job outside the home for our needs to be met. I think my father felt emasculated by this because my mother became the primary breadwinner, and as a result, she made most of the decisions that would have been either joint decisions or his alone to make. Sexism through stringent sex roles had forced my father into a role that didn't fit him and that had great personal cost for him. It also made me more vulnerable because he no longer protected me as he once had.

It is only with the benefit of hindsight that I can recognize the impact being born a female has had on my life. My marital status, career choice, and many life experiences are directly related to being female. Also directly related is my contemporary concern for professional recognition, future financial stability, and health issues including the type and kind of medical care I can receive. Although I cannot address all of these issues in the space allowed, I will talk about sexism and how sexism relates to financial stability, professional recognition, and personal safety.

Sexism has affected me in profound ways. The irony is that I have not always been able to recognize the unequal treatment as sexism. Because I am a product of the society in which I was raised, this nonrecognition was very much a part of the problem. For so much of my life, I just accepted things as a matter of course. There are some things, however, that one cannot simply ignore. The first story that follows is a revelation of what I would call the cocoon phase of my development, the second is the larva stage, and the third is the full-fledged butterfly phase.

MY METAMORPHOSIS IN PERSPECTIVE

The cocoon stage: waiting for life to happen

As a junior in college majoring in education, I met, fell in love with, and married David Langer. I was supposed to get married; that's just what one did—at least that's the message I received from society, my parents, and my peers. All of my friends were getting married, and although I was attracted to David, I didn't make a conscious decision to get married based on what I really wanted. I married because it seemed to be what I was supposed to do. Part of my reason for getting married was related to the wedding event itself: the white dress, the veil, the honeymoon. Romance was sold in *Modern Bride*, and I was definitely in the market for romance. I wanted to be like the brides I saw on the magazine cover, even though I don't think my husband was at all fascinated with looking like a groom. I was 19 years old.

Within our first year of marriage, I gave birth to our first child. Having children was never a conscious choice for me. One simply had children if one was married. It was a matter of course during the 1960s. I wasn't a hippie, so I received the message that I was to be responsible, get married, settle down, have a family, and be a productive member of society. People sometimes cringe when I say I never made a conscious choice to have children. They automatically assume that I wouldn't have had them if I'd had a choice. On the contrary, I just would like to have known that I actually had a choice. In the era in which I was raised, if one was married, one had children or people would whisper, "There must be something wrong with her." Sometimes the gossiper would go so far as to say, "I wonder if the problem is with him or with her?" If I hadn't married, I would have been called an old maid or a spinster. If I hadn't followed the wedding ceremony with a baby shower or two, I would have been labeled selfish or barren. That's the way the world worked in that place at that time. I was 20, a senior in college, and the mother of a 4-week-old baby boy.

Within the next five years, we had two more sons. David was light years ahead of his generation of males in terms of male roles and behaviors that were acceptable in the 1970s. Males in the 1970s were supposed to be the primary wage earner, were not supposed to show emotions other than anger, and most definitely did not help with child care or housework, at least until the child was of school age. I'm reminded of the television classics *Ozzie and Harriet* and *Leave It to Beaver* when I describe the marital and parental relationships we developed. David did change diapers and rotate feedings, but he didn't do laundry or housework. I'm positive he did his own laundry prior to our marriage. I remember the time he asked me to do his laundry for him; this was a huge event in my mind and indicated the depth of our commitment. Ironing his shirts was initially a labor of love. After our marriage, when he no longer did any laundry or his own ironing, the warm glow of ironing with affection wore off. During our nearly 10 years of marriage, I began to understand more about his behavior. He wanted what he perceived to be a traditional marriage, including sex-based division of labor. Conversely, I wanted a marriage based on who had the skills to do what needed to be done. This disparate perception of marriage never became a bone of contention, however. His job required him to travel a great deal from the time our oldest son was six, so I did everything for the home, including changing the oil in the vehicles, mowing and fertilizing the lawn, painting and cleaning the gutters, and dealing with all of the financial issues of the household. This was good practice for what was to follow—my more androgynous role was required for our survival.

From 1971 to 1973 when both of us were teaching high school, I was making $6,400 a year in part-time employment. I am not aware of comparable male salaries, but I am aware that the perception was that the male was the primary breadwinner and the female income was considered fluff, disposable income. The full-time salary scale for someone in my position was $12,000 annually. Teachers' income was based on their number of hours of education beyond the bachelor's degree and their years of teaching experience. On the surface, this sounds equitable. However, if one was expected to do child care and manage all household responsibilities, taking additional college credit courses was more difficult and had to be reserved for summer; and then child care was needed because the children were out of school. These factors alone made additional hours prohibitive for women with such responsibilities. Additionally, most male faculty could subsidize their annual income by coaching, an avenue not open to most females. In fact, most of the women who were teaching in the high school where I taught from 1971 to 1973 were elementary teachers. Most of the secondary teachers and all of the administrators and board members were male.

In 1976, to increase our opportunities, we moved from the rural area where both of us were teaching to a mid-size Nebraska city of nearly 25,000 residents. This is when David assumed the position that required extensive travel.

That same year I, a college-educated, professionally attired, and articulate professional, interviewed for a position as a bookkeeper. The questions I was asked included "How many days do you miss a month for, well, you know?" "Do you plan to have more children?" "What kind of birth control are you using?" As I sat there, trying to answer these questions, I became increasingly frustrated and uncomfortable. On the one hand, I needed the job to help support my family because we had underestimated our increased cost of living in the new area, so in that sense I felt vulnerable and trapped. On the other hand, I felt the questions were none of his business. I felt humiliated and objectified and I was intensely angry thinking that if my husband had been the one having the interview those questions would never have been asked. I felt violated. I don't even remember being asked about my qualifications for the position. The only comment I remember that might be related to my competence was something to the effect of "Well, the college degree you have at least lets me know you can learn." I left that interview prior to its conclusion, thinking I wouldn't work for this man if he did offer me the job. I called the state's Department of Labor and was told that there was "nothing they could do" because it was "my word against his." It seemed to me that things were just that way and I did not know how to further pursue the issue.

I was soon hired as a secretary-receptionist for a family-planning clinic. My husband was traveling and child care was frequently an issue. I used to take the two littlest sons to work with me and put them in a playpen in the waiting room. Many clients commented about how this was probably the most effective rationale for birth control that they had considered. I think this whole scenario was another example of the impact of sexism on my life. The position of secretary-receptionist was held largely by females in 1976 and I'm certain that my husband could not have taken the children to work with him, nor would he have been able to take a day off to care for them. His income was twice as much as mine, so we could not have afforded for him to miss work. Meanwhile, I continued to juggle child care, work demands, and household duties. Some nights I was so exhausted that I couldn't even remember going to bed.

David died in 1979 at age 33. I was 29, and a widow with three young sons to raise. It became imperative for me to find a better paying position so I returned to a dream: an advanced degree.

The larva stage: being and becoming

I went back to college and earned a Master of Social Work degree. While I was working on that degree, I worked part-time as a cost accountant and part-time as a home-based tutor for the public schools. Plus I cleaned the grill at the local Dairy Queen from 2 a.m. to 4 a.m. I would probably be arrested today for neglect because I left my three sons home alone during the times I cleaned the grill. Cleaning the grill allowed me to avoid free lunches for my school-age son and allowed a little fun money for the kids such as a weekly McDonald's drive-through.

In 1986, I began teaching part-time at a four-year liberal arts institution. I worked full time as a school social worker and part time as a medical social worker. My position at the college gradually increased to full-time, tenure track. My starting salary was $18,600 annually. I felt rich compared to all of the time I had earned part-time income, but in reality I was still not being paid the same as my husband had been paid in 1979 without an advanced degree. I worked at this institution for six years before deciding to leave. My reasons for leaving were tied to issues of sexism.

- I was forced to work on my Ph.D. by contract while a male in the computer science department had no such restrictions.

- The school hired a male athletic trainer with just a bachelor's degree, at a salary $6,000 greater than mine was after six years of service (according to the faculty grapevine).

- I served on six committees, I taught four classes per semester, I had four preparations, and I was both a freshman advisor and an academic advisor. I asked to be relieved of some of my committee work because I was driving quite a distance to night classes twice a week, and my mother had a stroke and I was the only surviving child to see to her care. I was told, "You're just the kind of person we want interacting with our students. There are people on this campus who we don't want near our students." My annual review usually included comments such as, "Needs to learn how to say no."

Thinking that my experience in higher education was probably universal, I left college teaching in search of another career. I moved to a community about an hour away and assumed a managerial position for a weight-loss center. The year was 1992.

Getting wings: the butterfly stage

I connected on a personal level with Bob, a man I'd known in high school. He seemed charming, witty, attentive, and stable. Bob had been my mother's real-estate agent for nearly five years and we talked frequently over the course of those five years. We began our serious relationship in early 1992 and married in September 1992.

Within the first month of our marriage, Bob held me captive in his home. Basically, I was supposed to stay home, cook and clean, and be ready for his return from a hard day's work. He secretly sold the items I had in storage and did not allow me to have car keys; however, two of my sons were teens and both had cars. My oldest son was in college in another city. Since my sons were in school, I tried to find a job. If I had an interview, Bob would call me before and after my scheduled appointment. I found part-time employment as a home-health, quality-assurance technician. The area where we lived was fairly isolated and had a high rate of rural poverty so jobs were scarce. I could not afford my prescription medications and Bob would not put me on his insurance. He would not allow me to call my mother unless I paid for the call because it was long distance.

I remember clearly the day that I asked if I could have a can of diet Coke that I had purchased. Something snapped inside me and I began laying the groundwork to leave. I began to save every cent I could and I investigated the cost of renting a U-Haul truck to move our remaining items. I could not have predicted how soon I would have to use this information, though. Before, my plan was fully in place, we needed to leave for our safety.

My youngest son was in another state at a choir retreat with a school group. My other son and I were home with Bob on a rainy fall evening. Bob had just bought a purebred chocolate lab. He was trying to housebreak the puppy. The puppy had just gone outside in the rain, but when Bob brought her back inside, she squatted and urinated on the floor. This infuriated Bob and he began shaking and hitting the puppy. My son asked him to stop, and Bob aggressively turned on my son, threatening him in no uncertain terms. I intervened, put myself between them, and told my son to go to the car. We left immediately with only the clothes on our backs. We stayed overnight at a motel in the nearest town and rented a truck the next morning. We didn't know where we were going until we were forced to give a destination. I have no siblings and had no other family nearby. We returned to the place where I had originally taught college courses. We were homeless. We put our items in storage and stayed with friends until we collectively earned enough to rent our own home. The year was 1993. I had stayed with Bob nearly a year.

I again began teaching as an adjunct at that college and both sons worked part time to help with expenses. They both eventually graduated from high school. My oldest and middle sons completed college. I returned to college and completed my Ph.D. in 2000. I was a telemarketer and a college admissions representative to support myself and assist my younger sons as much as I could.

CONCLUSION

It is an undeniable truth that one's sex at birth—biology—begins a process of socialization resulting in one's gender—the social role. In the 1950s, being male or female resulted in clearly defined social roles. As a female born during the 1950s, I didn't see very many choices for myself. As a result, I did what I thought I was "supposed to do"—I followed role-appropriate behaviors. Sexism is unequal treatment because of one's sex. Because of institutionalized sexism, my life story plays out in several important ways. First, my retirement income will not be the equivalent of a male counterpart because my salary has been less. This smaller "nest egg" will be reflected in both my personal retirement and Social Security income. I will have to work longer and save more than my male counterparts with equivalent professional training and jobs. Second, my education and training did little to balance my opportunities in the face of institutional inequality. I was powerless as an individual; however, I believe that positive change can happen with organized groups of educated individuals.

While I was writing this chapter, a colleague and I had a brief discussion of my use of the term *sex* as opposed to *gender*. He thought that I should be using *gender* because social implications are at issue. The point in my choice of terms is that the human biological level of sex has influenced my destiny. Gender, on the other hand, is what I can make of my life from this point forward. My colleague then questioned my use of the term *female*, saying he thought it was more empowering for women to identify as *woman* than as *female* (I am woman, hear me roar). My response to him was that I spent most of my life being "just a *woman*," doing "*woman's* work." Now, I prefer to think of myself as a human who happens to have been born female and all possibilities are open to me as a result. My basic biology is fundamental to my personal empowerment, no longer a limitation.

Biology is not destiny, and using biology as destiny should not be allowed to govern the expectations for women or men. My personal and professional growth has taken place across time. Recognizing and combating sexism has not been an overnight development. It is a journey I'm still taking. As for my sons, their life experiences have allowed them to become very supportive and nurturing males, husbands, and fathers. As teenagers and young adults, they witnessed the inequitable salaries I received. They did not have positive male role models in their lives and they each missed that sort of interaction in unique ways. The oldest son now has two children and values very much the time that he spends with them. He remembers times when he and his brothers were ill at the same time and there was just mom to tend to their needs. He finds it incredible that one person could do what needs to be done. He cooks, he cleans, he irons—he does whatever needs to be done. The middle son missed having someone to show him how to throw a football and change the oil. Even though I played catch with him, I didn't have the knowledge to throw a perfect spiral. He recently told me that he blamed me for that for a long time. Now that he is married and a first-time home owner, he realizes that throwing a perfect spiral was not as important as learning how to budget time and money and hearing, "I love you." He never fails to tell me that his wife is extremely grateful to me for raising a son with no fear of talking about his feelings. My youngest son is also married. He treasures his life partner, makes a great beef and broccoli stir fry, and openly cries if he feels he needs to. He is still struggling with choices about his life's work. Because my sons experienced firsthand the results of sexism on my life and theirs, they have vowed not to repeat patterns of inequality.

DISCUSSION QUESTIONS

1. Explain how "blonde jokes" are sexist. Someone in your usual crowd begins telling a blonde joke. What do you do?

2. What are the reasons that a woman might stay in an abusive relationship? How do these reasons relate to sexism?

3. Can men be feminists?

4. If women don't recognize that they are victimized by sexism, how might it be pointed out to them? Should this be pointed out?

5. How does pornography contribute to sexism?

6. Is it sexism to have assigned role responsibilities based on sex? Why or why not?

7. In what ways has your sex shaped your life?

REFERENCE

Bernard, J. (1989). The good-provider role: Its rise and fall. In A. Skolnick and J. Skolnick (Eds.). *Family in transition: Rethinking marriage, sexuality, child rearing, and family organization* (6th ed.) (pp. 143–162). Glenview, Illinois: Scott, Foresman and Company.

✳

Are We There Yet? ... Not Quite

Introduction to Part II

"**A**re We There Yet? ... Not Quite" contains a solo article titled, *The Journey to Understanding Privilege* by Middleton, Banning, Anderson, and Paguyo. Several years ago Sharon and Val began explore the question, "Was there a common pathway or a typical journey that helps people begin to understand their point or points of privilege? Was there a common path or journey within these stories?" With these questions in mind, the four authors began an exploration of these stories.

This article uses a meta-narrative approach to tell a collective story of the journeys the aforementioned authors went on to understand and dismantle privilege in both their personal and professional lives. This article includes the analysis process used to create a collective story and the commonalities that might inform a framework for individuals coming to understand their own privilege. The following questions guided the exploration. How do agents in the majority, be it race, religion, class, gender, ability, or sexual orientation, come to understand their privilege statuses that result in the oppression of others? Are there defining elements (experiences and/or conversations) that help people progress beyond defensiveness and toward understanding? If so, is there a common journey to understanding? And finally, is there a state of full understanding?

16

✳

The Journey to Understanding Privilege

VALERIE A. MIDDLETON,
JAMES H. BANNING,
SHARON K. ANDERSON, AND
CHRISTINA PAGUYO

How do agents in the majority, be it race, religion, class, gender, ability, or sexual orientation, come to understand their privilege statuses that result in the oppression of others? Are there defining elements (experiences and/or conversations) that help people progress beyond defensiveness and toward understanding? If so, is there a common journey to understanding? And finally, is there a state of full understanding?

To address these questions and honor the work of those who provided stories for *Explorations in Privilege, Oppression, and Diversity* (2005), we contacted as many of the contributors as possible and asked for permission to include their story in our analysis for the purpose of identifying possible commonalities that might inform a framework for understanding privilege. We analyzed each story using two approaches. First, we viewed the story from a holistic-content frame (Lieblich, Tuval-Mashiach, & Zibler, 1998), giving attention to its content as the contributor had written it. Second, to guide this focus, we employed a categorical/coding approach (Lieblich, Tuval-Mashiach, & Zibler, 1998) examining each story from the perspective of a journey metaphor (Anderson & Banning, 1998; Lakoff & Johnson, 1980). We highlighted aspects of the stories in terms of journey concepts such as paths, signposts, destinations, guides, and the like. We then brought the codes of each story together using cross-case analysis (Miles & Huberman, 1994), specifically looking for common key elements across the stories. Banning conducted the initial analysis and the remaining authors subjected the coding to peer debriefing (Lincoln & Guba, 1985). We used Riessman's (1993) criteria for validation or trustworthiness, reviewing the persuasiveness of the interpretations by checking to see that the results were plausible, reasonable, and convincing. We gave attention to coherence by checking that the data supported the interpretations. The results follow.

In their narratives, contributors spoke to the ongoing nature of the interactions with and intersections of privilege, oppression, and diversity. We chose a journey metaphor as the vehicle by which to analyze the narratives and integrate them into the collective.

Before they began their journeys, many contributors describe a propensity toward equity, but in retrospect the propensity was toward a misconstrued notion of equality. "Like many of my white contemporaries, I was raised to see myself as a 'color-blind' individual living in a cultural mosaic … No one I knew would ever admit to racist thoughts or actions, notions of White superiority, or fear of 'the other,' but the subtext was often there (Zetzer, 2005, p. 3)."

Important aspects of each journey are the *critical incidents* that propelled each contributor into a state of cognitive dissonance, which refers to the arduous stress resulting from holding on to incompatible thoughts, acting in contradictory ways, or believing one way and acting another (Festinger, 1957). This discordance prompted a conscious effort toward resolution which generally meant recognizing their privilege.

Introspection, another aspect of the journey, goes beyond experiencing and recognizing the discordance and related emotions to clarifying the options that serve to resolve the disequilibrium (Ormrod, 2008). One option is a change in behavior and/or thought through reflection and intentional processing (Sinatra & Pintrich, 2003). Another option is to ignore the discomfort. A third option is to question or disbelieve the new information that brought the dissonance. Most often, the contributors chose the path of active reflection or introspection coupled with self-disclosure as the road to resolution.

The discordance and introspective experience needs to be processed in myriad ways and specifically with enlightened others. Without the opportunity to react and articulate the dissonance and the new thoughts/attitudes, the momentum might be lost and no new ground gained. The opportunity to process came in different ways. Many of our contributors had what we call *difficult dialogues* with those who did not share their privileged status. These individuals, who often experienced oppression, served as dialogical guides to enhance understanding and help the contributors move to a deeper level of awareness. In addition to difficult dialogues and constructive conversations, contributors referred to readings and other media as less direct, yet stirring avenues for positively impacting their level of comprehension and ability to think through and come to terms with their privilege.

Destinations are not necessarily an end to the journey, but a place of new understanding and more-informed actions. At this point in our metaphor, the destination represents recognition that each new experience with privilege is an opportunity for further understanding and growth. One possible outcome of this part of the journey is movement from an ethnocentric and self-centric perspective of privilege to an ethno-relative/self-relative understanding. Upon reaching this destination, one is afforded the opportunity to examine ethnorelativity which is the ability to appreciate and respect other viewpoints that are different from one's own.

Other destinations were personal transformation leading to personal action, and societal transformation leading to participation in social action. The terms *personal transformation* and *social action* are loosely based on Banks' *An Introduction to Multicultural Integration* (2002), and on Fraser's (Fraser & Honneth, 2003) discussion of affirmation and transformation: "Affirmative strategies for redressing injustice aim to correct inequitable outcomes of social arrangements without disturbing the underlying social structures that generate them. Transformative strategies aim to correct unjust outcomes by restructuring the underlying generative framework (p. 74)." When injustice is addressed, affirmative strategies target end-state outcomes and transformative strategies address root causes.

Personal transformation means that the function/structure of the person is changed to enable an uprooting of privilege in one's everyday life. Personal transformation does not necessarily indicate a willingness to journey outside of one's own personal life to address issues of privilege and oppression. "I will admit that, at this point, I do not have the energy or enough sense of social justice to demand change in the physical environment ... I am presently at a stage at which I continue to learn to challenge my own internal attitudinal barriers (Priester, 2005, p. 54)." Although our contributors' narratives speak to their commitment at the personal and transformational levels, it is conceivable that persons could participate at the societal level without addressing their own issues at the personal level.

Ideally, in societal transformation, the person is not only changed, but also engages in social action to seek changes at the societal/systems level. "I have had the experience of being an ally and of benefiting from the efforts of allies ... Both experiences have consistently reinforced for me McIntosh's (1988) assertion that one of the most important privileges that dominant community members have is the privilege to confront prejudice without being seen as self-serving. Taking on the role of an ally—deciding in advance that I will not tacitly support injustice with my silence—has helped me find the courage to speak up when opportunities arise (Liddle, 2005, p. 175)."

SUMMARY

The contributors who shared their stories contend that these narratives and many others lived and told will inform and educate others about the issues associated with privilege and oppression. The idea of a collective narrative emerged through a discussion of our own personal stories and those of students, peers, and colleagues with whom we work. The notion of a collective narrative also brought with it a concern about losing the individual experiences and voices that often get left out in a process of making voices collective. To address the notion of collective voices without the loss of all individual experiences, we allowed individual voices to be heard and stories to be told by including scenarios taken from the original narratives.

We chose a journey metaphor to bring together the individual stories because many of the authors speak to the ongoing nature of the moment-to-moment interactions with, and intersections of privilege, oppression, and diversity. These stories speak to how the contributors came to be more cross-culturally aware and cross-culturally competent as they traveled along their paths from obliviousness, to awareness, to open-mindedness, to personal transformation, and ultimately for some, to social action. The contributors speak of the discordant events that brought thoughts, emotions and even livelihoods to a screeching halt; and those that allowed them to keep chugging along until they stalled in the middle of nowhere. Some writers sought to blame the person, situation, or circumstance for their uncomfortable and oftentimes embarrassing predicaments until they realized they had to look inside themselves. Introspection got them back to a place of comfort and understanding only to discover that intellectual capacity and self-talk was not enough to get them to where they truly needed to go. From that point on in their journey, they called on friends, family, colleagues, experts, and even strangers to help. They talked, laughed, cried, pushed, and pulled each other along until the naïve among them asked, "Are we there yet?"

Some answered that question affirmatively and definitively, as various models in the literature suggest end statuses or goal lines toward cross-cultural competence. However, it appears that for most, the question "Are we there yet?" can best be answered with "Not quite." For when we think we have arrived, the only thing left to do is unpack the knapsack and revisit the privileges that got us started on the journey in the first place.

So the journey continues; each and every story or incident of privilege and oppression enlightens it. Help-oriented professionals doing multicultural work with diverse subject matter and diverse clientele come face to face with critical experiences that lend credence to the ongoing journey metaphor; these experiences in turn, reinforce the notion of cycling or spiraling through a journey of becoming aware, learning and unlearning, teaching and being taught.

FURTHER DISCUSSION

The personal stories examined in this meta-narrative study and the questions that remain point to a never-ending story and a never-ending journey. Many more voices will need to be added to the conversation as we continue to move toward understanding the role of privilege on a personal, professional, and societal scale. As the journey for understanding privilege continues, varying aspects will continue to come to the surface, and many questions remain. Since the first edition of *Explorations* (2005) was published, we have added more contributions at the request of readers who felt other stories needed to be told. Understanding and addressing privilege continues to be a work in progress.

As such, the contributors to this article and text submit the following toward continuing the dialog.

- How is story important to the process?
- Whose stories are not being told or heard?
- If there is only one story, does that story count?
- What stories can be added to the visible and invisible privilege statuses?
- What is the role of personal identity development in the process?
- What makes a transformative experience that leads to an immediate cognitive paradigm shift, versus a more gradual and incremental shift?
- What are the components of a transformative experience that makes it such?
- Are the stories that end with affirmative positions rather than transformative positions equally valuable?
- What is the role of readiness in any part of the process and can one "be made to be ready"?
- What are the costs of making this journey?

REFERENCES

Anderson, S. K. & Middleton, V. A. (2005). *Explorations in privilege, oppression, and diversity*. Belmont, CA: Thompson Brooks/Cole.

Anderson, S. K. & Banning, J. H. (1998). Creating an ethical environment: A journey looking for a road map. *Journal of Student Affairs, 7*, 26–34.

Banks, J. A. (2002). *An introduction to multicultural education*. Boston: Allyn & Bacon.

Festinger, L. A. (1957). *A theory of cognitive dissonance*. Stanford. CA: Stanford University Press.

Fraser, N. & Honneth, A. (2003). *Redistribution or recognition?* London: Verso Publishing.

Lakoff, G. & Johnson, M. (1980). *Metaphors we live by*. Chicago: University of Chicago Press.

Liddle, B. (2005). Tales from the heart of Dixie: Using White privilege to fight racism. In S. K. Anderson & V. A. Middleton, *Explorations in privilege, oppression, and diversity*. Belmont, CA: Thomson Brooks/Cole.

Lieblich, A.; Tuval-Mashiach, R; & Zibler, T. (1998). Narrative research: Reading, analysis, and interpretation. *Applied Social Research Series*. Vol. 47. Thousand Oaks, CA: Sage Publications.

Lincoln, Y. S. & Guba, E. G. (1985). *Naturalistic inquiry*. Newbury Park, CA: Sage Publications.

McIntosh, P. (1988). *White privilege and male privilege: A personal account of coming to see correspondences through work in women's studies*. Wellesley, MA: Wellesley College Massachusetts Center for Research on Women. (ERIC Document Reproduction Service No. ED 335 262.)

Miles, M. & Huberman, A. (1994). *Qualitative data analysis*. Thousand Oaks, CA: Sage Publications.

Ormrod, J. E. (2008). *Educational psychology: Developing learners.* (6th ed.) Upper Saddle River, New Jersey: Pearson, Merrill/Prentice Hall.

Priester, P. (2005). Dirty secrets and unholy unions: Disability-based oppression and privilege. In S. K. Anderson & V. A. Middleton, *Explorations in privilege, oppression, and diversity.* Belmont, CA: Thomson Brooks/Cole.

Riessman, C. K. (1993). *Narrative analysis. Qualitative Research Methods. Vol. 30.* Newbury Park, CA: Sage Publications.

Sinatra, G. M. & Pintrich, P. R. (2003). The role of intentions in conceptual change learning. In G. M. Sinatra & P. R. Pintrich (Eds.), In *Intentional conceptual change* (pp. 1–18). Mahwah, NJ: Erlbaum.

Zetzer, H. (2005). White out: Privilege and its problems. In S. K. Anderson & V. A. Middleton, *Explorations in privilege, oppression, and diversity.* Belmont, CA: Thomson Brooks/Cole.

✳

Stories of Assumed Privilege—Racism, Heterosexism, and Ageism

Introduction to Part III

Part III includes *Stories of Assumed Privilege*. In this section, we follow up on the introduction to privilege by asking our readers to further analyze and dismantle privilege by acknowledging that privilege exists, that oppression exists because of privilege, that we participate in such oppression either consciously or unconsciously, that we benefit from privilege regardless of the oppression we experience as targets, and that privilege is reinforced at institutional and societal levels. We also ask our readers to recognize that knowledge is nothing without personal action and that choosing not to take an action is in actuality an action. Our hope is that those reading, sharing, and reflecting on our stories will add their voices to co-construct their own narratives and make learning relevant by exploring issues from both privileged and oppressed positions.

In each of the stories within the *Stories of Assumed Privilege* section, the authors are assumed by others to be different than the way they identify themselves. These authors talk about having a "choice" to share or not share components of their "real" or "true" identities. Barsky in "Assumed Privilege: A Double-Edged Sword" speaks to being a school-age child with the expectation of reciting Christian prayers and being in Christmas plays. Teachers who thought themselves more enlightened would also ask him to speak to the rites and rituals of being Jewish by asking him questions about the Old Testament or to sing a

Chanukah song. Although Barsky was sometimes closeted and outed regarding his Jewish heritage—thereby at times being sometime privileged and sometimes oppressed—he also experienced similar issues while coming to recognize his identity as a gay man. Deines and Delgado-Romero share a similar story of not looking Mexican or Latino, respectively. Deines in "Who, Me? White?" states that her story is not one of "passing;" while in the story "*No Parece*" Delgado-Romero questions the privileges he received. Both address their struggle with how others view their identities as people of color. Peila-Shuster joins this second edition with "*Ageism: The "-Ism" We Will All Face One Day*" sharing her story as it relates to ageism.

17

❉

Assumed Privilege

A Double-Edged Sword

ALLAN E. BARSKY

BACKGROUND

According to cliché, "You don't know what you've got until it's gone." This seems to be true in the case of social privilege. If you are born into society such that you are fortunate to benefit from mainstream or majority status, you are less likely to be aware of social privilege than if you come from an oppressed or minority background. In my situation, I did not know what I had until I slowly came to the realization that I was part of an oppressed minority group. In fact, the oppression was so strong that I hid my minority status for many years, living in fear about what life would be like without privilege.

I am 42 years old, White, male, Canadian, able-bodied, employed, and well educated. In other words, I have a background that has afforded me many privileges. I have not had to endure ageism, sexism, racism, ableism and so on. Educationally and career-wise, many doors have been open that I have generally taken for granted. Yet there are two areas of my life in which perhaps I am not quite so privileged, though some say I am twice blessed (Balka & Rose, 1991).

As a Jewish person who grew up in a small prairie city with few Jews, I have experienced a number of forms of discrimination throughout my life. As the only non-Christian in my classes, I was expected to recite Christian prayers and songs, participate in Christmas pageants, and eat food that went against family traditions. Although our family did not keep strict rules of kashrut (religious dietary laws), I still remember a Christmas party at which I bit into something and said it was the strangest beef I had ever had. My friends laughed at how I did not even know what ham was. I can still feel the blush in my face even though I did not really have anything to be ashamed of. There were times when teachers acknowledged my Jewishness, but that was often worse than when they ignored it.

Once I was asked to play Jesus in a school play because Jesus was Jewish and so was I. Initially, I wondered whether this meant they wanted to crucify me. The play was not as traumatic as I thought it might be, but it did reinforce that I was different, not quite fitting in with everyone else. Another memory that still haunts me is being asked to sing a Chanukah song at the Christmas pageant. I think the teacher meant to be sensitive to my religion, but once again the experience felt alienating and embarrassing. I also remember being asked questions about the "Old Testament," with the teacher assuming I would be an authority on this because I was Jewish. I wanted to say, "What do you mean, Old Testament? There is only one testament." It seemed easier to comply rather than to confront. Most of my classmates had little knowledge of Judaism so most of their insensitivities could be chalked up to ignorance rather than intentional meanness. One told me that I could not be Jewish because I did not have horns. Another told me his parents would not let him come to my house because we were Jewish, although he did not know why they had this rule. Others used the phrase "I got jewed" (meaning cheated) without even knowing this was an offensive phrase. In spite of these incidents, my overall experience of being Jewish has been quite positive. I have felt strongly supported by my family and by the Jewish communities I have been associated with. With few exceptions, my opportunities to make friends, to be admitted to educational programs, to participate in cultural events, and to get jobs have not been limited by my being Jewish. Though Christian privilege still exists in Canadian and American society, more and more opportunities seem to be open for non-Christians.

My other experience of being a minority is a bit more complicated. I am gay and believe that being gay is something I have always been. However, being gay is not an aspect of myself that I was always aware of. From my earliest recollections about sexuality in my childhood until into my early adulthood, I assumed I was heterosexual—I lived a heterosexual life and I benefited from living with an assumed heterosexual identity. I was free to date women and be seen with them in social situations, without fear of being harassed verbally or physically, and without fear of losing a job, family, friends, or other support systems. At the time, I was not aware of the privileges I had. As I came to realize my identity as a gay man, however, all of this privilege came into doubt. I had to make some decisions about the life I would lead, the risks I would take, and the privileges I would have to leave behind.

THE PRIVILEGE OF THE CLOSET

When people ask me about my being in the closet, most assume that this was a horrible part of my life. In hindsight, parts of this closeted lifestyle were horrible—living in fear about being found out, not wanting to disappoint or embarrass my parents, doubting who I was, living a double life, feeling as if I was living a lie, wondering whether suicide was the answer. However, for several years my closet was actually quite a comfortable place to live.

Although I was gay, people assumed I was heterosexual, and I benefited from heterosexual privilege. Most of my mannerisms, interests, clothes, and so on were not stereotypically "gay." In grade school, I was sometimes teased for not being the most coordinated or athletic kid, particularly during competitive team sports, but I was not the last one chosen for the team or the one who was called "fag" or "fairy." In retrospect, perhaps I should thank a couple of classmates for taking much of this abuse because I could have just as easily been the recipient. As someone who generally fit in, I could talk hockey and football, play sports, drink beer, party, and do most of what "ordinary guys" did with their peers. Although I was somewhat shy and awkward with dating, that did not identify me as gay because many young straight men go through a phase of being shy and awkward when they are dating women.

Although I was surrounded by homophobia and heterosexism, I was not aware that those biases had any direct relevance for me. I was still deep in my closet, even if I was called a fruit or mocked for having long, curly hair, and this teasing did not go to my identity because I still thought of myself as a "normal person." I hardly ever discussed sexuality—homosexual or otherwise—with peers or family. To avoid the embarrassment of having to talk directly about these issues, my parents strategically placed an old edition of the book, *Everything You Always Wanted to Know about Sex, but Were Afraid to Ask* (Reuben, 2000), on a bookshelf where each of their two preteen sons could read it in case we had questions we wanted answered. This was the first professional literature on homosexuality that I had ever read. Like most pre-1980s psychological literature on homosexuality, this book alluded to homosexuality as an illness. At the time, I did not know it was telling me I was pathologically disordered. In fact, the book seemed quite progressive.

My only other familiarity with gays came from Hollywood movies, such as *Dog Day Afternoon* or *Cruising*, in which gays were portrayed as promiscuous, dangerous, and deviant. I accepted that there was something wrong with being gay, and that it was something that required either punishment or curing. It was not until later in my life that I began to understand the oppressiveness of the media and of traditional mental health views on gay, lesbian, bisexual, transgender, queer and/or questioning (GLBTQ) individuals.

Throughout my adult education, I had very few role models, teachers, or professors who were gay-positive. Although law schools and social-work schools are more progressive today, many of my courses and textbooks still viewed homosexuality as immoral (something to be punished) or pathological (something to be treated and cured). The one professor who everyone "knew" was gay made deprecating remarks about gays, supposedly in jest. These jokes did not bother me. They were not mocking me because I was still not identifying myself as gay. Although some professors spoke of social justice issues for GLBTQ people, the curricula focused on sexism, racism, and cultural discrimination. I bought into the rhetoric and internalized the view that individuals who are GLBTQ choose their social condition and therefore do not fit into the same category as other oppressed groups.

As I began my professional career, still single, the comfort of my closet was starting to break down, and I had to make some choices—would I continue to live a life as if I were heterosexual, or would I start to admit to myself and others that I was gay, with all the risks that would entail?

BEGINNING THE PROCESS:
COMING OUT TO MYSELF

For myself, as for many other GLBTQs, coming out is a gradual process, including coming out to oneself, to the gay community, to straight colleagues at work, to straight friends, and finally, to family members. Each stage of coming out can be filled with fear and anxiety (Smith, 1997). For heterosexual adolescents and young adults, exploring sexuality can be a scary stage of life, fearing how the other person will respond to you and whether you will be "good enough" in spite of your inexperience. Yet as a heterosexual, society sends many positive messages telling you that intimacy with a person of the other sex is good, fun, and even expected. There are also many positive role models. For gays, many societal messages still tell you that same-sex intimacy is wrong, corrupt, dirty, or sick. When I had my first sexual and intimate encounters with other men, these were the messages I carried with me. Internally, something felt wonderful about this intimacy, but I also experienced an overwhelming sense of shame and guilt. I tried to rationalize, "Yes, I've had sex with men, but I can't be gay. I'm not effeminate like them. I'm just a bit shy with women."

Though I was not aware of this at the time, many social forces encouraged me to remain in the closet. As long as people assumed that I was straight, I would continue to be accepted by my family, my friends, my employers, and even people who hardly even knew me. In other words, I could access heterosexual privilege, so long as I played the game. I had a close friend whose parents cut him off from their lives when they discovered he was gay. He was emotionally devastated for several years. This could have been me. Most people from minority backgrounds are a minority within the community, but not within the family. But I felt alienated in my own family, afraid to ask for support from those who loved me most, out of fear of losing them altogether.

Professionally, I had many experiences that challenged the safety of my assumed heterosexuality. Having pursued careers in law and social work, I was supposed to be an advocate for social justice and promote equality for those in vulnerable situations. If I was too scared to advocate for myself, even within my own family, how could I be effective as an agent of social change for others?

MAINTAINING PRIVILEGE OR RISKING
SELF-DISCLOSURE

In one of my first social-work jobs, I worked with street youth, 14- to 24-year-olds who had either run away from home or been forced out of their homes by their families. Many of these clients, were gay, lesbian, bisexual, transgender, queer, or questioning. I felt incredibly queasy about working with these populations, still apprehensive that I was only starting to work through my own issues. I felt hypocritical trying to help GLBTQ clients feel better about themselves while I was still hiding so much about myself. On one hand, I risked losing the safety bubble of my assumed heterosexuality if I started to come out to my clients. On the other hand, I knew that being authentic with clients is one of the cornerstones of effective therapeutic practice.

Perhaps the most critical incident of my professional career came when a client presented to me in crisis, crying, perspiring, and trembling. Through a long and confused story, he divulged that he was gay, that he was just outed to his friends on the street, and that he would rather die than face them. Although he had slept with a few men, he did not have any gay friends or support systems. Incorporating what I knew from crisis-intervention training (Hammelman, 1993), I went through the protocols for suicidal ideation screening and intervention. He had a specific plan for killing himself-jumping in front of a subway-so I knew there was a high level of risk. Of Rogers' (1957) three core conditions for effective psychotherapy, I offered the client empathy and unconditional positive regard, but not genuineness. I felt that the client responded well to the understanding and respect that I demonstrated, but I also felt that had I been more authentic with the client and with myself, I could have offered much more. I wanted to let him know that he was not alone in his pain—that I had also felt the fear of being rejected by family and friends. Yet, how could I tell him this when I was still living in fear and not confronting it myself? I rationalized that I should not use the counseling situation to work through my own issues, so I should not disclose. I knew deeper down that I had internalized societal homophobia so deeply that I could not risk coming out to the client, even though he was gay and in need (Barsky, Barsky, & Laverdiere, 2000).

I tested the waters of coming out with people who I assumed had no connection with my family, friends, and co-workers. The easiest places to do this were in foreign cities and at gay venues in neighborhoods that were far from where I lived. I could continue to live as a heterosexual and enjoy the privileges this entailed, while beginning to develop relationships with people in the gay community. As I began to see more and more openly gay people, I started to visualize a realistic possibility of coming out. I would often ask people for their coming-out stories, expecting to hear the worst, but more often than not, hearing a narrative of triumph or freedom. My images of gays as being connected to being bashed, discriminated against, rejected, and destined to a troubled life were being replaced with stories of people who had accepted their destinies as being gay, who had gone through varying experiences of discrimination and rejection, and who ultimately were finding that being out and living without heterosexual privilege was far better than living a lie.

I still feel somewhat anguished for putting my parents through a period of misery when I came out to them. They also had to come out to friends and family about having a gay son. When I was in the closet, they did not have to be concerned about people's reactions to their son, who they saw as a source of pride. Once I came out, that privilege was lost. Who knew how people would react to news of having a gay son? They already questioned whether they were to blame. Interestingly, they never questioned whether they were to blame for the fact that their other three sons are heterosexual.

ASSUMED PRIVILEGE NO MORE

I have worked through many of my issues, accepting that each time I come out to someone I am taking a risk that a heterosexual person would not experience. Although many of my experiences have been positive, I continue to experience oppression in many realms of my life. I have had neighbors who would not speak with me because I am gay. I have had friends who cut me off from their lives when they found out I am gay. My partner cannot get health coverage through my university because the State of Florida does not recognize our Canadian marriage or our domestic partnership, even though it is registered with our county. Strangers ask about our daughter's mother and respond with bewilderment when we say that our daughter has two fathers. I have been chased by drunken teens and harassed by police because they thought I was gay. My partner's stepfather broke up with his mother because she allowed me into her house. I have had students accuse me of being "anti-Christian" because of my inclusion of GLBTQ content in the curriculum. Each of these incidents hurt me, making me feel angry and sad at times, but sometimes even more determined to do what I can to make life easier for those GLBTQ people who come after me.

As a social-work professor, I include GLBTQ content in my courses (Barsky, 2000; Bowser, Auletta, & Jones, 1993; Hartman & Laird, 1998; Martin & Hunter, 2001; Perez, DeBord & Bieschke, 2000; O'Neil, 1999; van Wormer, Wells & Boes, 2000; Roberts et al., 1994) because infusion of GLBTQ content in the curriculum has been found to reduce homophobic attitudes of social-work students (Lim & Johnson, 2001). I use inclusive language, such as "intimate partner" rather than "husband or wife" to promote language that validates the existence of GLBTQ people, rather than deny it. I use examples from my own experiences with doctors, social workers, and other professionals who had no clue I was gay and were therefore unable to help me with issues related to my gayness and the homophobia I was experiencing. Many GLBTQs are afraid to access help for serious concerns, including suicidal ideation (Tremblay & Ramsay, 1997), substance abuse (Howard & Collins, 1997), and domestic violence (Lundy & Leventhal, 1999; Mallon, 1998). I stopped seeing a doctor, for instance, whose intake questionnaire asked if I were homosexual; I feared how he would react if he found out I was lying and wondered what would happen to my health insurance if the provider found out. Using relevant examples from my own life not only demonstrates pride in who I am, but gives GLBTQ students permission to talk about their experiences with homophobia, in class or privately. I also invite students of other diverse backgrounds to relate their experiences with privilege and oppression. The class members learn to appreciate one another's experiences with privilege and oppression, which helps everyone to be more empathic and supportive when they are working with clients with similar issues.

I still catch myself, once in a while, fearing what others will think or do if they suspect I am gay. I know that accepting heterosexual privilege by not revealing myself to others can be a double-edged sword: Included with the benefits are costs, and these costs are simply too high.

APPLICATION

Consider the following scenario. Shauna is a recently hired assistant professor in a Women's Studies Department at a liberal-arts college. During her first year, Shauna has received positive teaching evaluations, published two research articles in credible journals, and taken a lead role in the department's curriculum redesign. What her department does not know is that Shauna was born as Shawn. Shauna had male-to-female sex-reassignment surgery shortly after she graduated from high school. She decided to start her life anew, which meant moving to a new town and not telling anyone about growing up transgendered.

Shauna has a number of reasons to fear disclosure. She lives in an area in which the majority of the population is very conservative in terms of religious and social perspectives. The laws of her state do not protect transgendered people from discrimination in the workplace or otherwise. She has not received tenure. She has heard other faculty in her department make disparaging remarks about gays and lesbians and she believes that the head of her department would nix her tenure if the faculty discovered her secret. Still, she has no proof that disclosure would impede her career.

Chris, a colleague from the psychology department, knows Shauna's history, having grown up with her. Chris tells Shauna that she needs to disclose her transgenderism to her department and to her students. According to Chris, Shauna is being dishonest. Chris and Shauna both see themselves as feminists, meaning that they believe "the personal is political" (Saulnier, 1996). Accordingly, Chris suggests that Shauna's transgenderism is not just a private issue, but also an issue that needs to be raised publicly to enhance awareness and social justice for all transgendered people. Shauna feels conflicted. How would you help Shauna with the following questions:

1. What aspects of social privilege has Shauna benefited from by being assumed to be nontransgender?

2. What are the potential risks to Shauna if she gives up the invisibility of her transgender background?

3. What are Shauna's legal, ethical, and moral obligations concerning disclosure?

4. Under what circumstances, if any, would it be appropriate for Chris to out Shauna against Shauna's will (Mohr, 1999)? Because Chris has grown up in a situation of privilege, how can she truly understand the oppression Shauna might face if she comes out or is outed involuntarily?

Consider the following questions from the viewpoints of Shauna (personally and professionally), the liberal arts college, the students, and general society.

1. Are the obligations of a professional any different if the person comes from another oppressed group (e.g., a lesbian or a light-skinned person with African American ancestry)? If so, what might justify the differences?

2. Do the answers to these questions depend upon whether the professional is a university professor, a social worker, a psychologist, a primary school teacher, or some other type of professional?

Consider the next two questions as they relate to the author of this chapter.

1. Reflecting back over the chapter, what aspects of the author's experiences surprised you? Why do you think these were surprising?

2. How could other professionals in the author's life have helped him with the coming out process?

REFERENCES

Balka, C., & Rose, A. (Eds.). (1991). *Twice blessed: On being gay or lesbian and Jewish.* Boston: Beacon Press.

Barsky, A. E. (2000). Archie's adoption (role-play exercise on advocacy involving a gay client). In A. E. Barsky, *Conflict resolution for the helping professions* (pp. 253–255). Belmont, CA: Wadsworth.

Barsky, A. E., Barsky, S. A., & Laverdiere, A. (August 2000). Crisis intervention with a gay Irish American man: Social work and interprofessional responses. In E. Geva, A. E. Barsky, & F. Westernoff. (Eds.). *Interprofessional practice with diverse populations: Cases in point.* Greenwich, CN: Greenwood.

Bowser, B. P., Auletta, G. S., & Jones, T. (1993). *Confronting diversity issues on campus.* Newbury Park, CA: Sage.

Hammelman, T. L. (1993). Gay and lesbian youth: Contributing factors to serious attempts or considerations of suicide. *Journal of Gay and Lesbian Psychotherapy, 2*(1), 77–89.

Hartman, A., & Laird, J. (1998). Moral and ethical issues in working with lesbians and gay men. *Families in Society: The Journal of Contemporary Human Services, 79,* 263–276.

Howard, B., & Collins, B. E. (1997). Working with lesbians and gay men. In S. Harrison, & V. Carver (Eds.). *Alcohol and drug problems* (pp. 293–318). Toronto: Addiction Research Foundation.

Lim, H. S., & Johnson, M. M. (2001). Korean social work students' attitudes towards homosexuals. *Journal of Social Work Education, 37,* 545–555.

Lundy, S. E., & Leventhal, B. (1999). *Same sex domestic violence: Strategies for change.* Thousand Oaks, CA: Sage.

Mallon, G. P. (1998). *We don't exactly get the welcome wagon: The experiences of gay and lesbian adolescents in child welfare systems.* New York: Columbia University Press.

Martin, J. I, & Hunter, S. (2001). *Lesbian, gay, bisexual and transgender issues in social work: A comprehensive bibliography with annotations.* Washington, DC: Counsel on Social Work Education.

Mohr, R. D. (1999). *Gay ideas: Outing and other controversies*. Boston: Beacon Press.

O'Neil, B. (1999). Social work with gay, lesbian, and bisexual members of racial and ethnic minority groups. In G. Y. Lie & D. Este (Eds.). *Professional social service delivery in a multicultural world*. Toronto: Canadian Scholars.

Perez, R. M., DeBord, K. A., & Bieschke, K. J. (2000). *Handbook of counseling and psychotherapy with lesbian, gay, and bisexual clients*. Washington, DC: American Psychological Association.

Reuben, D. (2000). *Everything you always wanted to know about sex, but were afraid to ask*. New York: Bantam (1st edition, 1969).

Roberts, H., Gonzales, J. C., Harris, O. D., Huff, D. J., Johns, A., Lou, R., & Scott, O. L. (1994). *Teaching from a multicultural perspective*. Newbury Park, CA: Sage.

Rogers, C. (1957). The necessary and sufficient conditions of therapeutic personality change. *Journal of Counseling Psychology 25*, 91–103.

Saulnier, C. R. (1996). *Feminist theories and social work: Approaches and applications*. Binghamton, NY: Haworth.

Smith, A. (1997). Cultural diversity and the coming out process. In B. Greene (Ed.). *Ethnic and cultural diversity among lesbians and gay men*. Newbury Park, CA: Sage.

Tremblay, P. J., & Ramsay, R. (1997). Gay and bisexual male youth: Overrepresented in suicide problems and associate risk factors. Presented at Third Bi-Regional Adolescent Suicide Prevention Conference, Breckenridge, CO. Available on World Wide Web at: www.virtualcity.com/youthsuicide/colorado.htm.

van Wormer, K., Wells, J., & Boes, M. (2000). *Social work with lesbians, gays, and bisexuals*. Boston: Allyn & Bacon.

18

✳

"Who, Me? White?"

The Process of Acknowledging and Challenging Racial Privilege

HELEN G. DEINES

UNDERSTANDING AND EXPERIENCING WHITE PRIVILEGE: HELEN'S STORY

My first week at college taught me an unexpected fact—I do not look Mexican. I grew up in San Francisco, the daughter of a Mexican mother and an Irish father. In my circumscribed immigrant neighborhood, everyone knew me as I knew myself—as both Elena (at home, a little Mexicana with braids) and Helen, one of a motley assemblage of children becoming Americans.

When I moved thirty miles away to attend Stanford University, my social identity changed practically overnight. What a mess! At 18 years old, for the first time in my life, I was identified as "White." I learned that most Americans equate fair skin and unaccented English with "White" and simply refuse to accept what to them is a contradictory term, "Mexican," or even "Mexican American."

This is not a story about passing—in 1960, I didn't even know that term. I tried to explain who I was "really," and I devised my own convoluted process of racial coming out. Most people, however, did not pay much attention to my efforts to explain myself. Over the years, I continued to grapple with building some clear sense of who I was, sometimes boldly asserting my Mexican roots, but at other times simply being unable to find a graceful way to challenge others' assumptions about my Whiteness. Two incidents stand out for me as pivotal to my identity development and my understanding of privilege.

Story one

I left California after college, moving successively further away from the part of the country where Mexican heritage is widely understood. In 1996, by then a social work professor in Louisville, Kentucky, I participated in the Lilly Conference on College Teaching at Miami University of Ohio. I walked across campus in a soaking rain to hear Trinity University's Distinguished Professor of Humanities, Arturo Madrid (1996), present a paper on Latino history. I was unsure of my motivation to hear the speech. I just knew it was sufficiently important to me personally to justify a thorough drenching.

I listened, for the first time, to my reality being described as an objective academic topic. Madrid used the words I had grown up with and long ago forgotten or suppressed—the demeaning *pachuca* (a poor street kid, and my mother's greatest insult, as in, "Elena, dress like that and people with think you are a *pachuca!*"), the mystifying *californianos* ("We are descendants of the Spanish conquistadors, you know!") rather than the charged *mexicanos* (the not-quite-respectable mixture of Spanish and "Indian"). Madrid's voice was slow and sad, I thought, when he used the homogenized, meaningless Hispanic. None of us, after all, ever came to the United States from a country named "Hispania;" we who are Latino/a carry the cultures of Puerto Rico, Cuba, Mexico, Ecuador, Spain, Chile, and so many more—each unique and each worth naming to the persons whose life the country shapes.

Most importantly, he described my interior life—that of a woman who looks White, carries an Anglo name, speaks Spanish like a four-year-old, but is nonetheless a Latina. He described the lives of people I had never envisioned—people who looked Mexican or Puerto Rican or Guatemalan, had Spanish surnames, but spoke no Spanish and grew up in totally Anglo cultures; nonetheless, they identified as Latinos and Latinas. I wept throughout the talk, realizing for the first time that my own confusion was a common experience among Latino/as in the United States. These were tears of relief. I felt expansive, deeply connected in a whole new way to people whom I had never met. Yet I also felt a fleeting sense of shame that I was so self-absorbed that I was blind to others' struggles. At that moment I did not realize how my Whiteness had exempted me from others' realities.

When I spoke with Madrid after the presentation, he responded to my emotional intensity and promptly gave me the Web site for the written text of his speech so that I might easily revisit all the new ideas. I left the hall feeling weightless. I no longer saw my confusion about identity as a personal failing. I was now confident that my individual struggle would be eased by awareness of faceless sisters and brothers who walked through similar challenges.

At the end of the conference I returned to Louisville committed to finding ways to reclaim my Latina roots. I began reading Latino/a authors. An anthology of growing up stories by Mexican American children (López, 1993) included narratives very much like my own and a Latino/a studies reader (Delgado & Stefanic, 1998) introduced me to complexities of identity I had never considered. The famous Richard Rodriguez (1982, 1992) whose writings explore how his brownness has shaped his life, was educated just as I, by the Sisters of Mercy and Stanford. Yet Rodriguez (1982, p. 130) notes that he "was the student at Stanford who remembered to notice the Mexican American janitors and gardeners working on campus." I had not.

As I became increasingly focused on my Latina identity, I studied Spanish and made plans to travel to Colombia as a human rights observer. I wanted to "try out" a Latin culture, but I was not quite ready for Mexico. A pervasive uneasiness suggested that "who I was" was not a simple matter.

Story two

Only a few months after the Lilly Conference, I was having lunch with an African American colleague. We were bemoaning the disrespect we experienced as women of color. I ached as I heard her description of being dismissed as "just one of those affirmative-action hires." She listened quietly as I described my frustration at repeatedly "coming out" to colleagues and students who most often responded by denying my claim of being Latina or joking about what might be an apt metaphor for a woman who is white on the outside and brown within. My friend was silent for a few seconds, finally saying, "But you always have the choice."

WHAT "HAVING A CHOICE" MEANS
AND WHERE IT LEADS

My friend's simple observation was what transformative educators (Mezirow & Associates, 2000) identify as a "disorienting experience," an event that causes a shift in one's most basic paradigms. Suddenly I knew that how I named myself mattered not a bit because the world saw me as White. I had, in fact, lived with all the advantages that accrue to Whites in American society. As I look back on the experience of leaving home for college, I realize that I knew I was White long before I acknowledged that I was White. Like any 18-year-old going off to college, I worried about many things—that I would not be smart enough, that I would be the poorest person in my class, that I would be the only Catholic in a Protestant world. Yet I have no memory of thinking that I would look or sound different from my classmates. For all my conscious thoughts about being Mexican, I knew in an unspoken, deeply visceral way that I would "fit." Race was not a worry.

That pattern has continued throughout my life. When a police officer stops me while I'm driving on the expressway, I assume I must have been speeding; racial profiling need never occur to me. I enter every professional job interview free to focus solely on my qualifications, never diverted by having to manage ethno-racial differences—people in power almost always look just like me!

Diane Goodman (2001) cogently describes the situation, "… oppression operates on the basis of how society (the privileged group) views and names individuals, not necessarily on the basis of how people define themselves" (p. 7). This is the insidiousness of privilege. I need not seek advantage. It is conferred through the ways in which our society distributes and uses power. Exercising privilege also requires no personal meanness. Silence and/or inaction maintain the status quo in which some are always unconsciously "ahead of the game."

My stories bear the "fingerprints" of privilege. Goodman (2001, pp. 25–31) describes three ways of thinking that she finds common among individual members of advantaged groups—lack of awareness of their dominant identity, denial of the existence of oppression, and a sense of entitlement to the advantages they usually experience. In retrospect, I realize that my gender, status as child of immigrants and nurturance in a social justice-oriented family masked my sense of Whiteness. I felt like an outsider, so I was quite oblivious to my identity as a member of dominant White society. Although my family ensured that I was aware of injustice and oppression, we never identified ourselves as the oppressors! Finally, I smugly nurtured in my heart a sense of being entitled to all the good experiences, opportunities, and relationships in my life. Did I have the advantage on an unequal playing field? Never!

My ultimate "white privilege" is to choose when and where to be a woman of color. Root (2000) offers a poetic "Bill of Rights for Racially Mixed People" that includes these lines: "I have the right to identify myself differently than strangers expect me to identify … to identify myself differently from how my parents identify me … to identify myself differently in different situations" (p. 121). Although in my mind I have always been Latina, I consciously decide, just like any person who "comes out," when to disclose my hidden identity. I try to be honest and practical, disclosing appropriately as friendships or collegial relationships develop, but not bothering grocery clerks with my heritage. I justify selective "secret-keeping by omission" as avoiding gratuitous debate. It was only after my colleague's comment about choice that I realized I was also protecting myself from painful discussions about whether I am "really" Mexican. I have the ultimate white privilege—I need never engage in America's contentious discussion of race unless I so choose. I am an active, yet sometimes unaware, participant in the racist "system of advantage and privilege which accrues to those considered White" (Basham, Donner, & Everett, 2001, p. 158).

That given a choice, I most often opt to describe myself as Latina should not be surprising. Goodman (2001) observes that people cling tenaciously to the disadvantaged dimensions of their identity (the place where they have known hurt) to defend against seeing themselves as advantaged in comparison with other groups. For example, White women tend to emphasize their gender, gay men their sexual orientation, and so forth.

To recognize myself as White has been an explosive piece of knowledge. Hardiman and Jackson (1997) suggest in their theory of social identity development that all of us begin as children with a sense of naiveté about race. Our culture teaches us the unwritten rules of domination and subordination. Eventually, we encounter landmines of contradictions that lead us to question, as I often do in my classes, "If we are all created equal and if we all are free to live the American dream, why are there so few people of color in my neighborhood ... or my child's classroom ... or leaders in my professional organization?" Ultimately, if eyes and ears stay open to contradictions and there is opportunity for value-focused reflection, individuals resist the long-standing "givens" that maintain the inequities that pervade our lives. Sustained, active resistance is possible only when one recognizes one's own place in maintaining systems of domination.

CONCLUSIONS AND LESSONS LEARNED

In this narrative, I have shared my struggle to recognize and challenge my own white privilege in a multiracial society. Antiracism education experts present my reality in coldly objectifying terms: "The already complex nature of racism is complicated further for people who identify themselves as biracial and whose families include both agents and targets [of oppression]" (Wijeyesinghe, Griffin, & Love, 1997, p. 85). My narrative is a more personal account, using Elena's/Helen's story to demonstrate the common human dynamic of clinging to an image of self as disadvantaged, oblivious throughout to one's own privileges and place in maintaining systems of domination (Goodman, 2001).

Considering my personal stories in the context of multicultural education and practice, I find two consistent applications. First, as social identity develops and changes through interactions across the lifespan, change agents need a "long haul" view in promoting individuals' recognition of their own privileges. I focus my work on precipitating those disorienting experiences and building spaces safe for exploration of the threatening world of relative advantage and disadvantage. I highlight the disturbing elements in student or client stories, poetry and fiction, videos, as well as multicultural exercises, encouraging participants to move in their own time through dis-ease. Immediate epiphanies are neither required nor encouraged. I reward critical, reflective thinking and tenacity in staying in the struggle.

Second, I believe that simply recognizing privilege is an insufficient measure of competence in the helping professions. Actions that dislodge longstanding patterns of domination and subordination are required. I foster skills in raising questions, visioning alternative ways of working and living together, and acting intentionally to resist injustice. My goal over that long haul is to foster a spirit of discomfort about life's inequities, uneasiness that calls forth sustained reflection, and, ultimately, deliberate action to unravel pervasive webs of privilege.

DISCUSSION QUESTIONS

1. Have you told your own racial and ethnic stories? With who have you shared them? How have they responded? Have you ever gone "below the surface" with a colleague, considering what difference your race makes and how other facets of your identity interact with your race?

2. When do you notice Whiteness? Do you assume that it equates with a European heritage? How do you ask White persons about how they see themselves?

3. When, if ever, do you discuss white privilege in your direct practice with clients? Have you ever suggested privilege as a topic for supervision or for "over-coffee" conversations with co-workers?

4. How do you respond to the feelings associated with a serious discussion of race—guilt and shame, anger, fear, and anxiety? Are you willing to take the personal risks involved in openly confronting your part in maintaining both racial oppression and white privilege?

5. How do you invite your clients to recount and explore the critical incidents that shape their sense of personal and social identity?

6. In an era of managed care and outcome-focused practice, how can you reserve time for in-depth reflection about race as a crucial dimension of individual and social functioning?

7. Does your agency or professional association include white privilege in its diversity trainings? If not, how can you help them provide a safe forum for sustained exploration of the realities of and challenges to white privilege?

CASE STUDY

Angela is a 45-year-old attorney referred to you for counseling for depression related to a recent diagnosis of Stage 2 breast cancer. During her second session with you, she reveals that she is a lesbian in a seven-year relationship with a local health professional. Angela describes her feelings this way: "It's not fair! I've worked hard my whole life, tried to everything that's expected. I've struggled with my sexual orientation, put up with my brothers' verbal harassment, and faced the fact that my family church doesn't want me! I volunteer in the community and help out my parents. I don't deserve this and I can't go through any more!" Imagine Angela as a White client; where would race fit in your treatment plan? What if she were a woman of color?

REFERENCES

Adams, M., Bell, L. A., & Griffin, P. (Eds.). (1997). *Teaching for diversity and social justice: A sourcebook.* New York: Routledge.

Adams, M., Blumenfeld, W. J., Castañeda, R., Hackman, H. W., Peters, M. L., & Zúñiga, X. (Eds.). (2000). *Readings for diversity and social justice: An anthology on racism, anti-Semitism, sexism, heterosexism, ableism, and classism.* New York: Routledge.

Basham, K. K., Donner, S., & Everett, J. E. (2001). A controversial commitment: The anti-racism field assignment. *Journal of Teaching in Social Work, 21* (1/2), 157–174.

Delgado, R. & Stefanic, J. (Eds.). (1998). *The Latino/a condition: A critical reader.* New York: New York University Press.

Goodman, D. J. (2001). *Promoting diversity and social justice: Educating people from privileged groups.* Thousand Oaks, CA: Sage.

Hardiman, R. & Jackson, B. W. (1997). Conceptual foundations for social justice courses. In M. Adams, L. A. Bell, & P. Griffin. (Eds.). *Teaching for diversity and social justice: A sourcebook* (pp. 16–29). New York: Routledge.

López, T. A. (1993). *Growing up Chicana/o.* New York: Avon Books.

Madrid, A. (1996, April). *Juntos y revueltos*: The U.S. Latino population at the end of the twentieth century. A paper presented as the Schomburg Memorial Lecture, Mount Holyoke College, Mount Holyoke, MA. [On-line] Available: http://www .mtholyoke.edu/acad/latam/schomburgmoreno/juntosweb.html

Mezirow, J. & Associates. (2000). *Learning as transformation: Critical perspectives on a theory in progress.* San Francisco: Jossey-Bass.

Rodriguez, R. (1992). *Days of obligation: An argument with my Mexican father.* New York: Penguin Books.

Rodriguez, R. (1982). *Hunger of memory: The education of Richard Rodriguez.* New York: Bantam Books.

Root, M. P. P. (2000). A bill of rights for racially mixed people. In M. Adams, W. J. Blumenfeld, R. Castañeda, H. W. Hackman, M. L. Peters, & X. Zúñiga (Eds.). *Readings for diversity and social justice: an anthology on racism, Anti-Semitism, sexism, heterosexism, ableism, and classism* (pp. 120–126). New York: Routledge.

Wijeyesinghe, C. L., Griffin, P., & Love, B. (1997). Racism curriculum design. In M. Adams, L. A. Bell, & P. Griffin (Eds.). *Teaching for diversity and social justice: A sourcebook* (pp. 82–109). New York: Routledge.

19

No Parece

The Privilege and Prejudice Inherent in Being a Light-Skinned Latino Without an Accent

EDWARD A. DELGADO-ROMERO

INTRODUCTION

I am a light-skinned Latino with no (Spanish) accent. My parents were born in Colombia, South America, and I was born in the United States. I am 100 percent Colombian, a Latino, a Hispanic, and a person of color. However, because my appearance and speech do not meet the stereotypical expectations of other people, I am often exempt from the prejudice and oppression that other people of color face. Worse, at times people will try to confide and involve me in their racist thoughts and beliefs. I am not quite invisible, nor am I a chameleon. Struggling with privilege and prejudice inclusion and exclusion has given me insight into the complex nature of the intersections of privilege, ethnicity, race, and oppression.

PROFESSIONAL CONTEXT

I am a licensed psychologist; my doctorate is in Counseling Psychology. I am an assistant professor in Counseling Psychology at Indiana University, Bloomington, after having worked at the University of Florida Counseling Center for five years. I consider myself a "self-taught" multicultural Counseling Psychologist, given that my doctoral program offered only a 6-week seminar on multicultural issues. I am indebted to Dr. Beverly Vandiver (who was then a counseling-center psychologist) and the pre-doctoral internship at Michigan State University, especially the Multi-Ethnic Counseling Center Alliance (MECCA), for helping to advance my training in multicultural issues.

PERSONAL BACKGROUND AND
CRITICAL INCIDENTS

My skin is not really that light. My son, who is half-Colombian and half a Dutch/Irish/English/Russian/Norwegian mix, has skin so fair that it seems translucent. His eyes are blue, as were mine when I was born and before they changed to brown. My skin is light brown, darker than White but not quite brown or black. My parents, whose strong Spanish accents subject them to prejudice to this day, drummed any trace of a Spanish accent out of me. My parents saw their accents as a source of shame, and they made certain that their children would not stand out as "different." Thus, visibly and audibly, people do not often identify me as being Latino or Colombian. This perception is not limited to White people; many times, other Latinos and even other Colombians do not think I look Latino. This hurts the most.

> I was walking around the streets of downtown South Bend, Indiana, during the international festival, wearing my Colombia T-shirt that symbolized my newfound pride in my heritage. A young Latina woman approached me and asked, "*¿Colombiano?*" I eagerly answered, "*¡Si!*" She looked at me, wrinkled her nose, and said, "*No parece*" (you don't look like it). And then she faded into the crowd, leaving me alone with my shame and anger.

Often people will mistaken me for Italian or Arabic, if anything, but mostly it seems my ethnicity is invisible, often leaving me feeling left out of both majority White and Latino cultures. I have often been so distressed by this cultural invisibility that I have asked my mother whether I was adopted, whether she is "sure" that I am Colombian. She is offended every time I ask her. Being ethnically ambiguous (in my case being able to pass for White) has its privileges. I can go where I want without the fear many people of color have regarding how they might be treated.

Although I grew up in Atlanta, Georgia, my exposure to other people of color (outside of my immediate family) was limited. I lived in a predominantly White suburb and attended predominantly White (middle-class) Catholic schools. The nuns who taught me in grade school were socially progressive and they taught me to desire social justice. We learned about the Civil Rights movement and were taught not to hate others based on the color of their skin. When we left the safety of our suburban school to visit the Martin Luther King Center in downtown Atlanta, we had to pass through poor neighborhoods to get there. Everyone in those neighborhoods was African American, and they stared at me in my new school bus, full of White nuns and priests, White teachers, and White friends in their Catholic school uniforms. I began to feel guilty; this was not Martin Luther King's dream.

My hardworking mother kept me anchored in reality. We did not have much money because my father would spend money faster than he could make it. I knew that attending Catholic school was tenuously dependent on my mother being able to earn enough money babysitting, sewing, and cleaning other people's houses. My father would have sent me to the dreaded public schools in an instant. My father firmly believed that his children should assimilate to United States culture, and to him that meant we should be White. He also encouraged me to turn down minority scholarships for college (including a letter from Harvard inviting me to apply based on my PSAT scores and minority status). Instead I took out more than $50,000 in student loans to attend a prestigious institution where elite southern families sent their children. His perspective mirrored that of others.

> "Ed, you don't want to go to this college; it's not very good," my guidance counselor said. I knew "not very good" meant too many blacks went there and therefore the college was second rate. Southerners have a secret, coded language to avoid the appearance of being racist. "Plus, you want to get into college on your own merits, not due to some minority scholarship." I wondered whether she told that to athletes, or to children of alumnae? I knew the answer.

Every day I was confronted with the privilege that my college classmates felt was as natural as air. For example, my roommate was a descendent of one of the founding families of Atlanta, and he was literally a millionaire. The large iron gates that surrounded the school reminded me that not everyone was welcome on campus. I began to wonder what I had done to deserve this privilege. What was so special about me that I deserved to be at this overwhelmingly White private university while literally steps from the university gates, was a city that was 60 percent African American? Furthermore, surrounding this urban, African American city were small farming communities that were stringently segregated by race. I felt guilty for living in my privileged world while people beyond the gates, including my mother (my father had finally left us when I went away to college), struggled to make enough money for food to eat. The following is an incident I experienced while attending the private university.

> My college girlfriend took me to her small hometown to introduce me to her family. When she introduced me to her grandmother, the matriarch of her family, she said, "This is Ed; his family is Spanish, from Spain." Her grandmother nodded in approval and later I found out that she was pleased that I was not Mexican and thus not a migrant worker. I was Spanish, therefore European, therefore White, and therefore acceptable.

I went from a small private school to a large private Catholic school for my graduate studies. Despite qualifications that were equal to or better than my classmates, I was viewed by many people as a either an "affirmative action" admission (not qualified but a minority), a Spanish/European (academically qualified but not a "real" minority), or my ethnicity was ignored altogether (a White guy with a Spanish surname). Consequently, many people would "trust" me enough to share their real opinions regarding racial matters. I do not think that people were trying to be offensive or malicious in telling me their real opinions. Rather, I think that they were so comfortable with me that they considered me a person with whom they did not have to be politically correct. For me, part of my privilege was hearing what some White people "really" thought.

> A colleague congratulated me on my graduate minority fellowship. "Good for you," she said. "You aren't even a real minority! I mean, you don't speak broken English or have an accent!" I think she genuinely meant to congratulate me on what she saw as a way for me to manipulate the system.

> While I was shopping for fruit at my local grocery store, an elderly White employee giving out samples of kiwi struck up a conversation with me. She noticed that I was looking at the avocados and stated, "Those are from Mexico." She then looked around to make sure no one else could hear her. "A lot of things in the U.S. are from Mexico, if you know what I mean. I feel sorry for those poor Mexicans. I used to live on the border of Texas and Mexico and I tell you, it's sad. Plus most of those Mexicans are on dope."

This knowledge often made me suspicious about the motives of Whites, especially as I sensed that it was only a matter of time before I became a target.

In graduate school, I was taught about social justice, feminism, and equity. My clinical training motivated me to take a closer look at myself and at the themes in my life. I realized that I needed to come to understand myself as a person of color, because for many years I had let others define me and be the judge of whether or not I was a "real" person of color. However, this was a painful process. For example, at a local conference, I was invited to a "students of color only" meeting and I went begrudgingly and left as soon as possible. The leader of this meeting was an African American student who seemed ready to take on the world. She talked about the need to unify and our common destiny as people of color. I was scared of her words, but the things she said continued to echo in my mind for quite some time.

As I continued my clinical training and continued to read about race, oppression, and multiculturalism, I began to make connections in my life, and I began to notice injustice and prejudice that surrounded me. As hard as it was to realize, I had to go no further than my graduate program to notice inequity. We had no professors of color, few graduate students of color, and limited training in multiculturalism. As a graduate student, noticing these things was difficult. I lacked the power to make any real change and my status in the program was dependent on the very faculty I was criticizing. Around this time, I read

The Autobiography of Malcolm X (Haley, 1964) and I began to understand institutional racism and was able to center my feelings about race within a broader context. I became inspired to reclaim my Latino heritage and asked my mother to take me to Colombia. I put a great deal of energy into consciously being Latino, and I devoted my free time to outreach and retention efforts with minority students. As Janet Helms (1990; 1995) might say, I immersed myself in being Latino.

By a fortunate twist of fate, the graduate student who had inspired me at the "students of color only" meeting accepted a job as a Counseling Psychologist at my university during my third year, and we became instant friends and colleagues. My fervor and energy for multicultural issues were amazing, but my friend could see some of the holes in my identity. Although I was connecting with Latino heritage, I was still very prejudiced, privileged, and homophobic.

> "Ed, just because you are Hispanic doesn't preclude you from being prejudiced. Did you know that Hispanics owned slaves too? You can't exempt yourself from the legacy of slavery by saying you are Hispanic. I mean, Colombia had some of the biggest ports for slave ships. Brother, you have to get yourself together."

She was right. I had too easily identified with the oppressed. In my zeal to appease my guilt for having privilege, I had assumed an identity that was not authentic. "Getting myself together" was, and is, a continual process of acknowledging my privilege, of not negating having received unearned assets due to privilege, of not so easily identifying with those who are oppressed, of critically examining my authenticity as a person of color, and of ferreting out the more subtle impacts of racism and oppression that linger in my subconscious.

The first step was to realize that consciously giving up my privilege was not the same thing as never having had privilege in the first place. For example, my mother had come to this country with nothing, but her light skin and family connections allowed her to quickly make something of herself in the United States. People in projects such as Chicago's Cabrini-Green, or migrant farm workers picking fruit in Michigan would likely never have the opportunities I had, no matter how hard they worked. This process of self-examination has turned out to be a life-long process. A friend mentioned to me that I have an easier time dealing with the White, Spanish, and oppressive side of me than I do accepting the indigenous, racially mixed, and oppressed side of me. This seems to be my growth edge.

PROFESSIONALLY ORIENTED PERSONAL
STRUGGLES AND TRIUMPHS

After internship I took at job at the counseling center at the University of Florida where I worked from 1997 until 2002. Moving to Florida from the Midwest was another lesson in privilege for me. Although Florida has a large Latino population, Cubans and South Americans predominate while Mexican Americans are a small minority, all of which is a stark contrast to many other areas of the United

States. Consequently, there exists a hierarchy of Latino heritage with Mexican Americans consistently being at the bottom. Earl Shorris (1992) referred to this racism within Latino culture as *racismo*. As a result, I had to confront anti-Mexican prejudice and educate students about the political activism of the Chicano movement as a model for Latino activism.

I was not prepared for the tension that existed between African Americans and Latinos in Florida, especially amongst faculty and administrators. It seemed that Latinos were viewed as competing for traditionally African American resources and African Americans were viewed as wanting exclusive rights to diversity and multiculturalism. The rise in numbers and power of Latinos is a growing political reality, and it seemed to me common sense to build coalitions between minority groups, but many disagreed with me. In the politicized battles over rapidly diminishing diversity resources, it seems that no one emerges victorious.

I became the faculty advisor for the Colombian Student Association (COLSA), and my work with these students gave me a chance to connect with both Colombian and other Latino cultures. I attended Latino cultural events, gave Latino music and dancing a chance (and grew to love it), improved my Spanish, read Latino literature, and watched Latino movies. I learned to insist that people use both of my surnames, which surprisingly forces people to view me differently. These things helped me feel more authentic as a Latino, regardless of what others thought. More often than not, people now identify me as a Latino, if not always a Colombian. Having other Latino friends to share my struggles and to compare notes also has helped me a great deal.

A main part of my work at the University of Florida Counseling Center was outreach with Latino students. I found that the multicultural literature does not offer much guidance in understanding and working with Latino clients, especially with those who are not from the demographically dominant groups (that is, Mexican American, Puerto Rican, or Cuban). In particular, I was unsatisfied with Latino racial/ethnic identity models (Delgado-Romero, 2001) that seemed to be too general to be of much use. Similarly, there is relatively little known about bilingual therapy and few programs that offer training to bilingual therapists. I believe there is much more to be learned about Latino people and the way that we are being changed by (and changing) mainstream American culture. The multicultural literature needs to move beyond generalities and deal with the specifics of each Latino culture. For example, I can verify from personal experience that Colombians often differ more from each other than they do from other Latinos. Colombia is an immense country with many ethnic, racial, and cultural variations within its borders, and it is only one of the Latino countries.

CONCLUSION

"NO SPICKS FOR PRESIDENT"—Graffiti painted on the side of the Institute of Hispanic/Latino Cultures on the morning of student-government elections in response to the first Latino presidential candidate, who was also one of my students.

The misspelled racial slur caught me by surprise. I had grown comfortable within my enclave of Latino friends and the small but powerful Latino student community. There was a sense of excitement as my student ran for student-body president. He was the first Latino candidate for the influential student-body-president position (the president directly controlled an eight million dollar budget), and there was hope that he could win.

The result of the slur was emotional and political upheaval. For the first time in their lives, many of the Latino students felt unsafe and singled out because of their ethnicity. Many people became "minorities" for the first time that day, especially those who had lived all their lives in predominantly Latino cities such as Miami. It seemed that because of recent numerical and political gains, Latinos were the new targets for backlash.

I wondered whether I had made the right choice in choosing to identify so strongly with my Latino heritage. I wondered whether my life and that of my half-Colombian son would have been easier if I had just continued to "pass" for White and lived a life wherein my Colombian heritage was an interesting factoid, but otherwise not important.

As I prepared to speak at the student-led rally in response to the racial slur, I looked out into the crowd. There were faces of every color and race, there were gay men and lesbians, and there were White people. All were united in a sense of common outrage and purpose. At that moment, I knew I had made the right choice and that, through examining my deep-seated prejudices, internalized racism, and homophobia, I was providing an example for others. Then I spoke....

DISCUSSION QUESTIONS

1. If you had a client or colleague who was struggling with cultural/ethnic invalidation, how would you deal with it?

2. You might be more prepared to deal with oppression than privilege; what might be some of the challenges in helping someone deal with privilege (especially if you don't have that privilege yourself)?

3. What happens when people tell you what they really think—when politeness and political correctness are stripped away, and anger and resentment surface? Can you work productively with these beliefs/feelings?

4. How prepared are you to work with Latino clients from different ethnic and national origins? What kinds of resources do you have, and what kinds of resources might you need?

5. Does working through privilege have to be a struggle? The author implies being "comfortable" is a negative thing. Do you have to be uncomfortable to examine privilege?

6. With so many differences within groups, how can we effectively teach multicultural competence?

7. Is multicultural competence a goal or an ever-evolving attitude?

REFERENCES

Delgado-Romero, E. A. (2001). Counseling a Hispanic/Latino client—Mr. X. *The Journal of Mental Health Counseling* (Special Issue: Counseling Racially Diverse Clients), *23*, 207–221.

Haley, A. (1964). *The autobiography of Malcolm X.* New York: Ballantine Books.

Helms, J. E. (1990). *Black and White racial identity: Theory, research and practice.* New York, Greenwood Press.

Helms, J. E. (1995). An update of Helm's white and people of color racial identity models. In J. G. Ponterotto, J. M. Casas, L. A. Suzuki, & C. M. Alexander (Eds.). *Handbook of Multicultural Counseling* (pp. 181–198). Thousand Oaks, CA: Sage.

Shorris, E. (1992). *Latinos: A biography of the people.* New York: W.W. Norton & Company.

20

✴

Ageism

The "-Ism" We Will All Face One Day

JACQUELINE J. PEILA-SHUSTER

INTRODUCTION AND BACKGROUND

I am a White, heterosexual, mostly-able-bodied, middle-class, Christian female currently serving as an instructor in higher education and working on my doctoral degree. I am in my forties. My life was fortunate enough to be blessed with grandparents who lived close by throughout my childhood and adolescence. Along with my parents, these individuals instilled within me countless values and morals. Their strength flows through me to this day.

When I was entering ninth grade, one of my grandmothers suffered a stroke and ended up living in a nursing home. I recall visiting her there and experiencing various fears and judgments of residents and of the various disease and disability processes with which they had to cope. One individual would walk around and slap the side of his head. Another would come up to me and whisper words that I did not understand. Furthermore, my grandmother was confined to a wheelchair or her bed most of the time and had difficulties speaking or feeding herself. However, the love in her eyes for her family always reassured me that she was, indeed, my grandma. Nonetheless, I decided then to never work with "old people in a nursing home."

As it turns out, during my years as an occupational therapist, I found my passion in working with patients who were older adults. I even worked in a nursing home where the individuals I worked with became real people with rich histories. One individual I worked with was a master quilter and another did incredible woodwork. One gentleman would sit and talk at length with me about fishing and ranching. Most of them were parents and grandparents that had negotiated many of life's travails. Even though their wisdom and outlook on life touched me, I was still wrapped up in my own youthful privilege. I saw the diseases and disabilities that these individuals had as processes associated with aging. I did not scrutinize the idea that processes often *associated* with aging were not necessarily *outcomes* of aging. For example, the actor Michael J. Fox was diagnosed with Parkinson's disease in young adulthood. Additionally, I have known young adults who have had to cope with the effects of having a stroke.

In my early thirties, I left the medical arena to further my education in the area of counseling and career development. Early on in that process it became clear to me that my passion for older adults was to play a part as I constructed the next chapter of my life. Consequently, I have focused various aspects of my education and my practice of counseling towards individuals considering retirement. My desire is to help them determine how they want to construct the next chapter of their lives. I also teach courses on adult development and aging, and on career counseling. Without delving further into my lengthy career story, suffice it to say that aging, retirement, career development, and counseling all flow seamlessly together as part of my future self and life plan.

During my graduate studies, I have often been pushed into times of both cognitive and emotional dissonance, prompting growth. The result is an increase in my understanding of privilege. However, I have also come to understand that privilege will always have blind spots. I am now more willing than ever to admit that as I learn more, I seem to know less. Thus, it is understandable that in the process of writing this chapter, I have continued to find it necessary to confront my privilege and assumptions about aging. This has caused me considerable growth, as well as moments of discomfort.

MY STORY

In 2001, I experienced the onset of pain and swelling in both of my feet. Almost two years later, I was diagnosed with rheumatoid arthritis. Although arthritis is the most common chronic condition among older adults, rheumatoid arthritis typically strikes in middle adulthood (NIAMSD, n.d.). In my case, it came about in young adulthood.

I have experienced many ups and downs with this disease and have become increasingly aware of what I took for granted in terms of my physical abilities. To be able to wear shoes of almost any type and walk with absolutely no pain are no longer realities for me. My exercise routine has changed dramatically. After doing simple gardening, my finger joints can become quite swollen. Additionally, due to the fatigue that is a large part of this disease, there are days when I simply cannot do that which I want or expect myself to do. In other words, my choices, independence and freedom in life are more limited now, an occurrence that often coincides with later adulthood. In fact, while referring to the work of Butler, Gruman (1978) stated that "... one of the greatest handicaps of aging is the decrease in the range of choice, a loss which results not only from physiological and economic limitations but also from the restrictive norms of a biased culture" (p. 363).

This loss of choice was brought to the forefront for me one day while at the gym. I was engaging in an exercise that I had adapted in order to protect the joints of my toes. A trainer at the gym came up to me and explained that I was doing the exercise incorrectly. To his credit, he was trying to protect other joints in my body that he felt were at risk. However, I just felt the painful blow of having another choice being taken away from me. This exercise was an example of one more thing that I should not or could not do. I was humiliated and disheartened. I was also angry that this individual had not taken the time to hear my story first and try to view things from my perspective.

This experience prompted me to reflect back to my time as an occupational therapist. There were many times I had suggested to an elderly patient that they complete their activities of daily living in a different manner. Of course, it was always done with the greatest intentions of keeping patients safe and sound, or improving their ability to function. However, did I ever stop to get their full story before I barged in with my youthful expertise? Did I ever give more than a cursory consideration of the ramifications of taking away "choice"?

Another experience that I have encountered more often since acquiring rheumatoid arthritis is that of dealing with others' assumptions. A poignant example of this was when I finally came to grips with the reality that I would have to get a handicap parking pass for campus. On the campus where I work, a handicap pass allows one to park in any lot regardless of whether it is designated for students or faculty. This would provide me with more opportunities to find a space closer to my office. Although walking is not always a hardship for me, there are some days when walking more than a couple of blocks causes the joints in my feet to swell and become very painful. Making the decision to obtain this pass was not an easy step for me. It meant that I had to admit that I could not do that which I had always done (for example, simply walk across campus).

With some reluctance, I went to the parking services office to inquire about the pass. The young woman behind the counter looked me over skeptically and declared I would need to go to the campus health facility and be examined by a doctor who would have to clear it. Embarrassed and angered, I informed her that I had a doctor who specialized in the disease and would obtain documentation from him. Fortunately, when I hesitantly returned with a prescription for the pass, a different woman, more sensitive to the idea that not all disabilities are visible, assisted me.

LESSONS LEARNED

One lesson I learned, very deeply, was that admitting I need help is a painful and sometimes embarrassing process. As a result, it is no longer surprising to me when older adults hesitate to ask for assistance or fail to admit that some activities are too much of a struggle. In general, our society does not reward or respect needing help and/or being dependent on others. We focus so much on independence that we may ignore, to our detriment, the positive aspects of interdependence.

I also learned, on a personal level, that appearances can be deceiving. My appearance had been deceptive to the employee in parking services. I looked "okay" to her and thus must be trying to get around the system. Likewise, it is also possible that the appearance of an older adult, with grey hair and wrinkles, may be met with assumptions. Various stereotypes of older adults are easily accessible: physically slow, inflexible, incompetent, less worthy of our belief. If an older adult does have a limitation, it may be met with the belief that it is just what comes with the territory of being old. A tragic example of this can be seen with the diagnosis of depression in older adults. According to the National Institute of Mental Health (NIMH) (2003), a contributing factor to the low rates of diagnosis and treatment of depression in older adults is the belief that depression is an acceptable response to other illnesses or hardships that may accompany aging. Unfortunately, too many in our society, including health professionals, do not realize that depression is *not* a normal part of aging. Thus, not only are appearances deceiving, but so are the strong pictures of aging (and what may come with it) that are embedded in our social consciousness.

It is with an eye toward dispelling preconceptions and misconceptions that I approach the courses I teach on adult development and aging. Information provided throughout the course focuses on the physical, cognitive, and socio-emotional development of middle age and aging adults. I work to reinforce facts and dispel inaccurate beliefs. Many students are surprised by the following information:

- Dementia, including Alzheimer's disease, is *not* a normative part of aging, but rather a disease.

- Older adults do have sex and do enjoy it.

- While certain aspects of memory, cognition and learning might diminish, other aspects improve.

- Certain features of personality tend to remain fairly stable throughout one's lifespan. Hence, age does not cause one to become "stubborn" or "set in their ways." This may be an aspect of one's personality that has always been there.

- Older adults are a diverse group of individuals, even more so than younger adults. However, the stereotypes of older adults do not give voice to this truth.

The power of stereotypes is strong. Even in the face of contradicting evidence, some beliefs are so deeply ingrained that students continue to revert back to them. Fortunately, there are also successes that leave me feeling inspired, hopeful and motivated to continue the struggle against ageism. Following are two such examples:

1. I started volunteering at the assisted-living facility on which I did [a class assignment]. Yesterday was my first day … and what a day it was! … One of my main jobs is to talk one-on-one with the residents and get their stories. I get to talk to them about simple things like what their

favorite color is or who their favorite person is. But, in those simple questions are pathways to the stories of their lives. Today I talked with a 90-year-old woman who has significant dementia and depression. We talked for an hour in the morning and every time I could get her to smile at an old, happy memory it was like the clouds parted and the sun shone bright and beautiful. (J. Lawrence, personal communication, May 6, 2009)

2. I went into the [Human Development and Family Studies] major wanting to work with kids … and taking your class changed my mind. I now want to work with older adults…. I think one of the videos you showed toward the beginning of the semester made me definitely change my mind. It had interviews of older adults and one of them said they feel invisible. I think older adults have so much knowledge and so many stories to tell and people in our society really look past that. (E. Knop, personal communication, May 4, 2007)

In sharing these excerpts, I would like to recognize the countless number of students that have touched my life and honored me with their experiences. These are just two of many students that shared their stories of *seeing* older adults, rather than letting them remain invisible. Accounts such as these give me hope of a world that values all life, in all its splendid diversity.

CONCLUSION

The introduction of the term ageism has been attributed to Robert Butler, M.D. (1969), and is considered to be "a form of systematic stereotyping and discrimination against people simply because they are old" (Butler, 2008, p. 40). The consequences of ageism are similar to those of other prejudices. Older people may feel ignored, not be taken seriously, feel invisible, and be patronized. They are often the subjects of physical, emotional, social, sexual and financial abuse (Butler, 2008).

Unlike other prejudices, though, it is extremely commonplace and accepted to see advertisements and greeting cards openly and unabashedly perpetuate ageism. Older individuals are depicted as less able, forgetful, dependent, sexless persons and in effect, to be avoided at all costs. In many ways, ageism is something people are unaware of as it is a comparatively new and subtle concept (Palmore, 2001).

Ageism is different from other "isms" in another profound way: **everyone** has the potential to experience it firsthand if they live long enough. Not only may one be the target of ageism from others, but it is very likely that one will have internalized negative messages about aging throughout their lives and thus engage in self-directed ageist thoughts and behaviors. This self-directed ageism hinders people from fairly and accurately assessing their own abilities, and from recognizing unfair treatment or assessment from others (Bodily, 1991).

My journey of self-discovery towards ageism is ongoing. On numerous occasions I must challenge myself to face my own beliefs, behaviors, and automatic assumptions about older people. This, then, allows me to really see the person and honor who she/he is.

DISCUSSION QUESTIONS

1. What immediately comes to your mind when you see an older adult? How often do you even notice older adults in public?

2. Take one, or all, of the Facts on Aging Quizzes by Palmore (1988) and utilize your scores and the correct answers to delve into the various aging stereotypes that emerge. (At the time of this writing, these quizzes could also be found online at: http://www.msstate.edu/org/gerontology/.)

3. What do you fear most about aging? Are your fears based on fact or stereotypes?

4. What will you have to give up if you stop believing _____ (stereotype about aging)? What pressures do you have to not give up this stereotype?

5. What will you gain if you give up _____ (stereotype about aging)? What will others gain?

REFERENCES

Bodily, C. L. (1991). "I have no opinions. I'm 73 years old!": Rethinking ageism. *Journal of Aging Studies, 5*(3), 245–264.

Butler, R. (1969). Age-ism: Another form of bigotry. *The Gerontologist, 9*, 243–245.

Butler, R. N. (2008). *The longevity revolution: The benefits and challenges of living a long life.* New York: Public Affairs.

Gruman, G. (1978). Cultural origins of present-day "age-ism": The modernization of the life cycle. In S. F. Spicker, K. M. Woodward, & D. D. Van Tassel (Eds.), *Aging and the elderly: Humanistic perspectives in gerontology* (pp. 359–387). Atlantic Highlands, NJ: Humanities Press.

National Institute of Arthritis and Musculoskeletal and Skin Diseases (NIAMSD). (n.d.). *Rheumatoid arthritis.* Retrieved May 5, 2009, from Medline Plus: http://www.nlm.nih.gov/medlineplus/rheumatoidarthritis.html

Nelson, T. D. (2005). Ageism: Prejudice against our feared future self. *Journal of Social Issues, 61*, 207–221.

NIMH (2003). *Older adults: Depression and suicide facts (fact sheet).* Retrieved May 30, 2009, from http://www.nimh.nih.gov/health/publications/older-adults-depression-and-suicide-facts-fact-sheet/index.shtml

Palmore, E. (2001). The ageism survey: First findings. *The Gerontologist, 41*, 572–575.

Palmore, E. B. (1988). *The facts on aging quiz: A handbook of uses and results.* New York: Springer.

✳

Stories of Internalized Oppression, Acculturation, and Assimilation and the Complexities of Identity

Introduction to Part IV

In the *Stories of Internalized Oppression, Assimilation, and Acculturation*, the authors (most of whom are people or color) present their stories about the impact of internalized oppression and the subtle nature of assimilation and acculturation in varying contexts. Choudhuri's, "Oppression of the Spirit," graciously offers the reader an opportunity to see the power of oppression in her interactions with Shania, who is institutionally classified as African American, but was culturally Native American. Choudhuri, an Asian Indian, also fails to rightly assess the background of Shania and the differences between herself and her client. Emotional chaos ensues for both in their interactions with each other as well as with those outside of their relationship. Our next author, Gonzales, also looks at "Acculturation and Identity" and shares his perception of psychological and economic privilege as it relates to Mexican American students who distance themselves from the Mexicans "across the border" and who exchange or try to exchange components of their culture, such as the values of their parents and their native language, to obtain the benefits of the dominant White culture. Lichaw and Howell-Carter "Unmask

Within-Group Prejudice" by exposing the sometimes subtle nature of assimilation and its impact on the relationship between a counselor of color and her supervisee. Much of the story addresses Mayra's issues as a light-skinned African American woman examining the ideal of meritocracy and its distortion by racism and other "isms."

21

✳

Oppression of the Spirit

Complexities in the Counseling Encounter

DIBYA CHOUDHURI

INTRODUCTION: SHANIA

Shania sat before me, face turned obstinately away, looking out of the window, her eyes both distant and angry. I leaned forward to make the plea I had made too many times before. "Shania," I said, "I know you can do it. I know how intelligent you are; all you have to do is try, but you're giving up before you even start!" This conversation was part of a familiar dance we would do throughout the academic year. We would have a productive counseling session in which she busily planned out her schedule, organized her time, and made commitments. Then, during the next session, she would disclose that she had not followed through on those promises and would retreat into silence when I pursued her. I felt sure she could succeed; she seemed sure she would fail.

Shania was a sophomore in the university, institutionally identified as African American. She was a grudging member of the Black Students Association, an enthusiastic, but erratic member of the Women of Color group, and passionately attached to the Multicultural Center where I worked as a counselor. Academically, she traversed heights and chasms. Each semester she would start out with A's and end up with Incompletes from sympathetic professors who wanted to give her a chance, but didn't get much work from her. She received failing grades from professors too busy or too disinterested to notice the emotional chaos in which she was enveloped. When Shania was interested, she was dazzling, with great flashing eyes and beaming smiles, her heart on generous display. She was obviously intelligent with a facility for taking passionate and insightful part in discussions of multiculturalism. Her faculty noted her brilliant contributions to class discussions but bemoaned her lack of follow-through in producing written work. Indeed, upon first acquaintance, Shania seemed an ardent, committed, and intelligent young woman of unlimited potential. When she crashed, as I later discovered, the results were oftentimes late-night phone calls from her, threatening suicide. After her first year, Shania had been put on academic probation and was mandated to see me for counseling. I had recently graduated from my master's counseling program and Shania was one of my first clients. I desperately wanted to help her live up to the potential she so obviously had.

INTRODUCTION: DIBYA

I am an Asian Indian woman and a first-generation immigrant. I arrived in this country for college at 17 years of age with my family left behind in India, and I was quite happy to make it on my own. I had always been rebellious, fervent in my support of socialist ideals, and encouraged by my family's tolerance of my activism.

When I came out of four years at an Ivy League women's college, I was committed to issues of diversity. There, I had been one of those students who chanted slogans such as "Racism is a disease." We marched and protested to fight for the institution's divestment in South African business and support of apartheid and for increased ethnic minority representation among the faculty and staff of our college. After college, I continued working in an academic setting, administering a community-service program. This employment kept me in touch with human services and I continued to work with people in homeless shelters and domestic-violence clinics, and via suicide hotlines. I decided to go on to graduate work to formalize what I felt was my intrinsic passion to help.

My graduate program in counseling honed my counseling skills and gave me some theories that I alternatively questioned and accepted. For instance, while I loved the empowerment and respect inherent in the person-centered approach, I also felt intuitively that this approach might not work too well with clients who might be in survival modes. I pursued my interest in multicultural counseling with little support or guidance from faculty. I would read widely, following the work of scholars such as Pedersen, Sue, Ivey, and Arredondo, and would often find my faculty unfamiliar or unaware of the issues I then raised in classes. I attended workshops and conferences at which I could get some of the training and I used my electives to take classes in women's studies and anthropology. In spite of my efforts, I was woefully unprepared for Shania.

SHANIA REVISITED

Theoretically, I framed Shania's issues in a social and familial context (McGoldrick, Giordano, & Pearce, 1996). The narratives we form about the ethnic histories and group identities from which we emerge pattern how we organize to meet the changing contexts of our environment. In a sense, we are lived[1] by the stories of our race and place. Our stories inform us in togetherness and separation.

Shania's father was African American and she identified her mother as Native American, although she was unclear about the particular tribal affiliation, which is often critical to establishing identity (Sutton & Broken Nose, 1999). The first 10 years of Shania's life were spent on a reservation, but when her mother died, she was moved to a major city and placed with female relatives of her father.[2] Here, she grew up in poverty and was handed from relative to relative. In spite of the obstacles associated with poverty and her unstable living arrangements, Shania was able to attend college on a full academic scholarship. However, this college was a majority-White institution located in a cosmopolitan but small and mono-cultural town very different in community from both the reservation of her childhood and the urban surroundings of her youth.

Shania had absorbed the attitudes of women from her Native American nation, women whose position was of greater flexibility and power than in dominant society (LaFromboise, Berman, & Sahi, 1994). I believe that culturally Shania often gave the wrong cues and was subtly contradictory—looking African American, but acting in ways her African American peers didn't understand. When disturbed, she retreated into cold silence rather than in the expected manner of "in-your-face" confrontation.

Constantly confronted and frustrated by the issues associated with being a woman of color on a predominately White campus, Shania was likely in the throes of reconstructing her racial and ethnic identity. The Racial/Cultural Identity Development Model developed by D. W. Sue and D. Sue (1999) acknowledges similar patterns of adjustment to cultural oppression experienced by many members of minority groups, regardless of specific ethnic identity. In this model, the individual moves through five stages of development as he or she strives to come to terms both with the demands of the majority culture and the culture of origin, and the oppressive relationship between both. The stages delineated are conformity, dissonance, resistance and immersion, introspection, and finally, integrative awareness (Sue & Sue, 1999).

Shania seemed to be in the resistance and immersion stage with her passionate endorsement of minority-held views and her blanket rejection of dominant society values. Her anger toward White society, her conflicted empathy toward other groups of color, and most importantly, her reactivity were key identifiers to place her in this stage. One of the significant issues in such a stage is developing an identification with and immersion in one's own reference group of origin. However, Shania's struggles in this stage seemed complicated by the confusion

---

1. This is a postmodernist metaphoric phrase implying that unlike the notion of individuals approaching their lives independently, the social contexts and histories we inherit have far greater agency than we admit—we may not live them so much as they live us.

2. In African American families, often the female kin will be responsible for child-raising rather than the man whose offspring it is. He may offer financial support from time to time, but it is the grandmother and often older aunts who take over the day to day responsibilities. In Shania's case, she never actually spent much time with her father who migrated frequently all over the country.

about the reference group available to her. In this majority White, mono-cultural community, Shania's visible appearance identified her as African American, even though her inner ethnic and cultural reference group was Native American. She struggled with her connection to the Black Students' Association and the African American community because she felt like an outsider. However, given her commitment to activism and her upbringing by her father's family, she did not want to be perceived as rejecting the African American community. At the same time, trying to find a reference group that was similar to her inner experience was difficult given the distance of her original kin.

Based on messages she had received from her father's family, she feared she would also be considered an outsider among Native Americans because of her appearance. Physical appearance has often been a central part of social relationships, and this is particularly true for women. The physical ambiguity of perceived difference in appearance for mixed-race women can be particularly painful as a central part of self-worth (Root, 1994). Confronted by such dilemmas, Shania lashed out at everyone, sabotaging both her academics and her relationships. As Houston (1985) framed it in her poem about her own "Amerasian" mixed identity, Shania had "a soul composed of wars, mixed pride, and agony" (as cited in Root, 1994).

THE COUNSELING PROCESS

Shania and I worked together for a year in counseling. I began our work with providing a space in which she could speak. There were many silences, sometimes lasting half the session, but those I could take in stride given the cultural encounter (Herring, 1999). In my office, I had arranged the chairs so either one of us could look out the window to the trees beyond and Shania would spend long moments contemplating the vista while I tried to attend without staring intrusively (Sutton & Broken Nose, 1999). When she was particularly upset, she would take a shawl I had hanging and cover herself with it, as if in a cocoon. She would often miss sessions or come late. These times would be followed by the times when she contacted me every day with anguished refrains that evidenced her disintegrating emotional state.

Whenever there were such opportunities, I tried to bring her into contact with some of the local Native adults I knew who played leadership roles in the Native community. Many responded to her with warmth; but here too, she alternated between reaching out and withdrawing.

During a particularly harrowing period, when most of our interaction consisted of her either being silent or accusing me of not caring, I tried storytelling (Herring, 1999). Using the Ericksonian model of storytelling (Wallas, 1985), I carefully constructed for her a fantasy about a school in which a young girl learns to be a puppet master, only to discover to her shock that she and all those around her have strings attached to them. They too, are puppets. I detailed the girl's angry, shamed, and destructive responses and then led into her realization that the strings went both ways. She could dance to others' manipulations or she could use her connectedness to influence in turn and be interdependent. We didn't delve into the story or analyze it, but after that she seemed somewhat more thoughtful and less reactive. In our journey together, however, we seemed as lost as before.

My work with Shania brought my competence into question. Essentially, no matter how empathic I tried to be with her, I felt personally let down by her because I could not see why she was failing. I knew that she had encounters with racism on this predominantly White campus; but then, so did I. I had been followed and threatened, both verbally and physically. Through our sessions, I learned that Shania had conflicts with many of the other African American students, especially the men. In my mind, I framed the conflicts as her attempt to self-sabotage and alienate her own support group. My internal litany, especially obsessive after our counseling sessions, sounded something like, "Why can't she focus on the good stuff instead of the bad?" or "Why can't she let it go when a certain young black man talks about women derogatorily?" or "Why can't she hear that they aren't targeting her...?"

In spite of my apparent lack of success, Shania kept coming to our sessions with a willingness to give me and our counseling relationship another try. Perhaps she knew that despite my judgments and critical attitude (relatively visible despite the patina of my person-centered approach), I did care about her and believe in her. Where I failed her was in translating my awareness of the sociocultural conflicts she brought with her into a clinical approach that was effective.

DIBYA REVISITED

What I left out of the above clinical description was the exploration of my own privilege and oppression, a process that might have enabled me to understand Shania's impasse more clearly. Because I used my own identity as a woman of color as the focal point for understanding and interpreting her behavior, I assumed that Shania's emotional issues were based on the day-to-day harassment women of color face. When she related examples of being overlooked in class by the professor or of being asked whether she had really done the assignment by herself, I responded with understanding, but also with some underlying impatience. In my thoughts shaped by my own internalized oppression, I asked, "After all, wasn't this par for the course? One simply had to be twice as good to withstand the criticism." In doing this, I failed to notice the profound differences between us, differences my understanding could not encompass. One important difference between Shania and me was that for the first 17 years of my life, I did not live in a society in which I was the minority. I was raised middle-class and came from a caste background that gave me privileged access in my home country to almost everywhere I wanted to go. These differences in historical and lived experience profoundly affected the interactions and understandings that I brought into our counseling sessions.

As an immigrant of color, I understood the impact of racism in the present United States society, but I had little experiential understanding of racism as a generational force that operated to punish and confirm status. India, by its own history, still struggles with the impact of 200 years of colonization by the British and the legacy of internalized oppression that seeks paleness in its women, adeptness at Western cultural norms to denote competence and achievement, and infinite adaptability to oppressive conditions. My own internalized oppression led me to admire White people, because my attitude toward them was that they were absent conquerors who had left an admirable heritage. I internalized the "immigrant's optimism" and belief that struggle brought reward—the belief that if a person does everything twice as good as another, success is an inevitable outcome. After all, many others, including myself, have worked hard and become successful. I often wondered why the next person, in this case Shania, couldn't follow suit. My perspective of "I did, so why can't you?" caused me to overlook how messages of success have been defined by White, middle-class society for people of color in the United States. For some people of color, particularly Native Americans, the defined success may require directions that conflict with cultural lifestyle orientations (Tafoya & Vecchio, 1999).

I wanted Shania to succeed because she was a woman of color with whom I felt kinship; I wanted her to overcome obstacles because I cared and I thought she could do it because I had. I had no emotional understanding of the paralyzing traps she was in, traps in which failure and successes were one and the same. Although achievement and success were framed as desirable, they were defined in particular ways—as accessible through academic success in college using a language, stance, and process infused with White, middle-class values. If Shania did achieve that success, she faced losing her already-fragile membership in the communities of people of color. She had lost so much in her life already—her indigenous community, her mother, her father, her sense of family, and the norms and values she had come to know. No wonder she resisted when I asked her to risk losing what little she had left.

RESOLUTIONS: SHANIA AND DIBYA

At the end of her sophomore year, Shania told me that she was dropping out of school and planned to return to New York. I struggled with her decision, for she relayed no sense of future plans or purpose to go along with her decision. I foreshadowed a life of drifting that might end sharply, given my knowledge of her self-destructive attempts. I dreaded that I would someday hear that she had ended up in a series of positions that took no account of her amazing intelligence and generous spirit—or worse, that she had committed suicide. I felt a lack of competence in my abilities and viewed this act as failure by both of us, even though I argued and fought with her and for her, far more than I ever had with any other client. Nevertheless, she still left.

Two years after Shania left for New York and at a time when I was leaving my work site to go on to a doctoral program, I received a letter from Shania. In it, she detailed an incredible journey in which she had returned to the city, but then gone on to return to the reservation. She had made contact with some of her mother's relatives and reconfirmed her roots. She also ended up working with a youth-at-risk program. After having those experiences, she believed that she was ready to continue her education. During that time, she had been successfully taking classes at a local college to finish a degree in education, and she intended to get a graduate degree in social work so she could go back and work on the reservation.

In her letter she wrote that many things I had said to her during our counseling sessions were making more sense now, but she had needed to be at home to hear them properly. She did not elaborate with examples, so I can never know which of the many things I said to her stayed and which faded (and I suspect we might each have chosen different examples when pointing to critical moments). She finished with saying that although we had had our "fights," she wanted to let me know what was happening in her life because she knew I had cared. I cried when I read that letter. My tears were for the thankfulness I felt for her triumphs as well as for my own sense of relief and competence.

CONCLUSION AND LESSONS LEARNED

It has been many years since the experiences discussed here, but I have never forgotten the lessons. I am determined to stay conscious and humbled. To be framed in the role of expert who passes on the knowledge of multicultural counseling to others is a shaky endeavor. I realize we have much to learn about the convoluted nature of oppression and the resistance of privilege to self-scrutiny. The generations of learning and misinformation have deep roots, which can bear poisoned fruit that we ingest without ever knowing we are doing so. Knowing the theory of cultural competence is rarely sufficient to knowing the practice. Our own perspectives and worldviews, no matter how scrutinized through classes, theory, and academic experiences, still hold potency when we are challenged to reach across and be respectfully present and engaged with "an Other."

In counseling, it is in the spirit that we perceive the impact of oppression: the defeat and the despair, the self-hatred and the sabotage, the disjunction and alienation. In other roles, we can advocate and struggle against systems, but in the counseling relationship itself, I believe it is essential to work with the noxious messages that sicken the spirit. Effective multicultural counseling goes beyond theoretical knowledge of the stages of racial identity development (D. W. Sue & D. Sue, 1999) and a "culturegram" awareness of cultural customs (Culture-Grams, 2003). To infuse one's counseling and truly recognize the multicultural nature of every encounter is to become committed to interrogating the self in multiple contexts. If we can look at oppression as a powerful systemic force that shapes our worldviews, status, history, and experience, we must acknowledge that it permeates our practice. Every encounter invokes some aspects of oppression. The degree to which we can scrutinize both the client and ourselves and attend to the ways in which each of us brings to the mix our perspective of the world is the degree to which we can perhaps avoid replicating the toxicity of oppression. And because legacies of oppression and privilege are heavy with emotions such as shame, guilt, anger, and resentment, we must be prepared for the emotional upheaval of such scrutiny. Our reward for perseverance is that of the positive impact that uprooting the legacy of privilege and oppression has on both our clients and ourselves.

DISCUSSION QUESTIONS

1. How might you frame Shania's issues developmentally? Can you decipher ways of self-presentation that might be traced to her various cultural constituencies?

2. Are there any theories on multicultural counseling that might be helpful in practice with such a client?

3. In working with a client such as Shania, what issues of your own oppression and privilege might you need to explore and bracket?

4. What might the counselor have done here that could have been more helpful to Shania?

5. As a counselor, how can you manage your frustration and disappointment when a client is not helped?

REFERENCES

CultureGrams (2003). *Culturegrams: The nations around us, world edition.* Lindon, UT: Ferguson Publishing.

Herring, R. (1999). Counseling with Native Americans and Alaska natives: Strategies for helping professionals. *Multicultural aspects of counseling series 14.* Thousand Oaks, CA: Sage.

LaFromboise, T. D., Berman, J. S., & Sahi, B. K. (1994). American Indian woman. In L. Comas-Diaz & B. Greene (Eds.). *Women of color: Integrating ethnic and gender identities in psychotherapy.* New York: Guilford Press. 30–71.

McGoldrick, M., Giordano, J., & Pearce, J. K. (1996). *Ethnicity and family therapy* (2nd ed.). New York: Guilford Press.

Root, M. P. (1994). Mixed-race women. In L. Comas-Diaz & B. Greene (Eds.). *Women of color: Integrating ethnic and gender identities in psychotherapy.* New York: Guilford Press. 455–478.

Sue, D. W., & Sue, D. (1999) *Counseling the culturally different: Theory and practice.* (3rd ed.). New York: John Wiley & Sons.

Sutton, C. T., & Broken Nose, M. A. (1999). American Indian families: An overview. In M. McGoldrick, J. Giordano, & J. K. Pearce (Eds.). *Ethnicity and family therapy* (2nd ed.). New York: Guilford Press, 31–44.

Tafoya, N., & Vecchio, A. D. (1999). Back to the future: An examination of the Native American holocaust experience. In M. McGoldrick, J. Giordano, & J. K. Pearce (Eds.). *Ethnicity and family therapy* (2nd ed.). New York: Guilford Press, 45–54.

Wallas, L. (1985). *Stories for the third ear: Using hypnotic fables in psychotherapy*. New York: Norton.

FURTHER READINGS ON WOMEN OF COLOR
PERSPECTIVES AND PRACTICE

Adleman, J., & Enguidanos, G. (Eds.). (1995). *Racism in the lives of women: Testimony, theory, and guides to antiracist practice*. New York: Harrington Press.

Anzaldua, G. (Ed.) (1990). *Making face, making soul = Haciendo caras: Creative and critical perspectives by feminists of color*. San Francisco, CA: Aunt Lute Foundation books.

Anzaldua, G., & Moraga, C. (Eds.). (1983). *This bridge called my back: Writings by radical women of color* (2nd ed.). New York: Kitchen Table, Women of Color Press.

Bulkin, E., Pratt, M. B., & Smith, B. (1988). *Yours in struggle: Three feminist perspectives on anti-Semitism and racism*. Ithaca, NY: Firebrand Books.

Comas-Díaz, L., & Greene, B. (Eds.). (1994). *Women of color: Integrating ethnic and gender identities in psychotherapy*. New York: Guilford Press

Flores, M., & Carey, G. (2000). *Family therapy with Hispanics: Toward appreciating diversity*. Boston: Allyn and Bacon.

hooks, b. (1984). *Feminist theory from margin to center*. Boston: South End Press.

Hull, G. T., Bell Scott, P., & Smith, B. (Eds.). (1982). *All the women are White, all the Blacks are men, but some of us are brave: Black women's studies*. Old Westbury, NY: Feminist Press.

Jordan, J. V. (Ed.). (1997). *Women's growth in diversity: More writings from the Stone Center*. New York: Guilford.

Kim, E. H., & Villanueva, L.V. (Eds.). (1997). *Making more waves: New writing by Asian American women*. Boston: Beacon Press.

Lorde, A. (1984). *Sister outsider: Essays and speeches*. Trumansburg, NY: Crossing Press.

McGoldrick, M. (1998). *Re-visioning family therapy: Race, culture, and gender in clinical practice*. New York: Guilford.

Mohanty, C., Russo, A., & Torres, L. (Eds.). (1991). *Third world women and the politics of feminism*. Bloomington: Indiana University Press.

Romero, M., Hondagneu-Sotelo, P., & Ortiz, V. (Eds.). (1997). *Challenging fronteras: Structuring Latina and Latino lives in the U.S.: An anthology of readings*. New York: Routledge.

Rothenberg, P. (2000). *Invisible privilege: A memoir about race, class, and gender*. Lawrence, KS: University Press of Kansas.

Seeley, K. M. (2000). *Cultural psychotherapy: Working with culture in the clinical encounter*. Northvale, NJ: Jason Aronson.

22

✳

Acculturation and Identity
Intra-Ethnic Distinctions Among Mexican Americans
GENARO GONZALEZ

INTRODUCTION

I have taught psychology for fifteen years in the same South Texas area where I was born and raised, on the border with Mexico. If your cognitive road map conjures up San Antonio, you must still imagine driving directly south for another four hours, into *deep* South Texas.

During the past decade, the region has become one of the fastest-growing metropolitan areas in the country, yet it remains one of the poorest and least educated. My university more or less mirrors our demographics: of our 14,000 students, about 85 percent are Mexican American.

Being a native son, the Psychology Department hoped that I might serve as a role model. At a time when minorities were sometimes hired with only their race or surname to substantiate their status, my cultural credentials were authentic. My first years were spent in a family of migrant workers who followed the harvest across state lines. After my parents' divorce, my life became less nomadic, but still mired in poverty. Even after my mother remarried, my stepfather's wages as a taxi driver in a small town barrio barely matched her sporadic earnings in produce-packing sheds and fieldwork.

Both my father and stepfather were indifferent to my college plans and my mother's illiteracy could do little to counter their inertia. The region's dismal track record for supporting minorities in higher education did not help either and after two years in the institution where I now teach, I left for California where I eventually completed my doctorate in psychology. I turned down better teaching possibilities in order to return to this region and its university. Prior to my current position, I had also taught for several years in central Mexico in order to improve my Spanish and cultural awareness.

At first glance, my background would seem an ideal match with the student population. Certainly my personal history would not seem unusual for those of my generation. Nor is it that different from the backgrounds of first- or second-generation students who currently live in *barrios* or *colonias* (outlying, unincorporated communities with substandard housing). However, most of my Mexican American students now come from middle-class homes where English is often the language of choice. So, rather than resonating, my story comes across as a quaint tune. Despite our ethnic bond, my observations of growing up in the same place, but at a different time and in different circumstances, often elicits discomfort or defensiveness rather than ethnic solidarity. Perhaps their desire to gain acceptance in mainstream society requires that they ignore reminders that Anglo Americans might not welcome them with open arms. Thus, the disconcerting anecdotes of past local discrimination that I include in my Social Psychology classes, along with discussions on in-group prejudices based on skin color, make more than a few squirm uncomfortably.

I incorporate these anecdotes because any meaningful study of the Mexican American experience must examine prejudice and stratification, both historical and actual. But, a disturbing number of my students dismiss these issues as irrelevant, although in truth, a subtle yet complex denial seems at work. The uneasy nature of that underlying dynamic is a central aspect of this chapter.

More specifically I shall try to show how acculturation, by encouraging a blanket adoption of mainstream values, also ends up promoting mainstream prejudices against Hispanics. As a Psychologist, I am interested in the inner conflicts and doubts that this process may create in Mexican Americans, especially with respect to identity. Further, I shall explore the relationship between assimilation and privilege—how increased acculturation often goes hand in hand with added privilege, psychological as well as material. Indeed, a major incentive for acculturating is the accretion of social status, but as we shall see, one by-product of this process may be in-group prejudice. Finally, I shall touch on the occasional irony and paradox that comes with acculturation and privilege. For instance, acculturated Mexican Americans may find themselves on the "privileged" side of the stratification equation yet may end up as spokespersons or role models for the less privileged in their group. Such a redefinition of their status may force them to confront anew the culture they thought they had left behind, as well as their uncertain relationship to the nonprivileged members of their stigmatized group.

ACCULTURATION AND ITS DISCONTENTS

Although intrigued by findings that on average our Mexican American college students were quite "Americanized" (Cuellar, Arnold & Gonzalez, 1995), I first attributed the phenomenon to the changing times. The success of the Civil

Rights struggles spearheaded by my cohorts and I had paved the way for an acculturated generation who prefers English to Spanish and envisions endless opportunities ahead. My occasional reflections in my Mexican American psychology class of barrio life and migrant camps were a far cry from the middle-class world that most of my students and I now inhabit.

Before proceeding further, however, some aspects of acculturation, a central construct of this chapter, must be clarified. Acculturation, as first formulated in the literature (Redfield, Linton & Herskovits, 1936), described the process that occurs when two cultures come into contact. It does not presume that an acculturating individual will necessarily lose her original culture while adopting the new or host culture; when the latter does occur, the result is assimilation. In practical terms though, for ethnic groups during our country's history, acculturation and assimilation have generally gone hand in hand, regardless of which side one takes in the culture wars. That is, those who promote pluralism and diversity lament the loss of the native culture. Those who advocate a melting pot agenda lament that the shedding of the native culture and the acquisition of the host culture does not occur as fast or as thoroughly as they would like. For that reason, despite the conceptual differences, I shall use the two terms interchangeably.

Similarly, I am using the concept of identity in its broader, generic sense, including elements of self-esteem and self-evaluation. Various investigators (Cross, 1987; Rotheram & Phinney, 1987) have shown that ethnic identity is a complex construct, and that its relationship to acculturation and assimilation can be subtle and even relatively independent (Keefe & Padilla, 1987). However, these important and interesting nuances are beyond the scope of this chapter. I have chosen instead to examine identity in a more generic manner while still focusing on cultural themes and ethnicity.

I admit that my observations of what happens to my students are influenced by the nature of my own immersion into the larger society. While my contact was gradual, many of my students grew up in families already well immersed in the mainstream language and culture. While the lack of Latino success stories during my youth may have limited one's horizons and aspirations, it did make for a more clear-cut ethnic identity: Anglos were the "haves"; Mexicans were the "have-nots." By contrast today's ethnic stratifications are blurred, with Mexican American role models in greater abundance, especially those in the public eye. What goes unsaid is that the crossover performer or politician either expunges many of the ethnic elements from his public persona or else lacks them from the start, since by definition a crossover success must appeal to the mainstream. Usually this is not evident to my students, since the ethnic angle of these role models that is highlighted and promoted is often obvious (for example, a Spanish surname), yet trivial (for example, only a surname). The end result is a simulacrum; yet for many of my students this is fine since the recipient role model carries the imprimatur of the mainstream society. Here one can return to the earlier distinction between acculturation and assimilation, adding that while acculturation is largely a personal choice, successful assimilation requires that the larger society give the go-ahead through opportunities and access. Thus, for true assimilation, acculturation is necessary but not sufficient.

How then, does one assimilate? Through imitation of course, and like other forms of social learning this typically occurs through observation and interaction. But in a geographic area where barely 20 percent of the population is White and where even that small proportion tends to live within its own ethnic enclave, opportunities for observation and interaction can be problematic. One possibility involves vicarious or virtual interaction in the form of the constant multimedia portrayal of White America that enters almost every Hispanic home on a daily basis. Yet these sources depict a very distorted picture of mainstream America. Even "reality programs" portray the larger society in a way that is closer to hyper-reality. The result is that a border Mexican American growing up in an insulated environment ends up emulating the caricatures from the popular media. The corrective influence that might come from real and meaningful interactions with White people is often absent. Acculturation can have another unfortunate consequence. Mainstream views of Mexican Americans are often pejorative, so in seeking to enter that world, my students are pressured to incorporate a negative view of themselves, of family, and of friends.

Although I am not a clinician, my Psychology credential is incentive enough for students to drop by my office to talk about matters that usually transcend academic concerns. Once the discussion takes a turn for the personal, anxieties and insecurities over acculturation are not far behind. One familiar scenario with Mexican American co-eds centers on family tensions, and with slight variations, follows a pattern. She lives with her family, but the father disapproves of her weekend activities and returning at late hours. The mother, trying to mediate, merely antagonizes the father and exacerbates the conflict. Only gradually does the student see the clashing cultural dynamics. On the one hand she craves the independence of those media American coeds she seeks to emulate. Yet she also wants the emotional support and stability that comes with remaining "under her parents' wings," without realizing that such support comes with a price—following her father's rules, based on bedrock cultural attitudes. Oftentimes she simply tries to dismiss that world as "antiquated and out of touch" with modern times.

Although I hear such complaints frequently, for most of these young women, an objective analysis of the situation is neither obvious nor automatic since their premises are based on nonconscious ideologies (Aronson 1972, p. 178). She sees her need for personal privacy and independence as utterly natural; unfortunately her father sees *his* demands in the same way. The result is a recipe for culture clash with neither side realizing the implicit cultural assumptions of their respective views.

EDUCATION AND THE EXACERBATION OF INTRA-ETHNIC DISTINCTIONS

The theme of education is crucial to understanding both acculturation and identity among Mexican Americans. In fact, acculturation is re-education by the host culture. Although this new enculturation involves much informal and implicit learning, a large part is in fact formal. Therefore, educational institutions are crucial to acculturation and assimilation.

With "visibly identifiable" minorities such as Mexican Americans, one must realize that the very things that distinguish them as such are characteristics such as skin color and facial features. When one has these ascribed characteristics, there is little one can do to erase them. By contrast, educational attainment and its concomitant acculturation, resemble more an achieved status. As such, it offers the possibility of attenuating or minimizing one's minority status. It is no accident that efforts to allow Latinos fuller participation in mainstream society place an overwhelming emphasis on higher education. Beyond the obvious tools of knowledge and skills in the sciences or the arts that higher education provides, one must not underestimate its importance in "Americanizing" (that is, assimilating) the individual into a more homogenous cultural mold.

In addition to physiognomic criteria, Mexican Americans face other factors that accompany discrimination. For instance, even those with light complexions or more European features might still end up "aurally identifiable" due to distinct accents or limited English vocabulary. Here too, however, education offers a way out with its emphasis on language fluency.

The significance of education as a "cultural stamp of approval" may be difficult for White Americans to appreciate. After all, their formal education is largely an expansion of the cultural history, language, and attitudes already embedded in their early enculturation. For many Mexican Americans students, higher education legitimizes them to themselves and provides a ticket into a culture that views them as quasi-Americans. A college degree symbolizes their entry into mainstream culture. It not merely accredits their grasp of the arts and high culture; it validates their ability to navigate American lowbrow culture. Much has been made of the fact that the average college curriculum, far from being culture-free or culture-fair, often places those with nonmainstream enculturation at a disadvantage. For instance, Anglo instructors may pepper their lectures with American idioms and with references to popular culture. And yet this very same biased nature adds to the college diploma's worth. For some Mexican American students it affirms their enculturation into popular culture, including the latest fads and phrases making the rounds in mainstream America.

OTHER FACTORS THAT AFFECT IDENTITY

If I have painted a somewhat dismal portrait of the cultural orientation of Mexican American students at my university, one must remember that many do not resemble this generalization. Moreover, it is discouraging only if one advocates true cultural diversity and not simply the hollow paeans to pluralism one hears in academia, where cultural icons are trotted out on designated days while pluralism is left to languish the rest of the time.

To an extent, my concern lies in the eye (or ear) of the beholder. When I told a White colleague how quickly cultural awareness was eroding among my students, he first seemed genuinely puzzled. He then countered that he almost always "hears Spanish in the halls." I had to point out how often I *didn't* hear it, adding that perhaps his not being bilingual makes him overlook and forget the familiar (English) while remembering the foreign (Spanish).

The loss of cultural awareness and identity is all the more striking considering that our university is less than a half-hour drive to Mexico. This loss is probably worse the farther north one gets from "ground zero—the border," yet that proximity may paradoxically accelerate our acculturation. One reason is that Mexican American students here, despite their efforts to acculturate, are still more likely to understand and speak Spanish than those beyond the border area. Not that our students have greater cultural pride than others elsewhere; we simply live in Mexico's backyard so our exposure to its language and culture is overwhelming. An exodus of immigrants sees to it that our language and traditions are continuously replenished translating into a kind of cultural surplus rarely seen beyond the border. Whereas Mexican American youth elsewhere may find themselves fighting to retain diminishing traditions, our own students may unwittingly see themselves amidst a cultural excess and therefore entitled to squander some.

Yet were they simply shedding elements of their ethnicity due to a cultural glut, one would not encounter the cultural disparagement so often seen and heard. Here too, our proximity to Mexico plays a key role, since many find it difficult to identify with a mother country whose own people appear to be leaving in droves. To a social scientist, the reasons for the emigration are obvious— poverty, coupled with lack of opportunities. But many of our students, like much of the larger society, view these deficits as inherent conditions or characteristics rather than as causes. The end result is a pejorative perception of anything "Mexican," including their own ethnic origin.

A variation of this can be an intra-ethnic pecking order. For instance, a number of my native-born pupils criticize or disparage Mexican-born students (naturally, after first stopping to ascertain that *I* am not foreign-born). However, the prejudice does not end there. A first-generation victim may in turn point out that she lives here legally, while so-and-so does not. I have even talked to undocumented workers in the community who acknowledge their status, yet quickly add that they hold jobs, while their neighbors down the block are "not only illegal but on welfare." The aforementioned dichotomy of cultural adoration and cultural disdain fits Spicer's (1977) model of ethnic identity: individuals exposed to a culture with superior material benefits tend to embrace it openly. For instance, Spicer points out that such was Rome's prestige in the ancient world that its conquered subjects sometimes viewed their new status as a step up. Similarly, I regularly encounter immigrant "overshooters" who ape every mainstream fad and bend over backwards to appear more Anglo than Anglo Americans. In such an uneven playing field, their original culture is bound to lose prestige (Royce, 1982).

Unfortunately, acculturation may also encourage such individuals to adopt negative stereotypes about their group. So although recent Mexican immigrants bring positive in-group stereotypes, over the long-term they internalize the negative stereotypes of the larger society (Dworkin, 1965; Buriel and Vasquez, 1982). Juggling these prejudices requires considerable cognitive contortions. One favorite strategy with my students is to footnote their pejorative attitude with more positive exceptions (that is, themselves). Although research on this subtyping model (Webber & Crocker, 1983; Kunda & Oleson, 1995) centered on the prejudices of majority groups, I frequently find a self-subtyping variation among my students. While acknowledging that many Mexican Americans are poor and/or ill-educated, the acculturating individual carves out a more exclusive and desirable sub-category, referring to himself as Latino or Hispanic (supra-categories, actually). In sum, the person rationalizes that although s/he technically belongs to the stigmatized group, s/he nevertheless differs from the stereotype.

CONCLUSIONS AND A CAVEAT

Teaching at a university with a historical commitment to Hispanic students, I undoubtedly stress higher education for us. Yet my personal and professional observations also suggest that this view might be at cross-purposes with promoting ethnic awareness and identity. Even educators who have no qualms with assimilation must address the argument that as Mexican Americans move away from traditional values, they become more prone to deviancy and other social ills (Buriel, 1984). Offering college courses that validate diversity may help, but the token effort at most universities makes one wonder whether this really makes a difference. Ideally an additive approach to acculturation could provide the tools and skills to succeed without relegating one's original culture to ridicule or irrelevance. In reality though, we promote an educational process that impedes an affirmation of indigenous cultures.

A central theme of this book examines discrimination from the perspective of the privileged and/or oppressor. The draft of my original chapter contribution dealt more explicitly with the porous barrier between oppressors and oppressed, specifically Hispanics who first find themselves on the receiving end of discrimination; but later, through education and acculturation join the ranks of the privileged. This is not without cultural conflict and role strain. In fact, the issue is not limited to Mexican Americans who make a successful mainstream transition. Others from disadvantaged groups (for example, women and other discriminated minorities) make similar transitions and may face a crossroads with respect to identity and realizing that rather than leaving behind their status of visible minority, they now have a mutated status—*privileged* visible minority. This includes those whose new privilege anoints them as role models or as cultural contextualizers who work as ethnic go-betweens. The irony is that instead of lessening their cultural identity, it becomes even more salient.

In this chapter I examine not the end result—a privileged status—but the acculturation process leading to a privileged status including conflicts over identity that may carry over into the new status. In the trenches of the current culture wars, this sometimes translates into personal acts of resistance. For instance, some of my Chicano colleagues pay lip service to pluralism, but fail to follow through with congruent conduct. I have tried to do otherwise. Rather than let my first language wither, I forced myself to improve it in Mexican classrooms before firing squads of unforgiving undergraduates. Similarly, my refusal to neutralize or neuter my name ethnically elicits disapproval at times, and not only from Anglo Americans. I have done likewise with my child's name, realizing that it might narrow her options, not only within the mainstream, but among assimilated Hispanics as well.

And yet, whenever I hear Hispanic parents call out to their children with the hyper-Anglicized names that are all the rage in our community (Roberts, 1996), I try to restrain my cultural condescension. It is difficult to fault parents who reasonably believe that the strategy will enhance their child's chances in our country. I try also to remind myself that faulting them is a bit too facile, since my own brand of acculturation has already afforded me a certain degree of affluence. Still, I wish it were possible to convince them, along with my students, that one can master a second culture with minimal loss of the first or of one's identity.

DISCUSSION QUESTIONS

1. The above account describes a region where the minority status group is numerically the majority. Discuss how rather than producing a paradise free of prejudice, many Mexican Americans in the community practice their own brand of stereotyping. Explain what pressures, insecurities, and influences (for example, proximity to Mexico's poverty) might motivate them to do this.

2. Malcolm X once remarked that the mainstream society's greatest crime against African Americans was to teach them to derogate themselves. How might a similar argument apply to Mexican Americans with respect to their views of their own culture? What anxieties and emotional conflicts might be found in an acculturated person who, in "passing" from a stigmatized status to a more privileged one, tries to distance himself through a pejorative dismissal of his own cultural origins?

3. In some respects the internal "culture (civil) wars" that Mexican Americans often experience is merely a domestic variation of a drama played out globally among groups that are undergoing contact with American culture. Describe current or historical examples of other cultural groups who have undergone cultural conflict in dealing with another culture, either directly or indirectly (for example, through films, the internet, etc.).

CASE SCENARIO AND DISCUSSION

A graduate student conducting an interview in a Mexican American barrio asks how its residents view mainstream America and how they believe it in turn views them. In one home, the head of the house replies that although they may have experienced prejudice from White people, he is still proud of the fact that everyone in the house is native born, unlike the family at the end of the block. At that very next house the interviewer is told that while others may look down on them for being first-generation, at least they are in the United States legally, unlike the family two houses down. Upon being interviewed, that third family admits to its undocumented status, but quickly adds that at least they are all hard workers, unlike the family across the street, who is not only undocumented, but on public assistance as well.

1. In the above scenario discuss the statuses (generation level, employment, etc.) around which the intra-ethnic prejudice is crystallized.

2. Scapegoats are easy targets of discrimination due to their relative lack of power. How does the pecking order of the above scenario support this?

3. Discuss how the first individual interviewed responds to being viewed as a target of prejudice. Compare this to an approach that considers the larger societal forces that help create the prejudice in the first place.

REFERENCES

Aronson, E. (1972). *The social animal.* San Francisco: W.H. Freeman and Co.

Buriel, R. (1984). Integration with traditional Mexican-American culture and sociocultural adjustment. In J. L. Martinez, Jr. & R. H. Mendoza (Eds.). *Chicano psychology* (pp. 95–130). New York: Academic Press.

Buriel, R., & Vasquez, R. (1982). Stereotypes of Mexican descent persons: Attitudes of three generations of Mexican Americans and Anglo American adolescents. *Journal of Cross-Cultural Psychology, 13,* 59–70.

Cross, W. E. (1987). A two-factor theory of black identity: Implications for the study of identity development in minority children. In J. S. Phinney & M. J. Rotheram (Eds.). *Children's ethnic socialization: Pluralism and development.* Newbury Park: Sage.

Cuellar, I., Arnold, B., & Gonzalez, G. (1995). Cognitive referents of acculturation: Assessment of cultural constructs in Mexican Americans. *Journal of Community Psychology, 23,* 339–356.

Dworkin, A. G. (1965). Stereotypes and self-images held by native-born and foreign-born Mexican Americans. *Sociology and Social Research, 49,* 214–224.

Keefe, S. E., & Padilla, A. M. (1987). *Chicano Ethnicity.* Albuquerque: University of New Mexico Press.

Kunda, Z., & Oleson, K. C. (1995). Maintaining stereotypes in the face of disconfirmation: Constructing grounds for subtyping deviants. *Journal of Personality and Social Psychology, 68,* 565–579.

Redfield, R., Linton, R., & Herskovits, M. J. (1936). Memorandum on the study of acculturation. *American Anthropologist, 38,* 149–152.

Roberts, S. (1996, March 3). Forget Jose. There's an America of Kevin's and Ashley's aborning. *The New York Times,* p. E3.

Rotheram, M. J., & Phinney, J. S. (1987) Definitions and perspectives in the study of children's ethnic socialization. In J. S. Phinney & M. J. Rotheram (Eds.). *Children's ethnic socialization: Pluralism and development*. Newbury Park: Sage.

Royce, A. P. (1982). *Ethnic identity: Strategies of diversity*. Indiana: Indiana University Press.

Spicer, E. (1971). Persistent identity systems. *Science, 4011*, 795–800.

Webber, R., & Crocker, J. (1983). Cognitive processes in the revision of stereotypic beliefs. *Journal of Personality and Social Psychology, 45*, 961–977.

✳

Unmasking Within-Group Prejudice

A Case Study

FELICE LICHAW AND
MARYA HOWELL-CARTER

This narrative was written by two people: Felice, a supervisor in a community-based counseling center, and Marya, her supervisee. Their story highlights the impact of internalized oppression and the revelation of internal attitudes through good supervision.

INTRODUCTION: FELICE

I come from a Jewish, lower-middle-class family. My mother emigrated from Czechoslovakia with her family when she was quite young, and most of my maternal grandmother's family was killed in the Holocaust. My father was a first-generation American (United States) whose father had been persecuted as a Jew in Poland and Russia before World War I. I am the daughter of this union.

Having spent the majority of my 20-year career working with clients whose cultural contexts differed from my own, I was well down the road toward understanding the role of culture in treatment when I met Marya Carter, then a second-year doctoral student. Marya applied for an externship at our agency, a private, not-for-profit, community-based youth-service agency. The agency serviced a large and diverse area of Chicago including a historical port of entry for immigrant populations. The students at the high school closest to our location spoke a mix of 102 languages. Our primary population was African American adolescents and their families and I was looking for a student who would be available to interact within our clients' diverse cultural contexts. Marya was searching for a site at which to complete her externship and she had an interest in working with youth and families of color.

In our first interview, Marya presented herself as an open, enthusiastic, and idealistic young woman. She looked "fresh." She seemed surprised by some of my questions, but she gamely answered them, particularly the one I asked all students about what brought them to the agency and what they wanted to get out of the experience for themselves. I can't remember exactly what Marya said about her motivation for working in our agency. It might have been something about fulfilling the need to give back to her community or wanting to learn more about working with youth and families, but it was sufficiently self-motivated for her to be offered an externship.

INTRODUCTION: MARYA

My father is African American. Born in the 1920s of southern parents who migrated north to find work during the years following World War I. In the late 1960s, he married my mother, the daughter of a Caucasian German farm family in Central Michigan. I was born in Detroit, not long after the fires of the 1967 race riots destroyed much of our city. As I grew up, my father from time to time warned me about the legacy he perceived to be mine. "You are a Black woman; you will always be at a disadvantage. To be successful, you have to work harder and be smarter than everyone else."

I believed my father and identified with his admonitions—that is, Black women must do more and do it better, and they will never be given anything for free. What my father didn't realize was that, because of my light skin, I was insulated from many of the harshest realities Black women face.

When I decided to enter the field of Psychology, I made the commitment to work with People of Color. As the time for choosing training experiences approached, my graduate-school peers chose field placements in the affluent, White, and Jewish communities of Chicago's North Shore. I assumed that being Black, I wouldn't feel comfortable in those settings and that the people in those settings might not feel comfortable with me. I wanted to gain experience in a community of "my people," a community with "real problems," a community that needed someone like me—an educated, socially conscious, Black clinician.

My requirements for choosing a clinical placement were shaped by an additional assumption that I made about myself: that being African American, I could not exercise prejudice. Although I had been protected from the most blatant expressions of prejudice, I thoroughly understood the history of pain and disenfranchisement that Black people had endured as subjects of one of its forms—racism. I assumed that this awareness would protect me from engaging in any form of prejudice or discrimination.

UNDERSTANDING THE EXPERIENCE OF PRIVILEGE—
COMING TO CONSCIOUSNESS: MARYA

When I began my externship, I was totally unaware of the ways in which dominant cultural stereotypes had infiltrated my thinking about both about African Americans and other People of Color. I am now aware that the American myth of the meritocracy had pervaded my thinking. I had not yet examined how the ideal of meritocracy had been distorted by racism and other -isms. Despite my academic and family training about discrimination, I believed that those who are not successful are flawed either by illness, poor work ethic or a misunderstanding about the requirements for success. I thought that in becoming a therapist I would help my community by helping them to combat their "flaws" and achieve success.

I began my externship with Felice at Alternatives Inc. in the fall of 1991. During the first weeks there, my work seemed to be going well. I was making efforts to connect with my clients and it appeared that they were engaging in the therapeutic process. However, as time progressed, clients stopped regularly attending their therapy sessions with me. I became frustrated with their sporadic or nonattendance and started to look for an explanation.

The psychodynamic perspective I had learned at my White, upper-class university informed me that my clients were being resistant. In contrast, during supervision, Felice attempted to normalize the experiences I was having. We discussed the agency's client population and the factors that make nonattendance, sporadic attendance, and attendance only during acute crisis common. We also began to explore ways to change client expectations about attendance and counter the resistance sometimes associated with nonattendance. Yet I remained unclear about what kept certain clients engaged in the therapeutic process and not others and uncertain whether I was providing an appropriate therapeutic environment.

Looking for role models, I began to more closely examine the attitudes and practices of other therapists working at the agency and I noticed that my colleagues were not all equally skilled. While some were open, conscious, and sensitive in regard to the cultural contexts of their minority clients, others were ignorant, even offensive. I judged these to be poor therapists: People whose upbringing, race, and education limited their worldview and prevented them from connecting with our client population. At the same time, I realized that I shared something with this group. We had the same pattern of no-shows, cancellations, and premature terminations. I began to experience a growing dissonance between how I viewed myself and how my clients might be viewing me. As my recognition of my problem grew, so did my anxiety and confusion.

REFLECTIONS ON CHANGE: MARYA

Like the therapists I was so quick to judge, I realized that I too had failed to engage my clients by not creating a safe space where their experiences, strengths, and culture defined the context in which change occurred. Instead, I was attempting to replicate the values of the world in which I lived—particularly values around promptness, openness, and parenting. Without being fully aware of it, I expected my clients to tune into my values and to adopt those values as their own. I was replicating the experience of invalidation that they faced in their everyday lives.

I was an extremely reluctant supervisee as I struggled to understand why I was not having the success that I had expected. As the hour for weekly supervision approached, I experienced a pervasive feeling of heaviness accompanied by nausea. I attempted to avoid supervision by being late or "forgetting," and I gained a temporary reprieve from self-examination by diverting attention to my "acting out." The reason for my symptoms was the dissonance I experienced during supervision. I was being challenged to see my clients as whole people who were successful and productive in ways that I, as a product of the dominant culture, did not accept. I was being asked to view my clients not as the victims I perceived them to be, but as people living within a particular set of circumstances to which they responded adaptively. They were doing the best job that they knew how to do. I could not yet see my clients' strength, resilience, and integrity, a view that would enable me to effectively assist them in creating change.

The feeling in the pit of my stomach before every supervision session also came from the discovery that my cultural assimilation had been so pervasive that I was having difficulty meeting the expectations of my supervisor. Recognizing my middle-class status and embracing middle-class values made me different from the clients with whom I worked and impeded the therapeutic process. I also found it difficult to accept that a White, Jewish woman—both descriptors are important to me, given the history of interaction between these groups as I experienced them growing up in Detroit—had more insight into, and understanding of, the effects of economic deprivation and racism than I had. Fortunately, I was sufficiently engaged in the learning process to continue with supervision even though the dissonance it created was quite uncomfortable.

ENGAGING IN THE PROCESS OF CHANGE: FELICE

While Marya was working through this phase in her identity development, I was thinking about how I could help her to understand the context of the clients she was working with. Although it was true that Marya was biracial and had been raised in a predominantly African American community, it is equally true that there is a great amount of variability within African American communities (Ibrahim, 1991), and that relative privilege within does exist. She seemed to have a background that engendered that relative privilege. I knew that she had done her undergraduate work at a prestigious university and had won a fellowship for graduate study there. This led me to believe that in high school, she had achieved a degree of academic success which surpassed most, and that she also had managed to sustain her excellence through four years of undergraduate study to win a fellowship. When Marya and I began to work together, I did not yet understand how the dynamic of relative privilege would unfold within the process of her professional development.

It seemed to me that the best way to help Marya understand our clients and explore her own privilege was to acquire information regarding her context. When we began supervision, I attempted to establish a "safe" relationship. Establishing a safe relationship with a trainee is much like establishing a safe relationship with clients in therapy. The supervisor is required to maintain an attitude of acceptance and willingness to engage with the trainee's experiences, knowledge, mistakes, and criticism. If the expectation of the supervisor is that trainees will work within the contexts of their clients, the supervisor has to model this by working with the context of the trainee. Establishing a safe relationship also involves setting both norms for what is appropriate for discussion in supervision and having clear role expectations with the accompanying role accountability.

There were some important ground rules that I communicated to Marya at the beginning of the relationship:

1. Cultural identity is a valid and valuable tool for establishing connection with others.

2. It is important to accept and respect your own culture as well as others' cultural identities.

3. Discussion of cultural background, differences, and expectations is normal within the context of both the supervisory relationship and within the therapeutic relationship.

4. Respect for clients' cultural contexts is an important tool in establishing relationship.

5. Understanding context is an important part of understanding people's culture.

6. All cultures are adaptive in the sense that they are made up of components that help people get the work of living done.

7. Some adaptive cultural components may have outlived their usefulness yet still remain parts of the culture. These parts are usually referred to as dysfunctional.

8. Cultures' dysfunctional components offer valuable information about history and current functioning, and through implication, possible roads toward change.

Underlying these ground rules was my assumption that Marya came to our agency with her own set of experiences, beliefs, and assumptions about the world around her and the people in her world. These assumptions formed the framework that she would use in creating relationships. I asked Marya countless questions in an attempt to assist her in making her assumptions explicit. Explicit assumptions are more easily clarified and more easily shaped to include novel situations. I set out to assist her in developing an awareness of her own values, beliefs, and assumptions, with the intention of facilitating both the engagement process and her own counter-transference issues.

I was aware of the differences in our cultures and was deliberate in my attempts to understand and bridge the gaps in our culturally based understanding. I was curious about Marya, as I am curious about most people, and let my curiosity guide me in the process of uncovering the gaps and making connection.

I came to supervision aware that there is no single correct way of doing things or of seeing the world, and with the hope that I would model a good example within the supervisory relationship for working in treatment. I encouraged Marya to try new things and to make mistakes. I also encouraged confusion—in my experience the precursor to change. My goal was to assist her in ferreting out her "truths," and to challenge those truths when I saw them interfering with her efficacy in the development of therapeutic relationships. This formed the basis of our supervisory process. There is risk involved in this method—the student may be intolerant of dissonance or may not be developmentally or emotionally ready for change. Happily, Marya was ready to engage in this process. The stage had been set for her to begin to explore her identity as a therapist working with poor minority populations.

INTERNALIZATION OF CHANGE: MARYA

Clinical supervision furthered my understanding of my role with clients and my awareness of my own privilege. It helped me to see that I had been using my own cultural experience to infer my clients' cultural context. Although many things about Felice and her personal style spurred this change, the aspects of supervision that had most influenced me were the inquiries she made during supervision. She asked "How" questions about my clients, as well as about my own context and racial identity.

Felice asked me for information about how my clients experienced the world, and how their life experiences had affected them. Quite often, these were questions that I had never considered. I had learned to ask the "What" questions such as "What were the client's experiences?" Once I knew "what," I thought that my theory of psychopathology and my own ability to reason would provide me with the answer to "how" events had affected the client. Coming from a doctoral program that rarely addressed multicultural issues, I had not been encouraged to counsel ideographically. According to Ridley (1995), "The idiographic approach underscores the need to understand the personal meaning held by the client as a particular person, not simply as a representative of certain groups" (p. 83). By believing that I knew something about my clients because I was a Person of Color, I was ignoring individuality and within-group variation. As Ibrahim (1991) points out, "Treating any person as a stereotype of his or her cultural group violates the person's individuality and may lead to premature termination, with minimal therapeutic effectiveness, and possible negative outcomes regarding the client's perceptions of the counseling . . . profession" (p. 14).

The early stages of a therapeutic relationship largely consist of information gathering, assessment, and goal setting—what people's experiences have been, what those experiences mean about them, and how the process of treatment will proceed (Cormier & Hackney, 1987). After meeting with clients in these early phases, I would return to my desk, think through the information a client had given me and connect that information to the problem that had prompted the client to seek therapy.

For example, if an adolescent client reported that his mother was abusing drugs and that many of his friends were in a gang, I made the assumption that these factors were significant in his choice to be gang-involved. Gang membership provides adolescents with a substitute family. Based on this logical, research-based, well-intentioned understanding, I would create treatment goals and decide on a treatment approach. Before Felice inquired, I did not routinely ask a client how he or she interpreted life events or how had those events influenced the client's decision-making. My cultural encapsulation was so powerful, my socialization so great, and my education so narrow that I believed that I already knew the answers.

At the beginning of my externship and supervisory relationship, I was excited about the treatment-planning work that I had done for those clients because I *thought* I understood them; particularly those African American clients who I perceived were so culturally similar to me. However, as time progressed and attendance waned, so did my excitement. Fortunately, Felice's questioning of me regarding how life events had shaped my clients, and her insistence that I answer with what *they* had said about how life had shaped them and the meaning *they* made from their own experiences (rather than with assumptions and theories), prompted me out of my role as the expert who knew more about my clients than they knew about themselves. I began to understand why clients had cancelled, failed to attend appointments, or terminated therapy altogether.

My growing insight led to many discussions about the difficulty I experienced in asking clients the questions that were so critical to my forming a complete understanding. Often, I failed to ask the questions because I assumed I already knew the answers. As I learned to consciously question, to allow my curiosity to lead me, I had to constantly remind myself that the clients are the experts themselves and of their experiences. My work as a therapist is to assist clients in discovering their own paths toward change.

MARYA'S FINDINGS AND CONCLUSIONS

During supervision, I was asked how my life experiences had shaped who I was. This questioning led to conversations that made explicit my own strongly held cultural values, beliefs, assumptions, and counter-transference issues, and it helped me develop a tolerance for dissonance, ambiguity, and my own mistakes.

Since my work with Felice in externship, I have gone on to teach and train new counselors in multicultural counseling. The experiences that she and I shared in that formative year shaped the approach I have taken in training students to be culturally competent. This approach is consistent with the recent literature about multicultural competence in counseling (Arredondo & Arciniega, 2001; Vinson

& Neimeyer, 2000). The Association of Multicultural Counseling and Development (AMCD) identified three domains that are crucial in developing multicultural competence in clinicians: Counselor Awareness of Own Cultural Values and Biases, Counselor Awareness of Client's Worldview, and Culturally Appropriate Intervention Strategies (Arredondo et al., 1996, as cited in Arredondo & Arciniega, 2001). All of these strategies help to reduce the level of stereotyping, reduce the exertion of privilege, and eliminate the imposition of majority culture values that may occur in counseling.

DISCUSSION QUESTIONS

1. How are dominant cultural stereotypes perpetuated by organizational or institutional structures? How might this perpetuation affect an individual's ability to develop awareness about prejudice?

2. What are some of the values that you hold that might limit your ability to make connections with clients?

3. When a direct supervisor has difficulty accepting his or her own privilege, how might a supervisee work through his or her own biases? What resources might students draw from to further their cultural competence?

4. How might universities better integrate issues of multiculturalism, privilege, and racial identity development into both their curricula and training experiences?

5. Should universities have responsibility for overseeing multicultural training in off-site training facilities?

6. Although some people are ready to confront their prejudice, others are not. What methods, other than direct confrontation, can help people to uncover their prejudice?

REFERENCES

Arredondo, P., & Arciniega, G. M. (2001). Strategies and techniques for counselor training based on multicultural counseling competencies. *Journal of Multicultural Counseling and Development, 29*, 263–274.

Cormier, L. S., & Hackney, H. (1987). *The professional counselor: A process guide to helping*. Englewood Cliffs, NJ: Prentice-Hall.

Dukes, R. L., Martinez, R. O., & Stein, J. A. (1997). Precursors and consequences of membership in youth gangs. *Youth and Society, 29*, 139–166.

Gibbs, J. T. (1989). Biracial Adolescents. In J. T. Gibbs, L. N. Huang, & Associates (Eds.). *Children of color: Psychological interventions with minority youth* (pp. 322–350). San Francisco: Jossey-Bass.

Ibrahim, F. A. (1991). Contribution of cultural worldview to generic counseling and development. *Journal of Counseling and Development, 70,* 13–19.

Maxson, C. L., Whitlock, M. L., & Klein, M. W. (1998). Vulnerability to street gang membership: Implications for practice. *Social Service Review, 72,* 70–92.

Ridley, C. (1995). *Overcoming unintentional racism in counseling and therapy: A practitioner's guide to intentional intervention.* Thousand Oaks, CA: Sage.

Vinson, T. S., & Neimeyer, G. J. (2000). The relationship between racial identity development and multicultural counseling competency. *Journal of Multicultural Counseling and Development, 28,* 177–188.

✳

International Perspectives— Stories of Privilege, Acculturation, and Assimilation

Introduction to Part V

N ew to this edition is the section on "International Perspectives" where we read about the issue of privilege and oppression via the voices of individuals who were not born in the United States. These authors share similar circumstances due to practices in their own country and/or due to their immigration to the United States. In "Deprivations and Privileges We All Have," Tuason tells us about being born and raised in Baguio, a small city in the northern island group of the Philippines. Kawewe, growing up in Rhodesia (now Zimbabwe), shares with us how she "Navigates Oppression, Power and Privilege in Academia." Both Tuason's and Kawewe's stories share similar threads of living in poverty, but being able to obtain access to education via scholarships and chance occurrences. Both authors also describe the discrimination they incur in the United States because of their status as women of color. Chao, an Asian female psychologist, goes "Through Cultural Barriers in Counseling" as she brings to the forefront a scenario in which her client, a White female, feels that Chao is incapable of understanding her issues because of Chao's Asian ancestry. Chao finds few resources among her colleagues or in western literature and as a result, she (re)turns to her roots to address her circumstances with her client. In "Elaborating a Different 'Yes, But'" Riggs highlights the issue of Intersectionality Theory, which provides us as readers the scope to move beyond seeing identity categories as additive and instead conceptualize identity categories simultaneously. Although many of our previous authors have spoken to the topic of multiple identities amidst their dominant identity, Riggs—born and raised in Australia—focuses on the intersections of his identity as a white[*] gay male to tell his story.

The voices and stories of these international authors give us a glimpse into the language and culture of their own countries. The voices and stories also remind us of the fact that distance is no barrier to privilege and oppression.

---

[*]White is not capitalized as an ethnic designation in this instance at the request of the author.

24

✳

Deprivations and Privileges We All Have

MA. TERESA TUASON

INTRODUCTION

I was born and raised in Baguio, a small city in the northern island group of the Philippines. I am one of six children. My parents came from poor families and became teachers, a profession that does not pay well. We all lived in a one-bedroom apartment. We had no cars and no medical insurance, and subsequently, we rarely went to the doctor when we had an ailment. Before my parents could afford the apartment we rented, we stayed in my maternal grandparents' shack with my mother's four other siblings. We ran to the neighbor's house when there were typhoons or strong winds for fear the shack would be blown away with us inside.

I knew we were poor; it was evident by what we ate in school (that is, our lunch box from home almost always contained a serving of rice, one small piece of meat or fish, or a few pieces of vegetables; or on more difficult days, just rice with soy sauce or used oil for flavor), what clothes we wore, what toys we could not have, and occasionally by the fact that I was hungry on the days when we could not afford three decent meals a day. Although poverty was a common experience for those around us, I had always felt that we were poorer. We were six children to feed and we had to share and divide everything into six portions; including one chocolate bar. I knew we were poorer because my mother would do anything to augment the family income, including selling foodstuff and dry goods to her co-teachers. As children, we also sold candies to our classmates to save up for a much-needed pair of shoes. Compared to other families, my parents could not afford a maid to help in the house or take care of us. So even at an early age, we were cooking, hand washing and ironing our school uniforms, washing the dishes, and fetching water. I also know that we never traveled to another place and we never had family vacations.

Although my parents did not bring home much money as teachers, their profession helped us to become educated. For our elementary education, the religious congregation that ran and owned the university at which my parents taught, schooled all six of us. Because of this, we had obtained our elementary education for free. For high school and college, some of us obtained scholarships because we excelled in school. My parents paid for tuition fees for the rest of us with money directly deducted from their salaries. I knew from my mother's and father's paychecks that most of what they earned went to schooling us. My parents had prioritized education before food and clothing expenses.

UNDERSTANDING AND EXPERIENCING CLASS PRIVILEGE

As a result of obtaining a variety of scholarships, I earned a Bachelor of Science degree in Psychology and a Master of Arts degree in Child and Family Psychology from the same Catholic university in Quezon City. After having earned my B.S. degree and while doing my master's program in the evenings, I taught third-grade boys for three years as my income-generating job. After I obtained my master's degree, the psychology department asked me to teach undergraduate and graduate courses as an instructor. During weekends and several hours in the week when I was not teaching, I practiced psychotherapy. In the Philippines, because of a lack of instructor resources, M.A. degree holders were given a lot of responsibility. Because there is no licensing body and no ethical and professional standards to practice by, M.A. degree holders practiced therapy mostly because there was much demand for this. I was informally supervised in my psychotherapy practice only because I sought it. In addition to studying and working full time, I financially supported a sibling through college.

After finishing my master's degree and practicing psychotherapy for four years, I decided to apply to Ph.D. programs in the field of Counseling Psychology. I applied to counseling and clinical psychology programs in the United States and in Europe. This was hard to do from far away because the mail took much longer and all the application fees and test requirements—for example, Graduate Record Examination (GRE), Test of English as a Foreign Language (TOEFL), Test of Spoken English (TSE)—were expensive. I also applied for several scholarships knowing that if I did not obtain one, I would never have a chance to pursue my Ph.D. in a different country. I was disappointed and very angry when I did not get a scholarship and a program acceptance on the first try, but I applied once more thinking that the wisdom of timing could be on my side the second time around. I was rewarded with an opportunity to pursue my dream and I finished my Ph.D. in Counseling Psychology at the State University of New York at Albany.

Coincidentally, Albany provided me with my first experience of feeling and being different. In Albany and at the University of Utah where I completed a pre-doctoral internship and postdoctoral fellowship, people around me did not look like me and I realized that everyone around me reminded me of how different I was.

After two years in Utah, I went back home to the Philippines, hoping and expecting to bring back and share what I had learned in the United States. Unfortunately, my culture's high-power distance (that is, perceived inequality in a hierarchy between a less powerful individual and a more powerful individual [Hofstede, 2001]), traditionalism, and hierarchy, did not allow me to fulfill my dream of applying what I had learned. For example, I was told by the Psychology Department chairperson in the Philippines not to teach the course any differently from how it had been taught during the past 20 years. The chairperson reprimanded me for incorporating what I had learned in the United States and wanted me to teach as if I had never gone to study at the doctoral level. Additionally, the economic and political crises in the Philippines could not offer me a starting point for a professional life. Even with good intentions, advanced educational degrees, and hard work, I was not able to afford myself a decent life in the Philippines. So I moved back to the United States, and I secured a counseling center job in Illinois.

DESCRIPTION OF CRITICAL INCIDENT THAT INCREASED AWARENESS OF RACE PRIVILEGE

Having now lived in the United States for about 5½ years, my experiences with issues of diversity relative to race and socioeconomic status have increased. It is here that I have experienced what it means to be treated as different, as Asian, or as someone of color. When I think of this experience, it is definitely a mixed blessing because although it is my experience that I am treated differently because of my color, it is also here that I experience being empowered to work, to teach, to do clinical work, and to be a psychologist. I am not only working and doing what I love best; I am also, at the same time, earning and giving my family and myself a chance of a better life. Back home in the Philippines, I could work as a psychologist and a professor until I died and I still could not afford to buy myself a car, build a house, or educate my children. Here in the United States, with the occasional reminders that I am away from home, the opportunities make it a place to dream, to work, and to feel justified for working.

My most painful struggles with prejudice and discrimination have been precipitated by strangers, making me feel both hurt and unsafe. Most incidents have been based on reactions to my physical appearance as Filipino—that is, my having straight, black hair; small eyes; darker skin; and small build (at 5 feet 1 inch in height). For example, I was walking home when a car containing three young, White teenagers passed. They were repeatedly shouting, "Go away! You are not supposed to here! You are not supposed to be here! Go away! You don't belong here!" I was hearing this in my head all 20 minutes of my way home. I was so afraid they would come back and hurt me physically. I was scared and pained, and I was thinking, if only they would give me a chance to talk, to speak, I would let them know why I am here and let them know how hard life is where I am from. I also wanted to explain myself and tell them how I have likened being Asian in the United States to being in the middle of two worlds, not quite belonging to either world, but being in the middle. I am never here nor there. It was difficult to leave my family, especially my ailing parents, and it was difficult to leave my friends, especially those who I learned so much from and who are so endeared to me like family. If only I could tell these teenagers I am here now in hope of a better life. What I would hope for in such a conversation is that they would gain an understanding of the helplessness in my situation and the power and privilege in theirs. I also would hope they would see that I am not any different from their own grandparents, parents, or ancestors who may have come here to the United States for economic opportunities and freedom.

On a different occasion, I was at an intersection waiting for the stoplight to change in my favor, when five White teenagers occupying the car beside me shouted at me and spoke to me in what seemed to be an imitation of the Chinese language.

When I tell friends and colleagues about instances such as these, I typically get responses of disbelief, an apology for the actions of the offenders or remarks that ignore the pain and minimize the source. However, the more subtle discrimination I experience from colleagues, and the insensitive comments about socioeconomic status are still yet the most hurtful and the hardest to deal with. With the aforementioned experiences of overt racial discrimination, I pretend not to hear, I pretend not to look, I pretend to be unaffected. I process these within myself and then I try to forget. With colleagues, I wish to let them know what it means and feels like to be poor, what it means when deprivation is re-experienced over and over, and what they can do to be sensitive to these issues.

Although I no longer feel poor, working with clients who are poor and listening to colleagues' comments recycle these issues for me. At work, for instance, a colleague came back from vacation and mentioned how her back was aching. The colleague candidly commented on how she and her family slept in third-world beds and drove third-world cars on third-world roads. I did not immediately realize how much this statement hurt me—not until this colleague apologized to me, knowing that I was born and grew up in a third-world country, the Philippines, and still consider it my home.

I also feel hurt when other people complain about what they are deprived of here, when I know and have experienced deprivation in other parts of the world. For example, a colleague talks about the amount of money her family spent buying a horse and another talks about the amount of money she spent buying work suits. These are all comments about their reality and are not meant to be hurtful. I, however, cannot help but compare these amounts of money to the amount of money my parents need for medical care and to the amount of money I need to send home.

In another instance, a colleague asked me what she could do for a client who had no place to stay. I immediately told her of the city's homeless shelter, where it was located, what it was like, and I asked if she knew whether the client had eaten or even had something *to* eat. My colleague admitted that she did not know this and had not thought to ask the client. My heart sank at the lack of awareness. It would not have taken much to ask these questions, especially if the client had already admitted financial strife.

On yet another occasion, I presented a client case to my colleagues. As I talked about the client's cultural context, family-of-origin issues, poverty, difficulty trusting another, and struggle being in college, my colleagues agreed about how resilient this client was, and how therapy had benefited her. But then, someone blurted out that although this client might be helped in therapy, the client "would be killed anyway" when she went back to her neighborhood. I was appalled at the bias and the insensitivity. My colleague was clearly coming from her own fear and judgment about the culture. I was hurt when I heard this because this culture and this neighborhood is what my client regards as home. I told myself, it is because of people's ignorance and statements like these that my client would never tell anyone, even a friend, where home is.

CONCLUSIONS AND FINDINGS

What I am conveying is the same point that cultural scholars have reiterated: that it is important to be aware of one's own cultural background so one can be sensitive to and realize, understand, and accept the similarities and differences in culture (D. W. Sue & Sue, 2003; Brislin & Cushner, 1996; Gudykunst, 1994; Landis & Bhagat, 1996; Sue, et al., 1998), and even to celebrate and appreciate these differences and their beauty.

We cannot end discrimination unless we realize privilege. In many instances, the help of those privileged individuals will be required to lessen the acts of discrimination experienced by those who are oppressed. It is a danger to ignore culture (Pedersen, 1994) and also a danger to ignore the privileges we all have. We all are influenced by our culture because we all grew up in a form of a family, a community, and a society. We all are still experiencing everyday events that create us and that constantly hone our culture. As much as deprivations and disadvantages are part of our culture, so are our privileges and our histories. Intrapsychically and within culture groups, healing comes from an understanding of pain and also an acknowledgment of privilege in other areas of life—understanding and acknowledgment that eventually will envelope the hurt. Personally, this meant that I recognize that I am privileged in other areas such as having attained an education and having the drive to pursue my dreams, and the resilience that pulled me through, having the respect of friends and a wealth of friends. In essence, for the oppressed, movement comes from allowing the hurt and pained side to heal, and consequently feeling empowered by embracing the privileged and deprived aspects of the culture. Additionally, among groups and within the human race, healing also comes from the privileged people's acknowledgment of the status, power, and identity that dictate other people's lives. For instance, in my life, what I acknowledge as a catalyst to this understanding is having learned from a close friend that rich people can be good people too. I then experienced and felt liberated from my anger when at least one person from the oppressive culture made a deliberate choice not to oppress. In essence, it is for the privileged to realize how they can advocate lessening oppression and share empowerment and privilege with others.

I have found counseling sessions-individual, group, or both--to be safe places for one to talk about hurts and deprivations, and about privilege. It is when we talk about the prevailing inequalities, the historical beginnings and status, and our cultural identities that we begin to feel safe to move beyond oppression and recognize what power we have in changing. It is when we acknowledge power that has been bestowed on us by our roles, the color of our skin, and the origins of our birth and families that we extend ourselves and are able to understand somebody else's oppression. Then, we own our responsibility to end the oppression and advocate for equity, respect, and justice. The safe places to which we entrust these vulnerabilities and these movements are deep connections such as friendships, families, and therapeutic relationships.

CASE SCENARIO APPLICATION

The counselor is from a poor and Filipino background The client is depressed, middle class, and Caucasian with German heritage. The therapeutic relationship is good and there is apparent connection. However, there is a "stuckness" in the process that is clearly due to differences that remain undiscussed. In the sessions, assumptions and expectations about each other's backgrounds are heightened and cause a lot of tension. Yet, to make things easy for the two of them, the client and counselor go along and pretend that these things are not there. The counselor eventually decides to discuss the issues causing the tension. Both talk about what they were used to, and what their families' biases have been related to the culture and socioeconomic status. This discussion ultimately became the pivotal point in therapy (that is, when the client realized what she had, the blessings and privilege she had, and when she found her direction in terms of what she wanted to do in her life). It turned out that the client's deprivation of dreams (lack of direction and drive) was the counselor's privilege (having had to leave Philippines to strive for a better life), and the counselor's financial deprivation helped the client see her own resources that she previously took for granted.

CASE SCENARIO DISCUSSION QUESTIONS

1.   What do you know about Filipino and German cultures?
2.   If you were the counselor in the case scenario, what would you have done to facilitate talking about the differences that mattered in therapy?

3. How would the situation be different if the counselor is middle class and Caucasian with German heritage and the client is poor and Filipino?

GENERAL DISCUSSION QUESTIONS

1. How can you tell when race, class, or other forms of diversity are at play in the counseling relationship?

2. What are the privileges, deprivations, oppressions, assumptions, and/or expectations when one is poor? Rich? Of Color? White?

3. How might you address the issues of clients who feel that they must constantly prove themselves or earn respect and understanding because of their nonprivileged status?

4. When you are prejudiced or biased in your interactions with another, do you hurt yourself also? Do you lose part of your humanity?

5. Who are the people in your life that have opened your eyes to oppression? Enabled you to look at your own prejudices and act with more knowledge and empathy? Taught you to act with more humanity? Explain.

6. Do you have friends you care for who are Persons of Color? Of various socio-economic statuses? What strategies do you use to talk about those differences?

REFERENCES

Brislin, R. W., & Cushner, K. (1996). *Intercultural interaction. A practical guide* (2nd ed.). Thousand Oaks, CA: Sage.

Gudykunst, W. B. (1994). *Bridging differences: Effective intergroup communication* (2nd ed.). Thousand Oaks, CA: Sage.

Hofstede, G. (2001). *Culture's consequences* (2nd ed.). Thousand Oaks, CA: Sage Publications.

Landis, D. & Bhagat, R. S. (Eds.). (1996). *Handbook of intercultural training* (2nd ed.). Thousand Oaks, CA: Sage Publications.

Pedersen, P. (1994). *A handbook for developing multicultural awareness.* American Counseling Association, VA.

Philippine Statistical Yearbook, 2000. Annual per capita poverty thresholds and incidences of population by region. National Statistics Coordination Board.

Pollard, K. M., & O'Hare, W. P. (1999). America's racial and ethnic minorities. *Population Bulletin, 54*(3), 1–48.

Sue, D. W. & Sue, D. (2003). *Counseling the Culturally Diverse. Theory and Practice.* New York, NY: John Wiley & Sons.

Sue, D. W. (2001). Multidimensional facets of cultural competence, *The Counseling Psychologist, 29*(6), 790–821.

Sue, D. W., Carter, R., Casas, J., Fouad, N., Ivey, A., Jensen, M., et al. (1998). *Multicultural competencies: Individual and organizational development.* Beverly Hills, CA: Sage.

25

✳

Navigating Oppression, Power and Privilege in Academia

An International Perspective

SALIWE KAWEWE

I was born and raised in Rhodesia (now Zimbabwe) during a time when
Europeans had divided Africa into colonies in the way that a turkey is carved
out during an American Thanksgiving (Toler, 1998; Kawewe, 2001). I was born
in a rural area between Gweru and Kwekwe in the Midlands of a country that
had been colonized by the British. Through fraudulency and armed defeat of the
Black natives, Europeans imposed their will and power by pushing the colonized
into these designated semi-arid, overcrowded, impoverished tribal trust or com-
munal lands where I grew up until I reached school age. The relationship between European colonizers and the indigenous populations was that of rider
and horse (Moyo & Kawewe, 2002). The former had the power to oppress
and exploit the latter through the use of force and/or deceit. Many colonial
Whites referred to us Blacks as "*kaffirs*," which is as derogatory as using the
word "*nigger*" in the United States.

Colonialism introduced a cash economy through coercion; legislative discrimination controlling Black movement; residential segregation and initiatives aimed at the
"domestication" of Africans including a host of other physical, psychological and socioeconomic measures designed to disadvantage indigenous peoples and their social

systems. These entailed retribution and imprisonment for failure to pay taxes for such things as dogs, huts, cows, and so forth. These practices combined, forced young men to migrate to urban areas, mines, and White commercial farms in search of work to earn cash. Basically, colonialism institutionalized the capitalist system and its Western values. However, those values pertaining to freedom, human dignity and property rights were not accorded for Blacks and were reserved for Whites only. As more men migrated to the new cities, rural areas became mostly inhabited by women, children, those with disabilities and those identified as elderly.

Able-bodied urban men would visit their families during vacations, particularly during the newly introduced Christmas holiday. Similar to the rural arrangement, housing in cities was arranged on racial lines. It was general practice that European employers provided accommodations for the Black workers in high density areas and made sure that beer halls were in close proximity to their sleeping quarters. During colonialism, these workers were referred to as "boys" regardless of their age; thus, "boy" became synonymous with any servant even after women joined the workforce. For those working for White families, their living quarters were called "boy's kaya" meaning "boy's home" even when the employed occupant was a woman.

Initially, urban housing was designed for Black men to share military-like living quarters or barracks, making it difficult for conjugal or family visits. One-pit latrines for ten or more people also limited personal privacy. As time went on, some companies provided single-room housing for their workers while municipalities in Black townships built housing which ranged from one to four rooms thus making it possible for more rural dwellers to visit their kin in the cities. A few females who ventured into urban life during this time sought employment as house maids while males were often employed outdoors as "garden boys" or indoors as cooks, and sometimes as cleaners. In cases of injury or disability, the affected laborer would lose employment and be forced to return to the rural areas without any compensation, pension, disability benefits or medical care. In such a case, the worker had become the weakest link for the new economic system, capitalism. A sharp contrast existed between urban housing for Blacks and housing for European settlers. European settlers lived in low density areas, modern houses, or even mansions that were far away from where Blacks lived. The only Blacks lingering in their neighborhoods were house maids, nannies and garden "boys."

MY NEW ENCOUNTERS

I had neither been to any urban area nor seen a White person until I was about school going age when our maternal grandmother, the family matriarch, took me and my two brothers to Gweru, a city in the midlands and now the third largest city in Zimbabwe. She wanted us to visit our mother who worked as a housemaid in a White suburb before, proceeding to go and live with our aunt in the Black township.

As we entered the city, I saw a White man for the first time and then I saw a White woman on high heels. I wondered if these "Varungu," Whites, were people just like us except for their skin color. When I learned that they were "bosses" or seen as superior to Blacks, I did not question it. I actually envied them. We were among the few native children to be exposed to the city and to also have direct contact with a White family. On this visit to my mom, which lasted about a week, my brothers and I played with the White child there who was about our age. I was happy to have my newly found White friend and playmate that I spent a lot of time with while my two siblings mostly played with each other. Once when we were playing, I remember crying because I was upset about something and this White girl started singing, "cry baby cry," repeatedly. I neither knew what it meant nor suspected she was making fun of me, but thought she was singing for me to be quiet. After this encounter, I would sing this song whenever another child cried back home. I was proud that I could sing in English even though I did not know what the song meant and it took me three years of elementary school education to understand what it meant. Until that time, I just thought that whatever White people did or said was superior, nice, and kind.

Sometimes my White playmate brought treats that we had never tasted to the servant's quarters and my mother's employers would often give us leftover food, which we gladly accepted and enjoyed. It was European food and we thought it was better than the "sadza" and "vusavi" we were accustomed to. Generally, "vusavi" consisted of cooked soup bone stew with green vegetables, or green vegetables with peanut butter or cooking oil. On rare occasions we would have beef steak or chicken stew. Sometimes our White employers let their child come to our quarters and we offered her our food as well. She would eat and tell us not to tell her parents because they did not want her to eat native food.

Another visit took us to my father who was employed as a cook in another part of town. He brought us European food from his employer as he also lived in the servants' quarters. My father's employer was stricter than my mother's; therefore, we only stayed there for two days. We had to be quiet, which was very difficult and boring.

Although colonialism was about segregation between Black and White people in both commercial farm areas and low density White areas, White parents were not effective in preventing their children from playing with Black children and the same was true of Black parents. Even with strict monitoring, enforcement was nearly impossible as kids of both races would mutually find secret rendezvous to play as kids do anywhere else. Servants were generally not allowed to receive visits from their families, but my mother's White employers were either kind enough to let us stay and play openly or were not bothered by it.

EDUCATION AND THE AFRICAN GIRL CHILD

Our final stop was my married aunt's house in the high density Black neighborhood of the city where my older brother and I were to enroll in school. I had already been groomed to be a future "good wife and mother" as I was the best house cleaner, cook, and babysitter within both the nuclear and extended family system. Meetings were held to discuss circulating me among my mother's, aunt's, and grandmother's households to help them with chores. The initial plan was that I would spend a month with each one of the three families. My mother told them that I was her child; therefore, there was no need for such an arrangement. My grandmother and my aunt complained that they had helped raise me when my mother was working and that it was unfair for my mother to now want me to only help her with housework and so on. The resolution was that I would primarily live with my mom, but my aunt could have me whenever she had to go on cross-border trading trips so that I would take care of her family while she was gone. My grandmother would have me in the rural areas during school vacations: two three-week breaks and one four-week break during Christmas.

Once I was enrolled in school I was motivated to learn how to read and write and "know everything." For a long time I believed that education would allow me to "know everything" and I chased this dream until I got to college where I realized I would never know everything and that education was a privilege that many Zimbabwean girls did not have. I was the second born in a family of six siblings. As a girl, the odds for further education were against me in a patriarchal society that still values males over females. My family planned to end my education at the elementary school even though I had done exceedingly well and enjoyed education. My older brother had lost interest during his fifth year of elementary education and my younger brother was only a year behind me, but my parents decided that there was no value in educating a female because I would get married and then end up using my education to benefit my future husband's family. My grandmother is the one who vouched for me by telling my parents that since I was too young to be married and since I was bright, the best option for me was to proceed with education. My mom insisted that I would be handy to my grandmother in the rural areas and that since I had reached puberty, I was at high risk of being impregnated and becoming an unwed teenage parent, which would shame the family. Since in our culture, whatever the oldest family member decides is what is generally adhered to, my parents yielded and I was able to seek enrollment in high school. These discussions and debates took place while I was on my usual Christmas break with my grandparents. By the time everything was resolved, I had missed the registration deadlines, three weeks of school, and all my neighborhood schools were full. It was then decided that I would proceed to Zambia in order to enroll in school there. This was a time when Zambia had just become independent and Zambians were returning home. My stepfather was a Zambian immigrant and likewise was making plans for the whole family to relocate that year. I also had a maternal uncle who had migrated to Lusaka, Zambia with his employment company. The arrangement for me to go to Zambia would later turn out to be a blessing in disguise as it opened up better opportunities for me.

INTERNATIONAL EXPOSURE IN PURSUIT OF EDUCATION

At fourteen years of age I left Zimbabwe by train and headed for Luska, the capital town of Zambia, with two pieces of paper in my possession: my uncle's and the school's addresses. Upon arrival, my uncle gave me a warm reception even though there was no advance warning of my arrival. In our culture we just travel and visit each other without having to make an appointment. A person just shows up and gets taken care of. Similar hospitality is also accorded to strangers in my culture. I told my uncle that I had been sent to live with him so that I could go to school. I gave him the appropriate piece of paper with the address on it and I read the contents of the note. The heading read "Regency Correspondence College" and "correspondence" was a big word for my stepfather who had written and handed over two addresses to me before I left Zimbabwe. My stepfather had about three years of elementary school education which he acquired as an adult learner through night schooling.

Zambia had recently become independent from British colonialism and its government was very progressive. Its people were excited. I enjoyed being in a free African country. I quickly adjusted and made friends which enabled me to learn the local language, culture, and a variety of foods as well. Through my uncle who was politically active in the Zimbabwe African National Union, the movement to liberate Zimbabwe, I learned about the availability of high school scholarships sponsored by the African American Institute (AAI) whose branch offices were in Lusaka. After passing the AAI's educational screening test, I and two other Zimbabwean girls became candidates for joining a co-educational boarding school, Kurasini International Education center in Dar-es-Salaam, Tanzania. My uncle went up in arms opposing my relocation, but when I insisted that I wanted to go to school, the political party representatives supported my position. After a while, my uncle changed his mind and accompanied me to the boarding school with two other politicians. In June 1966, one year and a half after my completion of elementary school education, I arrived in Tanzania. I enrolled in the first year (Form 1) of high school in the middle of the academic year by passing the placement test administered by the school. I was the only one who passed the test and joined that year's cohort of students at midstream while my two companions would be a year behind me thereafter.

Most of our teachers were either Black or White Americans who were positive role models for me and allowed me to ask many questions on racial discrimination during this time period of the civil rights movement in the United States. My education was transformed when I learned for the first time that Europeans had neither "discovered" Africans nor various places such as the former Victoria

Falls. This was an educational awakening, which included us Africans as actors in history. Kurasini International Education center boarded youth and adult student refugees from all southern African countries (Angola, Malawi, Mozambique, Namibia, and South Africa) that were still under colonialism with the exception of those from Malawi. Later, a few students from independent Tanzania, Zanzibar and Kenya were included. Tanzanians were the most hospitable people I had ever known and still are. They were poor, but casual, gracious, and giving. As refugees, we were welcome in any part of Tanzania in which we stayed or visited and we never felt like "aliens." They taught us Swahili, introduced us to new foods, and invited us to their homes to share their meals. The school allowed us the opportunity to mix with diverse people from Tanzania and refugees from various African countries. In turn, this provided the opportunity for us to learn about each other and discuss struggles of our individual and collective experiences with oppression, dispossession, and homesickness due to loss of family linkages. Sometimes we cried and other times we debated about staying in school or joining freedom fighters. Some left for the bush wars where they perished, but others of us stayed in school.

Approximately seven of the first high school graduates from Kurasini, were sent to the United States and we escorted them to the airport to bid them farewell. I asked why they were going overseas to the United States and they told us that it was for further education since their motherlands were not yet independent. I told them that I would not stop going to school until I knew "everything." This had become more compelling after completing grade school when I realized that I did not know everything despite my ability to read and write in both English and Shona. I believed education meant knowing everything and I used every chance to read and learn about many topics. Watching the first graduates boarding a plane fueled my ambitions and enthusiasm for flying and going overseas some day.

I graduated from Kurasini and qualified to enter the University of Zambia in Lusaka and the AAI guaranteed me a four year scholarship. I majored in social work and encountered another diverse student population. Some students had never been to a city before and others had never used a fork and knife. We helped each other out regardless of whether we knew each other or not.

The most active branch of my political party was at this university of Zambia where we met and discussed Zimbabwean's liberation and had some freedom fighters address our regular gatherings. They gave us insights into the tribalism and witch hunts which led to the murder of innocents and infringements of human and civil rights within both the political parties and war torn rural areas of Zimbabwe. These aspects of the liberation struggle turned me away from joining politics fulltime after graduation. Instead, I was fortunate enough to be hired by the University as an Administrative Assistant in its various schools where I worked for approximately two years. I learned to speak two Zambian languages from my Zambian friends and workmates, worked and lived well in Zambia, and was able to help other Zimbabweans who were less fortunate.

My former Dean of the School of Social Work who had also taught me practicum and practice courses nominated me for a University-sponsored graduate study so that I could become a faculty member. She withdrew my name only after learning from the university registrar that I was not a Zambian. She told me that I worked and mingled so well with clients in the field and with faculty and student colleagues that she thought I was a Zambian. After the encounter with the dean, I applied for sponsorship from the AAI and I was awarded a two year graduate scholarship. Although I realized that I would never know everything, I still wanted to earn a Masters in Social Work, go to the United States and also to fly in an airplane.

EXCURSION/JOURNEY TO AMERICA
AS A STUDENT

I arrived in New York and proceeded to St. Louis where I attended George Warren Brown School of Social Work at Washington University. I found Americans to be easygoing and curious to learn about other cultures. I also noticed that when I was walking in the street, White strangers would say nothing to me but Black people would say "Hi!" There was just a connection there even if we were strangers. My life was primarily focused on books since I had a full scholarship. The learning environment was supportive and Black and White Americans and other International students interacted very well. We studied and discussed racism in classes, mostly in an intellectual way, as I really had not had much mixing with White people on an equal basis until I came to the United States I took additional classes on cultural diversity, the Black family, and had interactions with Black students which enlightened me on the dynamics of racism, power and oppression in this country. The international student office offered various programs and activities to help me learn about American culture and helped me feel at home. I was assigned a host and a guest family who took me to different places including their churches and also invited me to their homes during Thanksgiving or Christmas. They often picked me up in their cars and we drove on the highway and went to the most gorgeous neighborhoods of St. Louis. I only got exposed to poor neighborhoods when I chose to do my practicum on Community Development in a ghetto area. Had I not done this, I would have left the United States thinking that there were no such neglected and poor neighborhoods.

Soon after graduation, I went to Zimbabwe when it was in its transitional period between a colonial government and incoming nationalist government. Many Zimbabweans were excited to return home since the war had ended. I worked there as a Social Services and Probation Officer for about two years. I was the most educated person in our office, but the work was not challenging enough for me. I eventually returned to the United States to pursue my Ph.D. at Saint Louis University. This time I was working to pay for half of my tuition and living expenses.

During the first few weeks of class, I relied heavily on borrowing textbooks from my eight classmates (one African male who was married to a White American woman, one White male, and six White women). When I started doing better than them on tests, many were no longer willing to let me use their textbooks. Fortunately, I had managed to develop a network of part-time jobs ranging from babysitting, adult sitting, housekeeping and even part-time teaching of the culture of Zimbabwe in elementary and high schools in St. Louis. I was soon able to buy my own and I appreciated the fact that my classmates had initially been generous in lending me their textbooks when I could not afford them. Overall, we worked well together and were supportive of each other as a group. I was the first one to graduate from the program while the next would follow four or so years after me. My life as a student was simple and as students we worked in groups with people of all races without difficulty. While writing my dissertation, I worked as a Social Services Worker in St. Louis County and my workmates were great and supportive. Ultimately, I decided to join the academy with a wonderful American experience under my belt.

Whereas I had to struggle with sexism and other gender disempowering cultural traditions in Zimbabwe and to a certain extent Zambia, I had not come across blatant sexism or racism in the United States. It could have been covert or institutional, but for as long as I was viewed as being here temporarily, I encountered only a few barriers or obstacles. I always got what I put in. Many Americans showed great interest in Africa and my country. They often wanted to know when I was going back. According to them, it was a given that I had to take this American education back home and help my people. There was never any question as to whether my people might possibly reject my American education, neither was there any room for my own sense of self-determination to chose where to live or what to do with my education. In their view, there was never any room for me to serve here in the United States.

LIVE AND BE PART OF THE LAND OF THE FREE: PROFESSIONAL

Since I had lived and worked in Zambia after my undergraduate work and then in Zimbabwe after my masters, I decided I would work in the United States and gain some experience within the social system from which I had earned my highest credentials. I applied for academic positions and secured one in the south and taught there for three and half years. One White male faculty member from the Geography program, which was part of social work and two other departments, told me to return to Africa and not take jobs from Americans. He told me that I was supposed to return to my own country and not teach in the United States and that I did not have much to offer to American students. I simply told him that I had the credentials to teach, especially because I had interviewed for the job and was hired over a pool of American applicants. In order to diversify my academic experience, I eventually moved to a predominantly Black and small public university in the Midwest. I would later leave and work in two predominantly white public campuses, one in the East and one in the Midwest before coming to my current employer. I became the first female full professor with tenure in my unit within this Carnegie II university.

The American academy has been both a source of strength and strain. University campuses are supposed to be more open-minded, but I have found out that if you are of minority status and in my case, a Black woman, you deal with racial and gender issues. However, if you are also a foreigner, particularly from Africa, you also have to deal with issues of ethnocentrism. I have been told by people, even those who share my same skin color, that Africans come to the United States to "take our jobs." The issue seems to be that as long as I was going back to Africa, I posed no threat, but once I started competing in the United States job market, then it became a different story.

CONCLUSIONS AND LESSONS LEARNED

I currently teach at a large University in the Midwest and despite many trials and tribulations, my life is far better in the United States than it would have been had I returned to Zimbabwe and been a victim of the many horrific things that have taken place there. My life in the United States has put me, similarly to many in the Diaspora, in a better position to help those suffering in Zimbabwe by sending remittances (financial assistance). Many of my relatives and friends, educated or not, are refugees in either South Africa or England. They tell me that I made a wise move to leave the country early. However, oppression still exists for me and unfortunately my relatives, some colleagues, and students do not see the conditions that I often have to endure despite my privileged position of academic rank, level of education, and international background. Despite the various struggles that I face in the academy, similarly to many Black women, I continue to be inspired by the interactions I have with students, passion for my research on women and children and a commitment to human rights and social justice. To maintain focus and pursue my goals, I utilize Devore and Schlesinger (1999) premises that the present is the most important while at the same time being aware that ethnicity, and individual and collective history, affect how I tackle problems and challenges I encounter regarding diversity, oppression, power, and privilege in society.

DISCUSSION QUESTIONS

1. How did the imposed segregations and customs of the colonists such as Christmas affect family structures and their interactions? Do you think post-independence Zimbabwe has produced a different societal arrangement from one built on racial discrimination, geographic segregation, sexism, class distinctions, and power relations dominated by a White elite?

2. Children are primarily born to families and not just to individuals. As a result, major decisions may not reflect parent's wishes. Does this approach

differ from what you are accustomed to? How might this approach enhance or limit opportunities for youth in marginalized populations?

3. Consider the way the author was received and treated in Tanzania, Zambia, and the United States. How could the author's experiences as a foreigner in these countries affect her views of these nations and their citizens?

4. Why might the author's American hosts have shielded her from society's impoverished or neglected areas?

5. As you read the author's entrance into the American job market, what are your thoughts?

6. Explore how shared histories, ethnicities, power, privilege, oppression, and geographies affect how we perceive and treat those whom we deem like and unlike us.

REFERENCES

Devore, W. & Schlesinger, E.G. (1999). *Ethnic-Sensitive Social Work Practice* (4th ed.). Boston: Allyn and Bacon.

Gaidzanwa, R.B. 1996. The Ideology of Domesticity and the Struggles of Women Workers in Zimbabwe, In Chhachhi, Amrita, and Renee Pittin (eds.), *Confronting State, Capital and Patriarchy: Women Organizing in the Process of Industrialization*, pp. 273–289. London: Macmillan Press.

Kawewe, S.M. (2001). The Impact of Gender Disempowerment on the Welfare of Zimbabwean Women. *International Social Work Journal*, 44(4), 471–485.

Moyo, O. & Kawewe, S.M. (2002). The Dynamics of a Racialized, Gendered, Ethnicized and Economically Stratified Society: Understanding the Socio-Economic Status of Women in Zimbabwe. *Feminist Economics*, 8(2), 163–181.

Toler, D.L. (1998). Secrets and lies: Debunking the myths about Africa. *Essence*, 28(12), 74–79.

26

✳

Going Through Cultural Barriers in Counseling

RUTH CHAO

INTRODUCTION

As a minority[1] in the Counseling Psychology profession, I have met diverse cultural obstacles in my daily counseling. Culture and language differences are often interpersonal barriers that I have been challenged to turn into bridges.

My experience began at a practicum in a university counseling center. As a "non-white" counselor-trainee, I faced issues of "whiteness" on a daily basis. The program advocated multiculturalism; however, my supervisor was White, as were most professors, more than half of my peers, and most of my clients. As an Asian female in a Ph.D. program in the United States, I became used to thinking of psychology as "made in the West" and I thought I was at home in Western psychology until I met Mary.

CRITICAL INCIDENT

As part of my counseling practicum, Mary, a White, female client, came to me with issues associated with body image and romantic relationships. As she looked askance at me, I could tell by her body language that she was taken aback by having me, an Asian, assigned as her counselor. She affirmed my suspicions by saying, "But I don't think you would understand me. You are an Asian and

---

1. Being a minority person, I identify myself more with minority people than with the White majority. The following pages present me both as a minority person and as a counselor.

I'm not. I'm afraid you would judge me with your Asian, conservative values. I want a White female counselor."

Besides being suspicious of my inability to understand her culturally, Mary gave hints of worrying about my language ability. Specifically, she kept apologizing for using slang, idioms, and other culture-bound expressions. During our conversation, I repeatedly assured her that I thoroughly understood her words and their meanings. When those assurances didn't convince her of my understanding, I asked her if my accent disturbed her and was keeping her from accepting me as her counselor. At that point, she acknowledged a clear understanding of my English and instead stressed her concern about my "possibly conservative cultural values." She then expressed her desire for a White, female counselor with values similar to hers. I was shocked numb at this counselee's rejection of me and request for another counselor. I intuitively searched inside me for a way to respond to this client's judgment of my cultural background as a way to dismiss my qualifications in spite of my academic and counseling credentials. Because I could not change my birth or my accent to demonstrate my empathy and willingness to help, I was at a loss about knowing what to do with *myself*.

At this personally intimidating moment, I searched in my mind for resources to help me with this challenge. I ransacked my memory for readings on multicultural counseling, but unfortunately I found no "magic formula" to help me. However, I did remember what I was taught; that is, that a counselor's self-awareness of cultural values and backgrounds is an essential component in his or her multicultural competence. And so, after this session, to further my reflections on multicultural competence, I absorbed myself in multicultural literature. Because my encounter with this client was predominantly based on race and culture, I sought out the meaning of "multicultural competence." I poured over Sue, Arredondo, and McDavis' (1992) guidelines about "culturally skilled counselors" and compared myself with the examples they gave and with their suggestion that a culture-sensitive counselor has moved away from cultural naiveté to become aware and sensitive to his or her own cultural heritage. I felt competent with that guideline, because I already knew and felt how Asian culture differs from White, Western culture, and I recognized how much Asian culture had shaped my worldview.

Another guideline offered by Sue, Arredondo, and McDavis (1992) states that culture-sensitive counselors know how oppression, racism, discrimination, and stereotyping affect their work. Yet, my scenario was different from the ones described in the literature; it was not the counselor who was stereotyping and being racist, but the client. I continued searching these guidelines for support, but found nothing, no research or literature relevant to how a counselor of Color might counsel a White client when such cultural and personal issues arise.

Later when I met with my supervisor, she asked if I was angry with Mary. Surprisingly as it was with the supervisor, I was not angry with Mary because my experience with her was typical of interactions I have had with the majority of White people I had encountered; clients or not. Far from trying to resolve personal anger that was nonexistent, I was focused on how to work through therapeutically, the challenge Mary brought to the session; that is, the task of working through cultural differences between Asian counselor (myself) and White client (Mary), to effectively accomplish the therapeutic assistance to the White client.

In most cases, counselor-counselee dyads are White counselors working with clients of Color (Daniels, 2001), yet the reverse relations—counselors of Color with White clients—do exist and are on the increase. Counseling trainees of Color now occupy 30 percent of the membership in Counseling Psychology (Alexander, Heineman, Zarin, & Larson, 2002). Current multicultural theories facilitate White counselors in addressing their issues of racism and privilege when counseling clients of Color, counselors of Color are given little if any help in working through their prejudices or their clients' prejudices. Counselors of Color need to be culturally sensitive as well, struggling as they do *differently* from their White counterparts, and differently among themselves, in their quest to be culturally sensitive. I needed a theoretical guide to help me to help my client. My search of the literature, however, turned up few resources on this dilemma.

CULTURAL DIFFERENCES IN COUNSELING

Recognizing that most psychological principles derive from the West (Sue, 2001), I found no clear answers in Western counseling strategies. I turned inward to my own culture and upbringing for wisdom from the paradigms of Chinese sages (for example, Mencius) and other cultural paradigms (for example, Taoism, Buddhism) that inspired psychotherapy (Hayes, 2001). Somewhat intuitively, I fell back on my own culture and the significance of heartfelt concern for others—the "heart that cannot bear others to suffer ... seeing people hungry, I am hungry; seeing people drowning, I am drowned" (Mencius 1A7, 4B29, in Lau, 1984, 171). I also followed what Zen/Taoism says, "Don't push the river" (Chuang Tzu 19/22-24, in Graham, 1981).

In my initial session with Mary, I accepted her rejection as it was—not manipulating her distaste of me into my advantage, but following along and wrapping her rejection with empathy. I expressed my concern about her distrust of me and I *accepted* her comments calmly without degrading my professional dignity or position. I took her suspicion seriously and inquired her on her own ideal of a "White, female counselor."

In this situation, another factor that worked to our therapeutic advantage was that I did not take her criticism personally. As my Asian culture suggests, "Try our hardest and accept what comes, not prejudging future consequences." Yet another positive factor at work here was that my Asian culture also encourages letting go of "right" and "should," to be open and accommodating. Falling back on such old Asian values, I was ready to accept whatever my client questioned and criticized in the session with me.

Without guaranteeing that I would counsel her to find a suitable White, female counselor, I promised Mary that I would bring up her concerns at a supervision meeting. I tried hard to let her know that her distrust was also my concern. Although her suspicion and distrust hurt me, what I cared more for was her distrust as related to her needs. She was the center of my concern in that session. Seemingly touched by my good intentions, she decided to stay with me for one more session.

CONCLUSIONS AND LESSONS LEARNED

It is ironic that as I fell back on my cultural roots, the very factor of interpersonal obstacles provided an occasion for ubiquitous, compassionate empathy and acceptance of common humanity. Eventually, I was able to make a connection between my Asian sentiments and Western counseling skills, that is, listening, reflecting, accepting, and being client-centered. I realized that what was part of my response to accepting my client's reactions was also in line with what Teyber (1992) pointed out, "... not [to] act on initial impulse, which was trying to assure the client of therapist's competence and ability to help .... [I]t is even more essential to listen and respond to the client's concerns when ethnic/cultural differences exist between the therapist and client (p. 61)."

My living in two cultures—American and Asian—has provided me some fresh perspectives on cultural differences in counseling. My session with Mary and other similar experiences have taught me that cultural similarities and differences interweave to compose our complex world. Western insights on counseling today (for example, Teyber, 1992) and ancient Asian thoughts—what Chinese thinkers said so many centuries ago—can and should *mutually* echo, complement, and validate. This discovery of multicultural inter-enrichment vastly enriches and expands my counseling horizon.

Over time, mutual feelings of openness and serenity seeped into the sessions Mary and I shared. My anxiety and nervousness from her critical judgment shifted to calm, genuine acceptance. Mary also began to change. My accented English seemed to have turned less forbidding and more understandable. She found that my Asian upbringing would not prejudge her or shut her out. She laughed heartily as she watched me role-play her anger at her boyfriend, an imaginary interaction that showed her that I intimately and personally understood her anger, sorrows, and frustrated hopes. Slowly, we both came to experience a sharing of serious honesty, precisely through our cultural differences. She felt that I took her in, that I took her concerns with genuine seriousness. We both became motivated to build our cultural barriers into a bridge. We both began to *accept* our differences as we learned to understand—both each other and her initial mistrust. I learned to infuse my Asian cultural upbringing into my Western counseling strategies.

Such is one of many examples of intercultural experiences that have already vastly expanded and enriched my counseling. Cultural differences are not hurdles, but potential bridges-bridges to togetherness and mutual understanding.

DISCUSSION QUESTIONS

1. How do you cope with clients' stereotypes on your cultural background? Do you challenge clients, confront their stereotypes, or do you prefer not to address their stereotypes?

2. How do you integrate your cultural backgrounds with your professional training? Have you ever noticed yourself trying to blend your cultural wisdom with professional skills? Or do you think we counselors need to stick to our professional skills alone?

3. How do you connect yourself to your clients when you come from a culture different from theirs?

4. Do you think it important to be aware of our own cultural backgrounds? Why? If not, why not?

5. There are at least two types of cultural differences in counselor-client relations—[a] White counselors with clients of Color, and [b] counselors of Color with White clients. How similar are these two types to each other? How different are they each from the other?

6. What cultural barriers do you notice when you work with clients? How do your clients and you deal with them?

7. How do cultural differences influence counseling? Do you think cultural differences enhance or impair the counseling process? How? Why?

REFERENCES

Alexander, C. M., Heineman, C. J., Zarin, M. S., & Larson, L. (2002). Admission criteria to APA-accredited programs in counseling psychology over 10 years: Reflections of the specialty's values. *The Counseling Psychologist, 30*, 135–148.

Daniels, J. A. (2001). Conceptualizing a case of indirect racism using the White Racial Identity Development model. *Journal of Mental Health Counseling, 23*, 256–268.

Fuertes, J. N., & Gretchen, D. (2001). Emerging theories of multicultural counseling. In J. G. Ponterotto, J. M. Casas, L. A. Suzuki, & C. M. Alexander (Eds.). *Handbook of multicultural counseling* (2nd ed.). Thousand Oaks, CA: Sage.

Graham, A. C. (1981). *Chuang Tzu: The inner chapters*. London: George Allen & Unwin.

Hayes, P. (2001). *Addressing cultural complexities in practice*. Washington, D.C.: American Psychological Association.

Lau, D. C. (1984). *Mencius. Two volumes*. Hong Kong: The Chinese University Press.

Lin, Y. (1948). *The wisdom of Laotse*. New York: Random House.

Sue, D. W. (2001). Multidimensional facets of cultural competence. *The Counseling Psychologist, 29*, 790–821.

Sue, D. W., Arredondo, P., & McDavis, R. J. (1992). Multicultural competencies and standards: A call to the profession. *Journal of Multicultural Counseling and Development, 20*, 64–88.

Sue, D. W., Bernier, J. E., Durran, A., Feinberg, L., Pedersen, P., Smith, E. J., et al. (1982). Position paper: Cross-cultural counseling competencies. *The Counseling Psychologist, 10,* 45–52.

Sue, D. W., Carter, R. T., Casas, J. M., Fouad, N. A., Ivey, A. E., Jensen, M., et al. (1998). *Multicultural counseling competencies: Individual and organizational development.* Thousand Oaks, CA: Sage.

Sue, D. W., Ivey, A. E., & Pedersen, P. B. (1996). *A theory of multicultural counseling and therapy.* Pacific Grove, CA: Brooks/Cole.

Teyber, E. (1992). *Interpersonal process in psychotherapy: A guide for clinical training.* Pacific Grove, CA: Brooks/Cole.

27

✳

Elaborating a Different "Yes, But"

Intersections of Race, Sexuality, and Class in the Counseling Setting

DAMIEN W. RIGGS

Research drawing upon intersectionality theory has long taught us that we need to move beyond singular identity categories in our analyses of privilege, oppression, and diversity (Crenshaw, 1991). More specifically, such research has demonstrated the importance of examining the ways in which identity categories (such as class, race, gender, and sexuality) function in combination with one another to produce specific experiences of privilege and/or disadvantage. Importantly, intersectionality theory does not advocate for an additive model of identity *per se*, where identities are merely seen as a sum of their parts. Rather, it suggests that identity categories function simultaneously with one another and create an interplay between the many categories we all inhabit.

In my own work (Riggs 2006; 2007), I have drawn upon theories of intersectionality to examine the simultaneous privilege and marginalization experienced by white,[1] middle-class lesbians, gay men, bisexual and transgender (LGBT) people. In so doing, my interest has not been to deny the discrimination that white middle-class LGBT people often face, but rather to explore how experiences of marginalization on the basis of sexuality must be placed in a relationship to experiences of privilege on the basis of race and class. As such, my interest has been to elaborate what I term a different "yes, but." Typically, the "yes, but" I hear when speaking to white middle-class LGBT is: "yes I know I benefit from race and class privilege, but my nonheterosexual and/or nongender normative identity means that I am marginalized." The alternate "yes, but" I propose runs as follows: "yes, I experience marginalization as a nonheterosexual and/or nongender normative person, but I do so as a white middle-class person who benefits from considerable privilege."

The difference between these two "yes, buts" is not merely a matter of words, but rather is a matter of focus. In other words, presenting privilege and marginalization in the mode that I suggest is more likely to direct our attention to the complexities of white middle-class, LGBT identities, rather than to slip back into a sole or primary focus on marginalization. In order to exemplify these issues further, in the remainder of this chapter I first briefly outline the work I do as a family and relationship counselor, and then provide two case studies from my practice. In discussing these I explore how intersections of identity play out and provide some suggestions as to how issues of privilege and oppression in the counseling setting may be productively understood.

PRIVILEGE AND MARGINALIZATION IN PRACTICE

Issues of identity, intersectionality, and privilege always come into play when I work with clients. Despite our best of intentions, counselors and other practitioners in the "helping professions" sit in a relatively power-laden position in comparison to those with whom we work: we are typically positioned as those who hold the knowledge and skills, and whose role it is to "fix" the problems faced by others. Of course narrative and other similar therapies have sought to resist this model of the practitioner-client interaction and to recognize that clients bring with them valuable knowledge and skills that can sit alongside those of the practitioner (Denborough, 2002). Nonetheless, the dominant discourse

---

1. I have opted in this chapter not to capitalize the word 'white', as I do not solely use it to designate an ethnic or racial category (such as would be the case if I used the word 'Caucasian'). Rather, and drawing on work in the field of critical race and whiteness studies in Australia (for example, Moreton-Robinson, 2004), I treat the category 'white' as a cultural marker of a social location inherently marked by relative privilege, rather than simply by skin color.

surrounding the helping professions is one where those who seek services are positioned as in need of "help" and practitioners are those who can offer it.

In my practice I work with both heterosexual and LGBT clients, both individuals and couples. Initially, my interest as a gay man was to work primarily with LGBT clients. Yet despite this interest and my own professional development in relation to counseling LGBT people, I was quite unprepared for how challenging this would be. My interest in working with LGBT clients was three fold. First, I saw few public mental health services in my local area which specifically catered to LGBT people or employed LGBT practitioners. The second reason was more personal—I felt that working as a gay man may be "easier" if I worked with other people who experience marginalization on the basis of their sexuality or gender nonnormativity. This was due to my own relative gender nonconformity and the challenges this can present in working with heterosexual clients (who often view my self-presentation with suspicion). The third reason was a belief in the potential productivity of working with other LGBT people. I thought we would have a "shared ground" upon which to work. How wrong I was in my understanding of what "shared ground" meant to my clients and me!

In order to retain the confidentiality of the clients in these case studies, I portray their identities in very broad strokes (in addition to using pseudonyms). While the presentation of case studies in this way could be seen as drawing upon or reinforcing cultural stereotypes about particular groups of people, my point is to look at the simultaneous identity categories that both my clients and I inhabit and to explore how such simultaneities result in a dynamic between us where multiple forms of privilege and marginalization play out. My intention is to exemplify the complexities of privilege that we in the "helping professions" face and to further our understanding of privilege in order to better serve our clients.

CASE ONE

As a practitioner I have been fortunate to engage in long-term counseling with a number of clients during employment in my current position. This working with long-term clients brings many challenges as well as rewards, particularly in a public mental health system that primarily operates on a model of short-term interventions. Working with the first client I discuss here, who I will refer to as Daniel, has presented me with a range of challenges relating to my understandings of privilege and marginalization. Daniel is in his mid-forties and came to counseling to deal with issues related to childhood trauma. He was born in India and during his childhood migrated with his family to Australia. He experienced a great deal of racism as a young Indian-born child growing up in Australia, as well as much trauma related to his family. He is currently experiencing long-term unemployment and relies upon social security payments for his income. He does not have a clear diagnosis, but experiences ongoing negative mental health outcomes akin to those arising from complex-PTSD.

In our early sessions, Daniel was very reticent to open up to me due to the fact of identifying me as a younger man (more than fifteen years his junior) and as someone he verbally identified as "very different to him" based on our sexual orientation, race, and class. In these initial sessions Daniel often depicted me as removed from his life and unable to understand his relationships with women. As a child, Daniel's experiences of racism and marginalization intersected with his migrant status and living in a relatively remote area. This made his experience more extreme and socially isolating. The differing locales of our upbringing presented me with a challenge to recognize an aspect of my identity I had given little thought to before—that of living in a capital city. Whilst I was aware of research on the experiences of living in rural and remote areas and the impact of this upon mental health outcomes, I had not connected this to the socioeconomic privilege that came from living in a place where resources are abundant. Not only am I different to Daniel as a gay, middle-class white man who represents those who have discriminated against him, but I am also perceived as a man who has benefited from a childhood that was supportive and well resourced. This exemplifies how multiple identity categories intersect with one another and how my own self-depiction as an isolated gay child who experienced some marginalization bares little resemblance to the life of a racially marginalized child raised in a small town visibly shaped by norms of race and class. In working through these issues, we have often been faced with the very fact that the differences in our upbringings override any similarities (such as a sense of lack of connection to others around us as children).

As a response to these incommensurabilities, I have at times felt drawn to disclose aspects of my personal life that could demonstrate to Daniel some connection to his experiences, despite the fact that this is not a tool I generally tend to engage. In many instances this sharing of personal experiences has indeed served to enable him to feel a sense of shared knowledge with me. At other times, however, there have been complex interplays of privilege occurring between us where he has often rightly depicted me as privileged because of my whiteness and where he has in effect called me to account for my privilege. This calling to account has served as a salient reminder that any attempt at developing a relationship across differences is fraught by the possibility of falling into the trap of well-meaning liberalism on the part of those of us in positions of power. In other words, claiming that I have the capacity to connect with Daniel could easily be seen as ignoring the significant power differentials between us as client (long-term unemployed, Indian man) and practitioner (employed, white, middle-class man).

As a result of these complexities, my approach to connecting with Daniel has required me to go beyond simply recognizing his experiences and validating them. His experiences have forced me to recognize the broader social contexts in which they occurred and with which I am complicit, regardless of my distance from his personal situation. Regardless of my individual politics on race, sexuality, or class, I have needed to engage in a form of recognition with Daniel that moves away from being yet another "well meaning white person" who listens but does not connect his story to their own social location (as he suggested had been the case with previous practitioners). Instead, I have had to be willing to locate myself in his story as a participant in the broader society that formed his experiences of marginalization (i.e., in a society that privileges white Australians over all others). Importantly, such an approach does not involve martyring myself as a "bad white person" who individually caused his experiences of racism. Such an approach would only serve to maintain the focus on white people and our emotions. Rather, my approach has been about developing a relational framework in which we can recognize the interconnections of our privileges and marginalities.

CASE TWO

Mark and Andrew are two men in their mid-fifties, who have been living together for a year. Both men had been heterosexually married and had children in that context. Both had left their wives a decade ago. One of the men, Mark, had since then (until he began the relationship) enjoyed a very active sex life and had primarily engaged in anonymous sexual encounters at saunas or as a part of group sex activities. He also has a large group of gay male friends. Andrew, in contrast, had no sexual experience other than with Mark and had very little in the way of social networks with other gay men other than through Mark. Both of the men are white and both depict themselves as hard workers in relatively unskilled employment with little economic security.

From very early on in our sessions it became clear that the men had made a range of presumptions about what it would mean to have a gay counselor. Primarily, this meant that the men felt a certain liberty to discuss sexual matters that typically were not germane to our sessions about relationship difficulties (sessions that were not about sexual incompatibilities between the two men). In many instances the men referred to their genitalia or those of other men or to their sexual preferences, not specifically in a manner that was offensive to me, but certainly in a way that was not necessary in the context of the sessions. In most of these instances the men prefaced their comments with an inclusive "as you would understand." This rhetorical tool acted to render me in tacit agreement both with their worldview and with their presumption that I would welcome their sharing of this information.

As a gay man in his early 30s with three children (and not much of a social life as a result!) I could not identify with the sexual narratives they shared, but felt unable to resist these narratives on the basis that both men repeatedly stated how important it was for them to have a gay practitioner who "got" their situation. On the one hand, I felt compelled to allow their comments about sexual practices to stand in the off chance they were relevant to their relationship difficulties. I also sought to affirm to them that I did indeed welcome them as gay men and accepted their sexual practices despite them being quite different to my own. On the other hand, I felt a growing need to challenge their voicing of these particular narratives, particularly as they were often not central to the matters we were dealing with. My role as a practitioner with a particular injunction to be an empathetic listener was thus placed in direct competition with my own unease about being rendered complicit with the assumption that all gay men share a similar set of experiences. As a result, I repeatedly emphasized the different experiences that all gay men have (including the different experiences of the two men themselves), but the two men seemed very invested in collapsing those differences by endorsing an understanding of gay sexual practices as uniform.

Yet despite all of this, I was aware that as a younger gay man (in comparison to them), my experiences of coming out and of being proud in the face of homophobia were likely quite different from theirs and that this required sensitivity about our potentially conflicting needs in the counseling space. As I came to see, upon discussion in supervision and with other gay practitioners, perhaps part of the reason that the men placed such emphasis upon discussing sexual practices was precisely because there was an age gap between us, and that discussing their sexual practices as older gay men in the presence of a younger gay man may have been experienced as liberating or enjoyable. My point here of course is not to pathologize the men's desire to speak of their experiences, but rather to elaborate further upon how marginalization differentially played out between us as different generations of gay men, and that I had to take this into account in my work with the two men.

Kane (2004) identifies similar dilemmas in practicing as a gay man with gay clients and emphasized the need for clear boundaries with clients and the dilemmas of being engaged in multiple roles with clients (for example, in community settings and potentially through social contacts). Kane suggests that whilst issues relating to multiple relationships with clients must be recognized by all practitioners, they take unique configurations for those of us practicing with members of our own communities.

As this case suggests, whilst it is not unlikely that practitioners and clients may share some identity statuses, sharing an identity status does not mean shared experiences, belief systems, or instances of marginalization. In some instances these men appeared invested in asserting that we were "all the same," and in other instances they were clearly cognizant of our differences. For example, the men often framed me as a well paid professional, which they contrasted with a depiction of themselves as working men who have little understanding of the "helping professions." As such, I was positioned as a professional in possession of knowledge that Mark and Andrew did not have. As an individual, I was positioned as a middle-class gay man working with two working-class gay men. In addition to my status based on class, my politics on race (developed through academic engagement) sat a world away from those of the two men, who asserted their own politics were premised upon "real world experiences." Here I refer to an instance where the men began speaking on matters unrelated to the counseling issue at hand, drawing upon racialized stereotypes about Indigenous people in order to construct themselves as deserving of social security benefits in contrast to Indigenous people who they depicted as undeserving. When I attempted to speak of colonization as a possible explanation for what they were seeing as "special rights" for Indigenous people, both men very quickly asserted that I was speaking from an "ivory tower" and that as men in the "real world" they knew better. Again, these differences between us in terms of our politics required careful negotiation in order to maintain a focus on the purpose of the counseling sessions (i.e., their relationship).

PRACTICE IMPLICATIONS—LESSONS LEARNED

These cases highlight the complexities of working with clients positioned within and outside of one's own community and the complex ways in which privilege and oppression play out. Importantly, none of our similarities or differences can be understood in isolation from one another or outside of the social context. The differences between us and within each of us are intimately connected, so much so that it is very difficult, and I would suggest futile, to attempt to draw out their individual effects.

In my work with clients there continues to be complex interplays of privilege, providing challenges to building rapport across differences, as well as challenges resulting from clients' beliefs that may conflict with my own. At times I have felt silenced by normative statements about sexuality and gender, but certainly I haven't always been silent at those moments. On the whole, I have emphasized an understanding of our differences that requires me to be accountable for my privilege. As such, my interest has not been in letting anyone "off the hook" under some misguided form of benevolence; rather my point has been to position myself in a context of institutionalized racism, (hetero)sexism, and classism that shape all of our lives.

Furthermore, it has been important for me to recognize that despite my own relational approach to practice, there will indeed be instances where a relationship cannot be developed and that clients have the right to refuse the "goodwill" of practitioners and/or dominant group members (Ahmed, 2002).

Obviously the two cases I have outlined reflect my own analytic frameworks and beliefs about client/practitioner relationships and the degree to which practitioners can legitimately "challenge" clients. Certainly I am lucky in working for an organization that allows the space for practitioners to engage in social change through the style of practice that we engage in. Nonetheless, there are always opportunities to continue the work of thinking about how privilege and oppression play out, and to interrogate my role as someone positioned as a "professional" and the impact this has upon the work I do with clients. Certainly, the mental health professions will never be outside of power relations. As such, it is vitally important that those of us working in the field continue to examine both our own individual locations and the location of mental health practice in societies that typically privilege "professional" over "lay" knowledge.

CONCLUSION: A DIFFERENT "YES, BUT"

In this chapter I have explored some of the complexities that arise for those of us working in the "helping professions" when we engage across a range of differences. Importantly, my emphasis has been upon the need for those of us working in these fields to always locate ourselves within our own social contexts and identity positions. From there, I have suggested the need to develop an understanding of privilege and oppression that moves beyond a simplistic additive model to one that accounts for the intersections of identity categories and their role in relationship dynamics between clients and practitioners.

Reflecting back upon my own history of coming to understand privilege and marginalization I can see considerable changes in my own thinking and the shift I have made from an individualized account to a more relational under-standing of identity. For me, this shift has been central to applying the "yes, but" outlined in the introduction. Reflecting after many counseling sessions on how power dynamics related to age, class, relationship status, race, sexuality, gender, and ability have played out within sessions has been an important aspect of my own growth as a counselor, and has yet again provided opportunities to continue to develop my understanding of privilege and its operations. Importantly for me, my understandings of privilege always centre upon recognition of the fact that so-cial hierarchies, despite their historical contingency, are unlikely to disappear in my lifetime. As a result, my practice is always shaped by a desire to identify the role that cultural capital plays in shaping both my life and the lives of my clients, and in the interactions between us. Identifying cultural capital allows me to retain a focus on more than just the individual(s) in front of me, as well as locate us all in a relationship to networks of power that differentially determine who it is that will have a voice and who will not.

DISCUSSION QUESTIONS

1. In this chapter I have often located race privilege as requiring central focus in our everyday interactions. Discuss this in relation to your own life and views on the role of different identities according to your specific social context.

2. In this chapter I highlighted the possible benefits and disadvantages of working with members of your own community. Try creating your own list of pros and cons for working with your own communities, with an emphasis on intersectionality as it may affect your work.

3. If you work in one of the "helping professions," consider my discussion of the difficulties of developing a common ground with clients. How may this be difficult to achieve in the face of incommensurable differences between yourself and clients and how might you deal with this? Furthermore, how might you recognize the rights of clients to *refuse* a relationship with you?

4. In the chapter I drew a distinction between refusing to be either a "good" or "bad" white person. Nonetheless, I still advocated for a position in which ethical practice as a white person involves accountability for privilege (a praxis that is certainly not held by the majority of people in Australia). Consider how you have been positioned as a "good" or "bad" person in relation to your own practice and how these categories often serve to maintain the status quo.

ACKNOWLEDGMENTS

I begin by acknowledging the sovereignty of the Kaurna people, upon whose land I live in Adelaide, South Australia. Thanks must go to the clients and colleagues with whom I have discussed these ideas, and whose insights have centrally informed my writing in this chapter, and to Sharon and Valerie for helpful comments on an earlier version.

REFERENCES

Ahmed, S. (2003). In the name of love. *Borderlands e-journal* 2. Retrieved April 30, 2009, from http://www.borderlandsejournal.net.au

Crenshaw, K. M. (1991). Mapping the margins: Intersectionality, identity politics, and violence against women of color. *Stanford Law Review, 43,* 1241–1299.

Denborough, D. (Ed.) (2002). *Queer counseling and narrative practice.* Adelaide: Dulwich Centre.

Kane, G. (2004). 'The unintended use of a pronoun': Coming out in the counseling environment. *Out in the antipodes: Australian and New Zealand perspectives on gay and lesbian issues in psychology* (pp. 85–96). Perth: Brightfire Press.

Moreton-Robinson, A. (Ed.) (2004). *Whitening race: Essays in social and cultural criticism.* Canberra: Aboriginal Studies Press.

Riggs, D. W. (2007b). Recognizing race in LGBT psychology: Privilege, power & complicity. In V. Clarke & E. Peel (Eds.) *Out in psychology: Lesbian, gay, bisexual and transgender perspectives* (pp. 59–76). London: Wiley.

Riggs, D. W. (2006a). *Priscilla, (white) queen of the desert: Queer rights/race privilege.* New York: Peter Lang.

✳

Stories of Personal Compassion and Being Allies
Introduction to Part VI

Part VI "Stories of Personal Compassion and Being Allies," closes out this book with the authors sharing their insights into the process of standing up against privilege and oppression and connecting with someone different from themselves through compassion. Mock leads this charge in "Personal Compassion and Alliance Building" when he reinforces the notion that everyone should find the courage to stand up for self and others in need. Liddle describes herself as "a disabled, White, lesbian professor in the deep south—an identity that sometimes gives me mental whiplash" in "Tales from the Heart of Dixie." Liddle shares her journey and commitment to addressing racism in the community and classroom as a way to not fall prey to the oppression associated with several of her statuses. She makes it clear that as a White person, she will have more power to help other White people recognize their privilege. In "Yes, I See You're Committed to the Cause," MacPhee follows with his enthusiastic pursuit of social justice after growing up in a small, blue-collar town in Idaho and echoes the sentiment that there would be a greater acceptance of the social justice agenda if more White males were outspoken in their support. Gormley brings to the forefront a critical issue for People of Color—the issue of not being heard in a room of the majority. As is often the case, a White person has to "step up" and try to reach those who may be able to only hear White voices. In "A Multiracial Unity Group," Gormley joins all of our authors in tearing down the veil of obscurity to reveal a reality that needs to be changed for the sake of equity, fairness, and mutual understanding.

28

✴

Personal Compassion and Alliance Building

Observations of an Asian American Professor

MATTHEW R. MOCK

"Racism. Getting sick wasn't our fault.
But getting well is our responsibility."
(ANONYMOUS)

A STORY OF AN INCIDENT I OBSERVED

One day, after teaching a graduate psychology class, I went to a major department store to do some gift shopping for the holidays. I observed an incident that still stands out in my mind today. Although what I observed from close by took just a few minutes, I can replay it frame by frame as though it were happening in slow motion. Clearly, what I witnessed had an impact on me.

After a while of perusing the departments, I observed a man in his mid- to late-thirties looking in the cases of the jewelry department. The man appearing to be Asian American had also caught my attention because few Asian Americans live in the immediate and surrounding areas. This man was casually dressed and wore a trench coat because it recently had been raining sporadically. He seemed quite acculturated, perhaps even native born. I overheard his conversation with an Asian American woman and a child (perhaps his wife and daughter) agreeing to shop separately for a while. As soon as his wife took the escalator upstairs heading for another department, I observed the man become keenly focused on some earrings in one of the jewelry cases.

The jewelry cases were situated in a rectangle around the service and purchase area. On this particular day, the department store salesperson was a woman who appeared to be White and in her mid-fifties. Because it was the holidays, the store and jewelry departments were bustling. After careful scrutiny, the Asian American man seemed to make his decision about his purchase of some onyx earrings and waited in what was now a short line that was forming. He checked his watch. I thought that perhaps he was making certain that he had time to make his purchase before his wife and child returned to the shopping area.

Two other customers, one a man and the other a woman, both who appeared to be White, individually made their purchases. Now the only one left in line, the Asian American man waited for the saleswoman's attention and his turn to be served. However, instead of assisting this man, the saleswoman left the immediate counter and register and instead went to serve a woman, also White, who had just come to another side of the counter to ask a question. It was as though the saleswoman looked, but did not see the man, so she turned away! The saleswoman opened one of the cases at the female customer's request to show her some watches. She then proceeded to assist this customer in making her department store credit card purchase, as she had the previous male and female customers. Afterward, instead of returning to the Asian American man at the register, she answered the questions from a man passing through the department. Again, it was as though the Asian American customer was invisible or nonexistent. Despite the fact that these customers were being given attention and service out of turn, the man waited patiently.

Finally, upon returning to assist the Asian American man, this saleswoman made no mention that she had passed him by and put him off. He pointed to the earrings he had carefully selected and indicated that he wanted to also use his store credit card for the purchase. The woman stepped over to the register and swiped the card in the crediting machine, all the while studying the man up and down and carefully scrutinizing his face. After a pause, she came back to the man and requested his signature on the credit card slip. He routinely complied. She looked at the signature carefully, paused, and then commented, "I'm sorry. Please sign again." He signed once more, only to have her react with an audible sigh and then request, "I must see your driver's license or some other form of identification." In response, the Asian American man looked at her somewhat perplexed, but after a brief pause cooperated. After collecting his driver's license, stepping away and studying it against his store credit-slip signature, the saleswoman returned from the register. By this time, a small line had formed behind the man. The saleswoman said firmly in a lowered voice, drawing the man closer, "Please sign again. Only this time, make an effort to sign it like your license!" Clearly more flustered, the man complied once again, but first commenting, "I did not see you request this of the prior customers. And is showing a picture identification store policy?" To this, the saleswoman reiterated her stance for a "careful" signature. She responded assertively to him, but with careful, slowed, and purposely formed words, as though he might not understand English. Hoping to draw the man closer to her to not be within earshot of others, she spoke as though she were sharing a secret with him. At a near whisper she said in a patronizing tone, "Please, sir. This is for your own good!" Following this brief dialogue, the interaction finally broke off with the man hurrying away at last with his purchase, once again searching for the time on his watch.

REFLECTIONS AND CONSIDERATIONS

After reading this story, many of you will appropriately express some form of shock or disbelief at the way this man was treated. Others of you will recognize this type of treatment as personal to your own experience. Some of you will assume that there must be more to the story than was witnessed and recounted, for such blatant mistreatment does not occur without a reason. Still others of you may not associate this treatment with racial discrimination at all.

Consider *your* response. Also consider the following questions, some of which perhaps you asked yourself after reading this story: *How do you know the salesperson was discriminating against this Asian American man? Was this really a racist interaction? Was it about skin color or appearance, tone of voice, gender, facial expressions, perceived socioeconomic status, or was it something about this man's assumed attitude? Would it have made a difference if there had not been the earlier slights, invisibility, or acts of disrespect, dehumanization, or marginalization?* Finally, consider other questions you had that could be added to this list.

AN IMPORTANT REVELATION

There is an important sidebar to my story above and its concluding events. I was actually not just an idle witness to this event. I did not just observe this from afar. *This was an actual event that happened to me. I was that Chinese American man in the department store with my family, shopping like other families do. I felt the saleswoman had discriminated against me.*

By way of self-introduction, I am a third-generation, Chinese American, heterosexual man. I earned my bachelor's degree in Psychology with a child and education focus from Brown University and master's and doctorate degrees in Clinical and Consulting Psychology from the California School of Professional Psychology in the California Bay Area. I grew up bicultural in the company of many siblings, with few material or monetary resources, but with textured life experiences that enriched my growth and development. I recall that our family was one of the few Asian American families in the entire community, especially during my early, formative years.

Professionally, for more than 15 years, I have been Director of Family, Youth and Children's Mental Health in Berkeley, California, a program that provides services to the poor, working poor or those often most marginalized.

One of my other major roles is as system-wide ethnic services and cultural competency coordinator for the City of Berkeley.

Also, as a professor of Psychology and Director of the Cross Cultural Counseling program in the Graduate School of Professional Psychology at John F. Kennedy University in Orinda, California, I am committed to imparting knowledge to graduate students in ways that enrich their multicultural perspectives and their contributions to social justice. I give invited workshops and talks nationally and abroad.

As a Chinese American family, one of our core values is teaching and learning about compassion and empathy toward others. Living in the Bay Area of California, we are never lacking in situations that remind us of the great importance and imperatives of striving toward equality in how we, and others, are treated. Knowing and telling personal stories past and present, and creating future possibilities for us as a family are extremely important. I try to impart some of these stories as inspirations for my workshop attendees or graduate students. Whether it is in my personal or professional life, I feel I am addressing issues of combating racism and discrimination on a daily basis. Sometimes, personal and professional experiences closely interweave.

"THE REST OF THE STORY"

There is an addendum to my department store story. As I left the store and felt the coolness of the outside air, I had a moment of clarity and inner strength. I questioned what had just happened in just a few minutes' time. I paused to think about who I am and what I stand for: I am a professor and somewhat prominent multicultural psychotherapist who advocates for equality and social justice for others. I am a husband and a father. I am teaching my young daughter to speak up for herself as well as for others. I know all too well the historical legacy of Asian American mistreatment and what things might be done to help stop the cycle of discriminatory interactions. I thought to myself: For my daughter Rachel, my family, for others, and for myself, I cannot let this incident go by without having my voice heard. Now the coolness of the outside air contrasted with the warmth of my face and mounting renewed spirit.

With these internal, yet firm and grounded feelings hard to put into exact words, I trudged back into the large, bustling department store, past the fancy displays, sparkling boxes of costume jewelry and holiday-wrapped colognes and perfumes. As I got closer to the jewelry counter, the saleswoman with whom I had interacted had been joined by another saleswoman. The added representative was now helping customers on the opposite side of the counter to make their purchases. The saleswoman with whom I had interacted seemed to be counting receipts and perhaps preparing to take a break. As I walked toward her counter, she recognized me immediately and leaned toward me although somewhat cautiously from a safe distance. Summoning up my feeling of being more grounded and strong inside, I assertively said to her, "In that interaction before, you were not respectful to me. First, you passed me by as though I was invisible. Then you treated me differently than you treated other customers. As a professional, I sign many things. I question if you ask all of your customers equally for their signature multiple times, and for their identification or license, and then respond to them as you did to me. I did not appreciate your condescending demeanor. Please think about this." Although I kept a clear, calm, firm yet steady voice, her face registered some shock and dismay. If I had to guess, I think her reaction was because I had actually taken time to address her about what happened. Feeling satisfied with my verbal assertion, we parted ways.

Upon realizing that I was a bit overdue to meet up with my wife and daughter, I turned from the counter, taking a few quick steps away. Sweeping through the narrow aisle of holiday merchandise, my open trench coat caught some of the neatly displayed and stacked boxes of jewelry pins, tumbling all of them to the floor. Pausing to pick up the mess I had just made in my haste, I half-wondered if the saleswoman in witnessing this would mistake my actions and have her finger on the phone ready to call security. Suddenly, after apparently witnessing much of what had transpired, a White female customer knelt down beside me and helped me pick up the few remaining small boxes. Kneeling side-by-side, she gently said to me, "I saw what happened to you. I was shopping too and I was a few customers behind you in line. The way she treated you was not fair or right. I am sorry. I will also say something on your behalf." We stood together briefly sharing small smiles of personal, connected acknowledgement. I simply thanked her and we parted ways. To this day, when I think about this scenario, I feel warmth at the *personal compassion* of this anonymous woman, her words, and our nonverbal connection. I recognize an ally. We choose our battles and sometimes who will participate in the struggle. While I have gone to the store management in similar situations, during this one I let go to have an ally carry on where I left off. This partial ending brings me hope and renewed energy, even optimism.

CONNECTING OUR STORIES OF PERSONAL COMPASSION

We each have multiple identities, including ethnicity, gender, race, sexual orientation, religion or faith, professional status, abilities, and others. To be aware of which of these statuses earns us relative power and influence in different contexts is essential. There are many ways in which these interactions of enacted power become manifest in our lives. We can also understand ways to teach and learn what might be done in similar situations (Adams, Bell & Griffin, 1997; Creighton & Kivel, 1992). I share my personal scenario with the saleswoman, but I end with the female customer who took the time to help me as an ally, to emphasize the fact that even small acts of *personal compassion* have larger meanings in collective efforts to achieve social justice. Not only do the events themselves, but sometimes even the invalidation that can occur in the retelling, perpetuate feeling hurt. Small slights, like small nicks or cuts, lead to feelings of pent up rage or perhaps more appropriately, *outrage* for the continued injustices. It is cruitical for individuals to begin exercising *personal compassion*, getting them to understand at a deep, personal level what it means to be treated differently, and to understand how differential treatment is related to power and privilege (McIntosh, 1988; Pinderhughes, 1989), and to the conscious or unconscious perpetuation of acts of racism, discrimination, and oppression. We have to consider strategies to constructively address negative acts of others. For me, empowering people with a sense of hope and the ability to take personal action are the true meanings of what it means to be "PC"— *not* to be *politically correct* but instead to be *personally compassionate* (Mock, 1999; Mock, 2002). It is with small acts of one individual and the combined personal acts of hundreds that we can construct lasting alliances toward change.

FINDING OUR OWN PERSONAL COMPASSION TOWARD ANOTHER

The events of September 11, 2001, had a profound impact on us all. Like many people, I cancelled many flight plans right after that date, thinking about the planes that were used as projectiles to bring down the towers of the World Trade Center in New York City and all the people inside. I had been home watching television as that tragedy unfolded. Through my work, I tried to coordinate efforts through my clinic and school programs to help children and families to cope with all the feelings of profound sadness, fear, anger, loss, confusion, and anxiety.

As weeks passed, I found myself able to fly once again. On one of these trips to give a workshop presentation, I found myself on a full flight of passengers. As we all settled in, I noticed that one of the last individuals to get seated was a Middle-Eastern-appearing woman slightly younger than I. She sat two rows in front of me in a window seat. The flight proceeded without anything unusual, except midway through, when there was a slight bit of turbulence.

Shortly after this turbulence began, the Middle-Eastern woman got up from her window seat as though to go to the restroom at the rear of the plane. She walked briskly with downcast eyes. I noticed several people around me looking up from their reading or talking, acknowledging her passing. After several minutes, she returned. However, as the flight proceeded, she asked to be excused by her neighboring passengers once again to use the restroom. She had tissues in one hand and appeared to be dabbing at her face. After some moments of seemingly collective silence among those around her, she returned once more. The flight proceeded as expected, with the usual courtesies from the flight crew; and as the plane descended toward landing, the warning to be seated and secure seat belts was announced. A short time after the pilot made this announcement, the Middle-Eastern woman arose quickly once again, hurrying to the rear cabin restroom, this time carrying a small purse. Heads turning, several passengers seemed to take additional note, as did one flight attendant. After some moments ticked by, the flight attendant went to check on the woman. Finally, the woman emerged, returned to her window seat, and the plane landed with a near-perfect, smooth touchdown.

What had just happened? Why did I, and others, feel perhaps as we did? Was what several of us fellow passengers felt collectively yet silently "normal" under the circumstances? Was feeling uncomfortable or at least questioning, a reflection of fear, mistrust, or needing to be protected? How should we have voiced our concerns? And finally, what might the woman have been feeling and was she aware of how others reacted? I silently toiled over some of these and other questions as we got off the plane, walking on to get our baggage.

As we claimed our luggage coming off the turnstile, I noticed the Middle Eastern woman a few passengers away from me. We picked up our bags at about the same and then proceeded to the passenger pickup area outside. After sitting there side-by-side for a few awkward minutes, I finally broke the silence to say "hello" and make small talk. Within a few minutes, we had a readily flowing conversation, first about trivial matters of the day and then eventually to national and worldwide events. She told me how she too had been affected by the tragedy in New York, by the violence and loss. She had resided in the Bay Area of California all of her life, and her parents had lived there for more than twenty years. Shortly after September 11th, she was cautioned by some of her Muslim neighbors about wearing clothes more readily identifying her as Middle Eastern or Muslim. Her elderly mother, shopping one day as she usually did at her neighborhood grocery store, had her cart run into by another woman, supposedly as an "accident." Her mother stopped shopping there unless another family member accompanied her. A Muslim neighbor had also had an obscene gesture and verbal taunts made at her by teenagers as she was in her car at a stoplight.

With each of our rides due to arrive shortly, our conversation came around to her behavior on the plane of how she got up several times. She went on to explain how she had to get up numerous times with an upset stomach. She constantly felt the pressure of all eyes focusing on her, not just throughout this flight and other previous ones, but also by airport security who had carefully screened and checked her and her luggage twice before she boarded. She even told me that at times recently she had a bloody nose, perhaps due to increased stress and feeling the silent yet highly palpable tension of those around her.

As we talked and shared each of our stories, I felt a moment of closeness and commonality with this relative stranger. I expressed how badly I felt and how hard it must be for her, especially when others do not take time to acknowledge her or her feelings and experiences. I told her how I was glad that we had made brief contact to introduce ourselves to each other, to share brief snippets of our stories, especially in the context of tense times. What she shared next I will not forget. She expressed thanks for my taking time to speak with her, to check in about her welfare, and to engage her sincerely as a fellow human being with thoughts, feelings, and family history. She felt troubled with the silence of others, but validation through our brief yet meaningful engagement. Finally, as my ride arrived, we parted with short acknowledgements and each headed home.

Later that evening, upon reflection, I felt a mixture of feelings. At first, I felt badly for being one who experienced moments of tension on the flight. I also felt good for having taken the risk to engage this woman, which allowed us to get to know each other briefly, and to share my feelings of personal compassion toward her and her family's experiences. Last, perhaps most importantly for me, I was reminded how being an ally or successfully engaged with another person, even for a few precious moments, means taking risks, breaking from anonymity, finding and giving humanity, being aware of cultural humility, and discovering commonality across differences. That night, in the warmth of my home, reading with my daughter until she fell asleep, I felt hopeful.

CONCLUSION

I give multicultural workshops, presentations, and trainings to a wide array of people, from graduate students to seasoned health and related professional audiences who are primarily in mental health and related fields nationally and internationally. No matter how many times I present the material or how large the audiences to whom I give workshops on diversity and social justice, I often encounter forms of the same three questions. The first question is, "Is fighting racism and oppression for equality primarily the work of People of Color or of White people?" Another often asked question often is "The history of discrimination and oppression in the United States is so long and hard, and I am just one person. What can I do to make a difference?" One other common question might be, "What does someone need to do to make a difference when racist acts are still prevalent, covert and overt and at so many levels of our society?" Although these questions are common, moving toward answers is a continuous challenge.

Similar to what occurs in my classes, I hope the following teaching points have been articulated in this chapter:

1. Racism and discrimination have an impact on all people, no matter how much individuals have seemingly attained professionally;

2. Fighting racism, discrimination, and oppression for social equality are all of our battles, not just one person's or group's; and

3. We all need allies in this hard, ongoing struggle.

4. I am committed to take the daily position that "linking arms" strengthens stances against social injustices. I feel that not only should we take such a stand, but we must do so for our survival. We must move beyond simple political correctness to deep personal compassion leading to a better world for all present and future humanity.

DISCUSSION QUESTIONS

1. Discuss what you look to in order to decide whether someone's actions are discriminatory or not. At what point might you have determined that the saleswoman's behaviors were discriminatory towards the man?

2. Discuss the Asian American man's going back into the store. Do you feel he did enough to address the issue? What might he have done differently? If you were the man what would you have done? Would you have done more (i.e., go to management directly) or not? If not, why not?

3. Discuss the interchange from the perspective of the saleswoman and the man.

4. For the woman who was identified as an ally, what would you have wanted her to say to the store manager? What elements of her comments would be respectful of the man and be most beneficial?

5. What do you imagine might have been some of the thoughts or experiences of the saleswoman to get her to act the way that she did?

6. For the people who were targets of mistreatment in the earlier scenarios, what kind of conversations would you have with them?

7. Many of the scenarios can have additional aspects of focus including gender, immigration status, class, language, race, etc. Please discuss.

REFERENCES

Adams, M., Bell, L., & Griffin, P. (1997). *Teaching for diversity and social justice*. New York: Routledge.

Creighton, A., & Kivel, P. (1992). *Helping teens stop violence*. Alameda, CA: Hunter Press.

McIntosh, P. (1988). *White privilege and male privilege: A personal account of coming to see correspondences through work in women's studies (working paper no. 189)*. Wellesley, MA: Wellesley College Center for Research on Women.

Mock, M. (1999). Cultural competency: Acts of justice in community mental health. *The Community Psychologist, 32*(1), 38–40.

Mock, M. (2002). Cultural sensitivity, relevance, and competence in school mental health. *School mental health handbook: Strategies for successful implementation*. Baltimore, MD: Kluwer Press.

Pinderhughes, E. (1989). *Understanding race, ethnicity and power: The key to efficacy in clinical practice*. New York: Free Press.

29

✳

Tales From the Heart of Dixie
Using White Privilege to Fight Racism

BECKY J. LIDDLE

Wearing baggy gray sweat pants and an old sweatshirt with large pockets, I walked into a knitting supply store. An air filtration mask covered most of my face. I explained that I was looking for stocking stuffers and the clerk politely took me to a separate room filled with small items that would have easily fit into my many pockets. She showed me around a bit and left me alone there to browse.

This is a typical experience for me as a White woman. I wear a mask similar to those worn by people who mow lawns, because of my disability, Multiple Chemical Sensitivity. Each day I walk into businesses wearing my mask and on many occasions, I think how different my experiences in those businesses might be if I were a Black man instead of a White woman. Frankly, I wonder, if I were a Black man, would I have been mistaken for a robber and shot?

I am a disabled, White, lesbian professor in the Deep South—an identity that sometimes gives me mental whiplash, alternating as it does between disadvantaged and privileged group memberships. However, it is most often from my privileged status that I am able to combat racism.

Lacking certain privileges some of the time probably helps me to recognize those instances when I do benefit from unearned privilege (Treitel, 2000). Thus, my being female, lesbian, and disabled may make my white privilege easier to recognize because the notion of veiled discrimination or subtle advantage is not foreign to me. Akamatsu (1998) points out that those who have not experienced oppression may have a difficult time letting go of the myth of the level playing field. I have no illusions that we live in a meritocracy and so I have perhaps found it easier than some to recognize my own privileges. I do not see myself as unique or especially meritorious in my anti-racism work. I recognize that I fit the typical pattern of Whites who fight racism, described by Treitel (2000): I have been aware of injustice since childhood, recognize myself as a member of an oppressed group, and have long been involved in social justice movements. Perhaps most importantly, I view my work as an expression of my values (Treitel, 2000). Thus, I see my use of my faculty position to work against racism not as an act of charity, but as an act of integrity, which is its own reward.

Kappen (2001) points out that both persuasion research and social-identity theory predict that members of an in-group (in this case, myself as a White person) will have more power to help other members of the in-group to recognize their own privilege. She indeed found that White speakers were more effective in helping White listeners to recognize their own white privilege. Thus, in some instances, I, as a White counselor educator, may likely have more influence than my colleagues of Color in helping White people understand the subtle acts of racism People of Color experience every day.

STORY ONE

When I was first apartment hunting in Alabama (which the license plates still proclaim to be the "Heart of Dixie"), I asked my colleagues if they knew of any apartments for rent. Someone sent me to look at a delightful and remarkably inexpensive carriage-house apartment. I was about to take it when the landlady mentioned it had been vacant for several months. I expressed surprise because it was such a nice place. She responded, "Yes, but I can't advertise it. If I did, the nigras would be over here in two shakes." Stunned, I started backing out, explaining that I don't rent from racists. Realizing she was losing her chance to rent the place she hastened to explain, "It's not that. You see, it's furnished. You wouldn't want to sleep in a bed that had been slept in by a Black man, would you?" I said "No, I wouldn't care, and no, I don't understand," and sped away. If not for a slip of her tongue, I would have rented a lovely apartment for far below the going rate, while my Black colleagues were paying far more for less desirable units.

My experience in almost renting the carriage house was a clear and overt example of white privilege, but later that same week I may have been the recipient of white privilege that was much more subtle when I visited a large property management agency to look at the "apartments available" board. The receptionist at the property management agency observed my search, asked me what I was looking for, and then told me about a duplex that had "just become available." She said it was a really nice place and because they didn't want undergraduates trashing it, they were just telling people "like me" about it. I assumed she meant professionals or older adults. Since then, I have come to wonder whether she would have told me about the duplex if I had been a young Black faculty member instead of a young White faculty member. I loved that place, but I will always wonder whether it was good luck that I found it, or white privilege. Discussions of such (unanswerable) questions demonstrate the sometimes elusive nature of privilege.

The cost of being Black in the housing market was again made clear to me by an African American doctoral student whose accent does not betray her ethnicity on the phone. When she responded by phone to a house advertisement that did not list the rent, she was quoted one price, but when she showed up in person to see the house, the rent was suddenly $100 a month higher. Her price for that little bit of extra pigmentation amounts to $1,200 a year in disposable income, which over the course of several years would amount to a down payment on a house. This same student told me that while she was attending college in another state, the Black fraternities and sororities circumvented another discriminatory housing practice by developing a cooperative system whereby Black women would seek apartments for Black men. Otherwise, apartments were nearly always "just taken" when the men arrived. In this case, Black men lacked the privilege to find housing for themselves because of prejudices held by apartment owners.

I also cite research to show that discrimination in housing is still rampant. For example, fair-housing audits continue to show high levels of discrimination with African American auditors routinely being told units are not available, when in fact they are (Reed, 1991). Government audits in 76 cities showed rates of discrimination against Black auditors ranging from 10 percent to 90 percent in various cities, with the average being 46 percent. They are in a typical locale, Black apartment hunters have perhaps half as many apartments to choose from as Whites do.

STORY TWO

Several years ago, I was in a group that was considering two job applicants: one Black, one White. A White colleague said that although both candidates were qualified, he "just felt more comfortable" with one of them (the White candidate). I pointed out that if we make hiring decisions based on our comfort, we will likely perpetuate unintentional discrimination because we all tend to feel most comfortable with people who are similar to us in demographic characteristics such as race, gender, sexual orientation, and social class. Others agreed and we ended up hiring the African American candidate. After the meeting, the only African American person present thanked me for my comment saying that if I hadn't pointed out the issue, she would have had to. Unlike her, I had the unearned privilege of being able to make the point without seeming defensive. I still paid a small price because a few of the faculty saw me as a troublemaker, but my price was considerably less than hers would have been.

THE POWER OF ALLIES

Allies are sometimes more successful than targeted populations in changing attitudes because of the allies' privilege as members of the dominant group (Kappen, 2001). When I give lectures on lesbian, gay, bisexual, and transgendered (LGBT) issues in counseling, psychology, social work, education, and religion classes and challenge the students' views, I am seen by homophobic students as biased and self-serving. In contrast, a heterosexual ally who challenges their views might create more cognitive dissonance for them. Homophobic students' reactions to the ally's pro-gay attitudes might go something like, "Hmm ... I respect and identify with her, yet we disagree on this issue"; or "I thought only queers and militants were for gay rights, yet my instructor who has a husband is gay-affirmative.... How confusing!" (See Liddle & Stowe, 2002.) The words of allies are perhaps more difficult for homophobic listeners to write off, thereby provoking prolonged thought and the opportunity for more in-depth analysis before the listeners accept or reject the information. For example, I believe my most powerful and successful lecture on this topic was successful, not so much because of my own contribution, but rather because of the heterosexual course instructor's later discussion of my presentation. (See Liddle & Stowe, 2002.) During the class discussion the week after my presentation, the students at first reported only anger and discomfort. However, by the end of the discussion facilitated by the instructor who is a heterosexual ally to the LGBT community, there was evidence of substantive attitude change. Several students who had initially reported outrage at being forced to listen to a gay-affirmative lecture they felt was antithetical to their religious values, ended up saying things such as "I've completely changed my mind." It seemed that by having a safe place to explore their discomfort and perhaps by seeing the instructor and other relatively gay-affirmative classmates as role models, these students were able to incorporate the information from my lecture in a way they could not without the help of these allies.

Another advantage allies have in confronting prejudice is that they are more likely to witness some forms of prejudice than are members of the oppressed group. As an out lesbian, I am seldom confronted by open hostility. Perhaps this is because most people tend to be polite about their prejudices, at least when they are around people they know belong to those groups. However, people are not so circumspect when they are unaware that a member of that group is present. For example, a group of workers (one of whom was a closeted gay acquaintance) came to make a repair in my office. The workers were very polite to me, but I later heard from my gay acquaintance that, the minute they were out of earshot, they started making derogatory remarks about my sexual orientation. My friend did not dare speak out against this abuse for fear of arousing suspicion that he was gay. He did not share the privilege heterosexuals have—the ability to confront homophobia without fear of discrimination. Because it is legal to fire someone simply for being gay in 37 states, including Alabama (Human Rights Campaign, 2003), my gay friend might have lost his job if he had spoken up. If one of the straight men present had put a stop to the homophobic rhetoric, however, he would not have faced as great a risk.

CONCLUSION

Members of privileged groups can use their privilege to combat discrimination and oppression in both their professional and private lives. The first step is recognizing that privilege and discrimination still exist in our society. The next is deciding to use one's privilege in the service of reducing those injustices. Finally, it takes courage and practice to talk about these issues with one's colleagues and friends. The fact that I face fewer consequences when I act as an ally than would a member of the group being discriminated against makes me feel an obligation to speak up, rather than waiting for a member of that group to confront the problem. I have had the experience of being an ally and of benefiting from the efforts of allies to the LGBT community. Both experiences have consistently reinforced for me McIntosh's (1988) assertion that one of the most important privileges that dominant community members have is the privilege to confront prejudice without being seen as self-serving. Taking on the role of an ally— deciding in advance that I will not tacitly support injustice with my silence— has helped me find the courage to speak up when opportunities arise.

DISCUSSION QUESTIONS

1. You are spending time with two White friends. One friend tells a joke that you find racially offensive. Your other friend laughs.

   a) What do you do?

   b) Is what you would actually do different from what you ideally wish you would do?

   c) How are your feelings and your anticipated reactions influenced by your own race?

   d) How do you think your own race will influence how you will be seen by your friends?

2. Think of the last time you witnessed prejudice toward a group of which you are not a member. Picture the entire interaction including what happened afterwards.

   a) What was your role in this interaction?

   b) Did you respond constructively (in a way that would promote nondefensive self-examination in the offender)?

   c) If not, what stopped you, and in retrospect what do you wish you had done?

   d) What similar future situations are you likely to face and what can you do to prepare to respond constructively?

3. When in the last week do you think you benefited from privilege (for example, heterosexual privilege, white privilege, or male privilege)?

4. Do you feel any obligation either to give up some unearned privilege or to use your privilege constructively? If so, what forms might your actions take?

5. When have you had to choose between personal comfort and personal integrity? Which did you choose and what price did you pay for that choice?

REFERENCES

Akamatsu, N. N. (1998). The talking oppression blues: Including the experience of power/powerlessness in the teaching of "cultural sensitivity." In M. McGoldrick (Ed.). *Re-visioning family therapy: Race, culture, and gender in clinical practice* (pp. 129–143). New York: Guilford Press.

Ancis, J. R., & Szymanski, D. M. (2001). Awareness of White privilege among White counseling trainees. *Counseling Psychologist, 29,* 548–569.

Human Rights Campaign (2003). Gay, lesbian, bisexual and transgender workplace issues. [On-line.] Retrieved 4/5/03 from http://www.hrc.org/issues/workplace/index.asp.

Kappen, D. M. (2001). Acknowledgement of racial privilege, endorsement of equality, and feelings of collective guilt via ingroup versus outgroup influence. *Dissertation Abstracts International, 61*(9-B), 5056.

Liddle, B. J., & Stowe, A. M. (2002). A lesbian/straight team approach to changing attitudes toward lesbian, gay, bisexual, and transgendered people. *Journal of Lesbian Studies, 6* (3/4), 99–108.

McIntosh, Peggy (1988). *White privilege and male privilege: A personal account of coming to see correspondences through work in women's studies.* Wellesley, MA: Wellesley College, Center for Research on Women.

Reed, V. M. (1991). Civil rights legislation and the housing status of black Americans: Evidence from fair housing audits and segregation indices. *Review of Black Political Economy, 19*(3/4), 29–42.

Treitel, E. N. (2000). Anti-racist practice by White psychologists. *Dissertation Abstracts International, 61*(5-B), 2785.

30

✳

Yes, I See You're Committed to the Cause ... But Where's Your Credibility, and Why That Angst?

DAVID MACPHEE

C an a middle-class youth recognize his privilege without being immersed in a low-income environment? Can a White man comprehend racism viscerally if he has not been a visible minority in another culture or witnessed it in action?

BACKGROUND

Two figure/ground experiences in my youth had a formative influence on my perception of privilege. First, I grew up in a small, blue-collar town in Idaho that was dependent on mining and forestry, yet my parents were well-educated professionals. Second, many of the families I knew—all White—were regular churchgoers who believed in the Golden Rule and that God loves all people. Although they might sprinkle everyday conversation with ethnic jokes and slurs, paradoxically they gave to causes that served culturally diverse and low-income people. Most of them were generous and compassionate and would be offended to be called bigots.

Neither my ethnicity nor social class was obvious to me until I went to a private college where I was less worldly and wealthy. My battered 1954 bread truck advertised to all that I was a "hick from the sticks." I was in daily contact with People of Color for the first time, the novelty of which made me uncomfortable. Flashbacks to age five bubbled to the surface, when on my first trip to an urban, multicultural city, I pointed to an African American man in the grocery line ahead of us and asked my father, in a preschooler's stage voice, "What's that?"

This naiveté became more self-conscious in graduate school when I became good friends with a Black woman and several Jewish women. Paralyzing internal debates about protocol leaked out in ways that were probably amusing if not appalling. *How much can I ask about what it's like to be Black (or Jewish)? Is it acceptable to talk about prejudice and racism? Is "Jew" a slur, or do I always have to say "Jewish people?" Is it "Black" or "African American?" Am I an ignorant bumpkin or just garden-variety naïve? How can I become less naïve if I don't ask forthright questions? How much should I expect others to rectify my ignorance, even if my intentions are sincere?*

DEVELOPING AWARENESS

A handful of events shaped my perceptions of privilege as well as my commitment to equality and interest in diversity. First, few of my high school classmates attended a university and all were middle-class kids. The women had to fight much harder than I did for respect and success in school and their careers, especially if they went into law or engineering. I had assumed that I did well in high school because of native intelligence and hard work, not because I was middle class, White, and male. The social comparison processes that happened in college taught me that I had underestimated the role of opportunity structures (Bronfenbrenner & Ceci, 1994), those experiences provided by families, schools, and neighborhoods that allow certain predispositions to flourish. If my White, middle-class parents had not emphasized reading, encouraged involvement in extracurricular activities, and saved faithfully for college, I might have taken a different path in the woods.

Rural life shapes attitudes that are pertinent to everything from voting patterns to consumer habits, as well as perceptions of privilege. Brooks (2001, p. 62) observed, "… that most [rural] people don't think sociologically. They don't compare themselves with faraway millionaires who appear on their TV screens. They compare themselves with their neighbors" who tend to have a comfortable standard of living. As a result, there is little class consciousness. Attending a liberal arts college compelled me to think about social class for the first time because the framework for making social comparisons was so different there.

Another formative experience was religion. I was privileged to have several ministers who taught a gospel of caring for humanity, but especially for those who are oppressed. My maternal grandparents, both ministers, were outspoken opponents of the neo-Nazis who lived in a compound a few miles from their home. This moral compass was put to the test with other relatives who used the Bible to justify racism and intolerance for people who are gay. Such incidents crystallized for me the hypocrisy of professing belief in Christian principles while at the same time bestowing grace on only a privileged few, and that out-groups—all of whom were different from me—are a threat to some people.

My sense of White male privilege was honed by *Masculus hostilis*. This subspecies, the hostile male, vocalizes his displeasure with gender equity and multiculturalism in shrill diatribes (D'Souza, 1991; Schmidt, 1997), and in clippings posted on his office door that defend White male privilege in college admissions, hiring, and the exclusion of women, scholars of Color, and other disenfranchised groups from "The Canon." His table-pounding rants at faculty meetings are directed at those groups of people he feels are "given" too much that is not earned and he makes disparaging remarks about faculty research that focuses on gender and diversity. It is anger directed at those who threaten his status, not the angst of self-doubt. What I have learned from a few *Masculus hostilis* colleagues is that equality really does matter; otherwise, it would be a nonissue. Perhaps there would be greater acceptance of the social justice agenda if more of "us" (White males) were outspoken in support of it (see Smith, 1998).

INFUSIONS OF INSIGHT

As my adolescent self-awareness blossomed, I too wanted to be judged by the content of my character, not by my lack of sophistication in navigating a multicultural world with which I had limited experience. This is the nub of multicultural education for those of us from more privileged backgrounds: how to capitalize on interest in the topic—an interest motivated by relevance to one's career or by commitment to social justice—despite feeling inept in knowing how to behave and how to talk about it. When issues of privilege and difference have been relatively invisible in one's personal history, angst and stereotyping are predictable consequences of confronting such topics in the classroom or in social interactions with out-group people (Islam & Hewstone, 2001; Tatum, 1992).

My commitment and angst became more self-conscious when I participated in two curriculum-infusion projects at Colorado State University. The first focused on gender and the second on multicultural diversity. The faculty participants, virtually all White, wrestled with how to *talk*—not just teach—about prejudice, privilege, and the importance of diversity. If we were uncomfortable talking with colleagues who we knew to be committed to the cause, how could we face a class of students who might be dubious about, if not downright hostile to the principles we espoused?

These projects drew attention to issues of social class and culture and the undercurrent of power. The intellectual component was invigorating because a few fundamental processes explained disparate behavior patterns across people, class, culture, and time. Yet fieldwork with Hispanic and Native American families (MacPhee, Fritz, & Miller-Heyl, 1996), and with indigenous people in Australia and Belize, left a lasting, visceral appreciation for my privileged status. Inadequate housing and food, limited opportunities, and despondency often were rooted in patriarchy and colonialism, and by birthright I was one of the oppressors.

Despite this growing awareness of power and privilege, I have not completely relinquished my belief that the United States is a meritocracy (see Akamatsu, 2001; Banaszynski, 2001). I find myself suggesting to students that children from low-income families would have a brighter future if they just worked hard in school and their parents were more involved, which ignores a host of sociocultural forces arrayed against upward mobility (Lopez, Gurin, & Nagda, 1998; Molnar & Lawson, 1984). For example, children of less advantaged class origins need to show substantially more merit than advantaged children to achieve the same level of success as adults (Breen & Goldthorpe, 1999). One lesson for me is that my limited first-hand experience with oppression, hamstrings my ability to fully appreciate opportunities denied to others.

Membership in the privileged class has a hidden tax for the diversity educator—the emotional labor can be painful. I attended seminars in which White males became the scapegoat for a number of social ills and a conference workshop at which the only White person in the room (me) was humiliated as a way to "turn the tables." An occasional class went up in flames when a few vocal students were critical of the attention to diversity issues and I lacked the skill to defuse the tension (see MacPhee, Oltjenbruns, Fritz, & Kreutzer, 1994). Such incidents provoked in me resentment, frustration, and guilt—not exactly virtues. The literature on privilege suggests that these feelings, particularly collective guilt, are normal when in-group members think about their privileged status (Branscombe, 1998). In some cases, such angst may be adaptive because it links consideration of privilege with positive attitudes toward, and actions on behalf of social justice (Banaszynski, 2001; Doosje, Branscombe, Spears, & Manstead, 1998).

Credibility can also be a thorny issue for a professor from the privileged class. As a developmental psychologist, I have no formal academic training in women's studies, cultural anthropology, or sociology. On more than a few occasions, I groped for concepts and connections that were not yet second nature, but I found solace in the suggestion that multicultural competence requires professors to abandon their all-knowing façade and acknowledge their vulnerability and ineptitude (Vacarr, 2001).

More frustrating for me was the opinion of some students and writers that I had no business talking about issues with which I had little direct experience, regardless of my commitment to the cause. Recent commentaries on this issue assert that people from privileged classes must take responsibility for questioning beliefs and practices that support dominance and discrimination (for example, Boyle-Baise, 1995; Jacques, 1997). Research on social persuasion further supports a role for the White male teacher because attempts to influence others' understanding of privilege are more successful when made by in-group members (Kappen, 2000). It does seem self-evident that a person of dominant identity should refrain from talking about the *phenomenology* of oppression—how it is experienced personally—unless it is prefaced with "Other people report that ..." But I don't agree that lived experience is the only legitimate source of knowledge— a form of parochial reasoning (Brookfield, 1987)—even though it can enrich what is taught.

CONCLUSIONS

Why would a White male professor enthusiastically pursue social justice in the face of such obstacles? Edge (2002) argued that the ability to embrace diversity is necessary to experience compassion and compassion is a foundation of social justice. Aside from experience with diversity, the impulse for social justice also can be nurtured through community service, religious education, and discussions of moral and ethical issues. As well, certain values coincide with involvement in social justice activities, particularly the importance attached to influencing others and viewing one's work as an expression of beliefs and values (Treitel, 2000).

The conversion experiences I have described may also require some figure/ ground contrasts. For instance, can a middle-class youth recognize his privilege without being immersed in either poor or wealthy contexts? Can a White man comprehend racism viscerally if he has not been a visible minority in another culture or witnessed racism—such as slurs shouted from a passing car at a Black friend? Is a husband truly aware of patriarchy until there is marital conflict around his limited contributions to household labor? All of these examples suggest that power and oppression are relatively invisible to the dominant group until that privilege is challenged and for this reason it is inevitable that multicultural education provokes angst in students and teachers alike.

APPLICATIONS

The scenario and questions below are meant to help the reader think about some of these applications.

Scenario: You are a teacher in your fourth year. It is the third monthly meeting of a year-long multicultural education project that will teach instructors how to address issues of diversity, power, and privilege in their classes. The group includes 15 participants from diverse disciplines and different schools/departments and most are White. All volunteered; they were not coerced by an administrator. By now, you and your fellow teachers are moderately comfortable with one another: Everyone seems okay with sharing personal experiences and opinions.

The first two sessions covered "safe" topics such as project goals, terminology, student and societal demographics, and models of cultural awareness. Today's session is about how to sensitize students to issues of power and privilege. The first hour is devoted to self-exploration exercises that are supposed to help the participants become aware of this multifaceted issue and the remaining hour will be devoted to instructional methods. The discussion is rugged. Some of the men are getting defensive because all fingers seem to be pointing at White males for various social ills. Others look perplexed and wonder what all the fuss is about. They say, "I thought this was the land of opportunity," or "If you work hard enough, you can succeed." You express your doubts that you have the background to talk with authority about these issues in class. This comment triggers an anxious discussion about what will happen if the students feel blamed by the messages or worse, if they are overtly hostile and accuse the instructor of being "politically correct."

DISCUSSION QUESTIONS

1. Discuss how the "invisibility of privilege" might be made evident to professionals (teachers, counselors, social workers, psychologists, human services) from privileged backgrounds. Are there ways to create awareness without also fostering guilt (personal or collective) and defensiveness?

2. Should angst arise in a training seminar, how would you get to the source and how might it be addressed constructively?

3. Is it necessary to have firsthand experience (as a minority, with oppression) to teach with authority? If not, how do you bring these issues alive in the classroom? How might the White males in the group effectively work toward social justice? How are students likely to react to the topic of social justice in your setting?

4. A colleague says that he doesn't have the background in sociology or anthropology to address issues related to diversity and social status. How might you respond? What suggestions might you make?

5. How would you defuse a class that is "going up in flames"? Some students are making accusations of political correctness and asking why such issues are even being brought up; others are angry that some of their peers deny there is a problem to be dealt with; others sit tight lipped, with arms crossed.

6. Brainstorm teaching strategies that would illuminate ways in which (a) women have less power, and (b) youth of Color have less opportunity to achieve. Ideally, these strategies would help to personalize the issues for students (i.e., help them empathize), convey accurate information, and/or highlight implications for practice.

REFERENCES

Akamatsu, N. N. (2001). The talking oppression blues: Including the experience of power/powerlessness in the teaching of "cultural sensitivity." *Journal of Feminist Family Therapy, 11,* 83–97.

Banaszynski, T. L. (2001). *Beliefs about the existence of White privilege, race attitudes, and diversity-related behavior.* Unpublished doctoral dissertation, Yale University.

Boyle-Baise, M. (1995). The role of a European American scholar in multicultural education. *Theory and Research in Social Education, 23,* 332–341.

Branscombe, N. R. (1998). Thinking about one's gender group's privileges or disadvantages: Consequences for well-being in women and men. *British Journal of Social Psychology, 37,* 167–184.

Breen, R., & Goldthorpe, J. H. (1999). Class inequality and meritocracy: A critique of Saunders and an alternative analysis. *British Journal of Sociology, 50,* 1–27.

Bronfenbrenner, U., & Ceci, S. J. (1994). Nature/nurture reconceptualized in developmental perspective: A bioecological model. *Psychological Review, 101,* 568–586.

Brookfield, S. D. (1987). *Developing critical thinkers: Challenging adults to explore alternative ways of thinking and acting.* San Francisco: Jossey-Bass.

Brooks, D. (2001). One nation, slightly divisible. *Atlantic Monthly, 288*(5), 53–65.

Doosje, B., Branscombe, N. R., Spears, R., & Manstead, A. S. R. (1998). Guilty by association: When one's group has a negative history. *Journal of Personality and Social Psychology, 75,* 872–886.

D'Souza, D. (1991). *Illiberal education: The politics of race and sex on campus.* New York: Free Press.

Edge, R. (2002). One middle-age White male's perspective on racism and cultural competence: A view from the bunker where we wait to have our privilege stripped away. *Mental Retardation, 40,* 83–85.

Islam, M. R., & Hewstone, M. (2001). Dimensions of contact as predictors of intergroup anxiety, perceived out-group variability, and out-group attitude: An integrative model. In M. A. Hogg & D. Abrams (Eds.). *Intergroup relations: Essential readings* (pp. 383–395). Philadelphia: Psychology Press/Taylor & Francis.

Jacques, R. (1997). The unbearable whiteness of being: Reflections of a pale, stale male. In P. Prasad, A. J. Mills, M. Elmes, & A. Prasad (Eds.). *Managing the organizational melting pot: Dilemmas of workplace diversity* (pp. 80–106). Thousand Oaks, CA: Sage.

Kappen, D. M. (2000). *Acknowledgement of racial privilege, endorsement of equality, and feelings of collective guilt via ingroup versus outgroup influence.* Unpublished doctoral dissertation, University of Kansas.

Lopez, G. E., Gurin, P., & Nagda, B. A. (1998). Education and understanding structural causes for group inequalities. *Political Psychology, 19,* 305–329.

MacPhee, D., Fritz, J., & Miller-Heyl, J. (1996). Ethnic variations in personal social networks and parenting. *Child Development, 67,* 3278–3295.

MacPhee, D., Oltjenbruns, K. A., Fritz, J. J., & Kreutzer, J. C. (1994). Strategies for infusing curricula with a multicultural perspective. *Innovative Higher Education, 18,* 289–309.

Molnar, J. J., & Lawson, W. D. (1984). Perceptions of barriers to Black political and economic progress in rural areas. *Rural Sociology, 49,* 261–283.

Schmidt, A. J. (1997). *The menace of multiculturalism: Trojan horse in America.* Westport, CT: Praeger.

Smith, R. W. (1998). Challenging privilege: White male middle-class opposition in the multicultural education terrain. In R. C. Chavez & J. O'Donnell (Eds.). *Speaking the unpleasant: The politics of (non)engagement in the multicultural education terrain* (pp. 197–210). Albany, NY: State University of New York Press.

Tatum, B. D. (1992). Talking about race, learning about racism: The application of racial identity development theory in the classroom. *Harvard Educational Review, 62,* 1–24.

Treitel, N. P. (2000). *Anti-racist practice by White psychologists.* Unpublished doctoral dissertation, California School of Professional Psychology.

Vacarr, B. (2001). Moving beyond polite correctness: Practicing mindfulness in the diverse classroom. *Harvard Educational Review, 71,* 285–295.

✳

A Multiracial Unity Group for Graduate Students

BARBARA GORMLEY

CRITICAL INCIDENT

A memorable incident occurred in the late 1990s while I was working on a writing project focused on integrating women's issues with multiculturalism. The purpose of the writing work group was to provide students, such as myself, with an opportunity to meet faculty from other regions of the country with similar interests in order to establish mentoring relationships. The women were predominantly White, although the group included a few women of Color. Half of the women were faculty, including several who were highly influential in our field, and half were doctoral students. During this meeting, Sally, an African American student who was a friend of mine, spoke up about an important issue related to race. She wondered how effectively our final product would address multicultural issues with so few women of Color involved. She suggested seeking external consultation from women of Color. Not one of the 20 women in the room responded to her comment. The topic shifted to women's issues.

When there was a pause, I, a White woman, reiterated Sally's point. She had asked me to back her up this way if I ever noticed that she went unheard, or I might not have done so. Not only did the group focus on the concern after I brought it up, but a senior member of the group complimented me on "my" idea. Recognizing that I had not attributed the idea to Sally, I told the group that it wasn't my idea and that Sally had suggested it earlier. There appeared to be much embarrassment as many exclaimed that they did not remember hearing her say anything. This was not only a source of great pain for my friend, but also the beginning of the end of a group project that was never completed. Before this event, when People of Color told me that their ideas were often credited to

White people, I had not recognized the instances when this occurred, nor had I fully appreciated the destructive consequences of invisibility.

For 15 years preceding this event, I had embraced antiracist ideology, challenged my own and others' biases, advocated for Native American and Mexican migrant groups living in my rural area, and presented at conferences on diversity issues. I even won an award for cultural sensitivity in clinical practice. The emotional pain and trauma associated with repeated experiences of racism, however, remained a distant concept even when I heard about it from friends. I specialized as a practitioner in trauma related to violence, but emotional pain associated with race did not deeply affect me. When I went back to school to earn my Ph. D., the emotional process that I went through and the People of Color that I met led me to conclude that my protective emotional shield was White privilege.

FEELING THE PAIN

When I began my doctoral training, there was racial tension within my program. I tried to organize a White Awareness group based on Katz' (1978) model because I had been a member of such a group as an undergraduate in the early 1980s and I thought such a group would be helpful for me. A faculty member who knew Judy Katz was supportive, but response was poor. White students wanted to lead the group rather than join. I asserted that to be a participant before being a trainer would be helpful, but I lost some participants this way. If I could go back in time, I would ask them what it meant to consider being a participant instead of a leader. Perhaps students needed to examine the issue of power dynamics during recruitment instead of waiting until the group began, especially in light of the fact that I was a first year student trying to recruit senior students. In the end, insufficient interest was expressed to start a group. At one point during my attempt to organize the group, Sally, an African American student, wanted to know why the group was just for Whites. When I responded that the format offered Whites an opportunity to examine biased ideas in a safe environment, she asked how we would know which of our ideas were biased without any People of Color present. She had a good point and this was the beginning of an ongoing, fruitful dialogue. Sally later became my friend and co-facilitated our cross-racial dialogue group that I discuss below.

During my second semester as a doctoral student, a requirement of our multicultural course was to spend 15 weeks observing a cross-racial dialogue group that is one component of the Multiracial Unity Living Experience (MRULE; Thomas, Gazel, & Byard, 1999). MRULE is an undergraduate race-relations program at Michigan State University that emphasizes (a) a grounding in the lives of the student-participants; (b) the role of historical examples; (c) unity in diversity and the role of difference; (d) the centrality of race; (e) social constructions of race; (f) social constructions of Whiteness and White privilege; (g) exploring the dynamics of power relationships; (h) exploring the dynamics of genuine, authentic relationships; (i) the role of dialogue; and (j) the use of participatory action research to sustain, develop, and replicate the program (Gazel, 1999). A discussion group based on these principles is central; however, "field trips" that expose participants to different cultures and activities that require cooperation with racially different others are also paramount. The ultimate goal of the group we observed was to create opportunities for cross-race friendships for freshmen and sophomores. Forty undergraduate students from a variety of races and backgrounds learned to respectfully take risks while discussing difficult race-related topics. The group was moving and it inspired me to begin working with Jeanne Gazel, one of the group leaders, and several students in my program to organize a Multiracial Unity group for graduate students.

Again, there were strong reactions from students who this time reported feeling left out or judged if they didn't participate. Additionally, Black and Hispanic students recruited to participate did not want too many people from their cohorts involved because of trust issues. As a result, membership was established by word of mouth. Attempts to start these groups elicited strong emotional reactions and I became a focus of hostility for disgruntled students. One instructor told me that others had failed in similar efforts because they also had become the target of emotion surrounding a long history of racial conflict. My advisor pointed out that, by persevering, I stood up to people's projections, and in doing so, showed people that these projections can be survived. Several students who feared reprisals from faculty for expressing interest in the group observed that that this did not happen to Sally or me and they eventually joined the group.

That semester, the Multiracial Unity group for graduate students began. Jeanne Gazel helped facilitate the first session and she brought three students who volunteered to talk about their experiences in an undergraduate group. The graduate student group had a balanced mix of students of Color and White students, females and males, different ages, and different cohorts. The pain Black and Hispanic students expressed and the uncertainty that White students expressed about what to do about race issues moved many to tears. Consequently, we decided to begin by focusing on supporting each other to talk about our current experiences instead of jumping into social action. However, one outcome of these vulnerable conversations was action designed to try to change things within our program.

In the group, we learned to be honest, to take risks, to genuinely examine issues, to dialogue with each other, and to support each other through differences. The members of the group taught me the benefits of making mistakes and seeking new perspectives. I felt the pain of Black and Hispanic students who shared (a) current experiences of prejudice and discrimination; (b) heartfelt tales of wondering whether race influenced the way faculty treated them; and (c) reports that they could not be themselves in our training program. Their stories touched me deeply and I began to make an emotional connection to race inequity and to dismantle previously held beliefs about an educational system that is dear to me.

Another White member, after listening to the stories of how students of Color were treated, said that she would never be the same and that everyone in our program needed to hear these stories to understand what was happening.

I wished that everyone could hear these stories and I felt honored that I had. However, to expect a small number of students to educate the professional community also seemed an unfair burden.

I wanted to be part of the solution rather than part of the problem and I learned how to use privilege to benefit professional colleagues who do not have racial privilege. Specifically, I can break the silence or speak up about race and oppression when discomfort leads White people to change the topic to gender or religion or other personal characteristics that place them in the oppressed, rather than the privileged role. I can try to reach those who may be able to hear only White voices. I can support People of Color in their efforts to uproot racism and discrimination. I can speak up for those silenced by privilege and credit them for their ideas when others give the credit to me.

As I joined efforts to raise awareness in our training program around issues of oppression, discrimination, and privilege, I also had to work through the repercussions associated with social justice issues. On one hand, I was rejected by some of the White students in a way similar to how African American students were treated. On the other hand, sometimes my voice was heard over Black students who were saying the same thing I was. The complexity of the situation was overwhelming. Being heard was a privilege I would have liked to give up, but silence was a privilege I would not exercise. Instead, as I helped White colleagues see different perspectives, I learned to credit students and faculty of Color who for many years before I came along had diligently addressed race issues in our program. When faculty with evaluative power credited me with success in these efforts, I later wondered how much of the credit belonged to a long line of Black students and faculty in the program's history and whether I received the praise because I am White.

CONCLUSION AND LESSONS LEARNED

My efforts to alleviate racial oppression in my immediate environment led to experiences of failure, isolation, pain, confusion, and feeling as if everything was falling apart. I was credited with tolerating and overcoming these traumatic experiences, but what I suffered for one year seemed more like a vicarious experiencing of a lifetime of trauma or a collective traumatic experience with which many students of Color were expected to cope without acknowledgement.

Of greatest importance to me was the genuine contact with students and faculty of Color that resulted in a most enjoyable and facilitative aspect of my graduate training. The confrontation, camaraderie, guidance, and friendship of Jeanne, Sally, and others supported my exploration and facilitated a new degree of surrendering privilege. My previous individual efforts to address racial issues seemed insignificant compared to being immersed in a cross-racial community and actively working together. The emotionally connected, community-minded group provided opportunities unavailable in the hierarchical, individualistic, competitive educational structure.

One way students can produce effective dialogue about cultural influences, in spite of commonly experienced fear and anxiety (Constantine, 1998), is to create groups separate from evaluative settings, as we did. Another way is to collaborate with faculty within training programs or academic courses. Ponterotto (1998) recommended that trainees become partners in multicultural training and applauded a shift "from content to process, from knowledge to experience, from quantification to personal narratives" (p. 43). Personal narratives not only are cathartic but also must inform diversity efforts in training programs if we are to understand how student experiences differ by cultural background. In addition, White students need to practice giving up white privilege if they are to be able to work in diverse collegial groups.

There may be limits to how effectively these issues can be addressed in a classroom. Intellectual exercises seldom provoke the powerful affect that arises when the status quo or deeply held beliefs are challenged, and rarely do such exercises incorporate methods for strong emotion to be safely and productively processed. Trainers might expect intellectual decorum or unknowingly push trainees to adopt values like their own rather than encourage or tolerate a process of exploration. Enhancing awareness, confronting racist attitudes, and providing opportunities for processing related affect are difficult goals for training programs to achieve (Kiselica, 1999). Because of the power differential between faculty and students, trainees may comply with training expectations without expanding their awareness to accommodate other worldviews or changing their professional behavior (Steward, Neil, Breland, & Miller, 1999).

This power differential is especially daunting when a student encounters biased faculty members. Psychologists are ethically required to work to eliminate prejudice and to acknowledge discrimination that affects the psychological well being of students (American Psychological Association, 1993); however, faculty vary in levels of multicultural awareness and they are not always aware of discriminatory events. Students might not disclose experiences of racism within their training programs to their faculty, fearing negative consequences, even though students report experiencing racism in training programs when offered indirect opportunities for disclosure (Constantine, 1998). We all may be reluctant to link dynamics that arise to race. "Racism ... is not a dualistic (i.e., either/or) status but a pervasive, often subtle, set of attitudes that can surface in surprising ways for all of us" (Vasquez, 1992, p. 199).

APPLICATION

Imagine that you are a student in a graduate course with 20 other students. Besides you, the course includes two African American men, one African American woman, one Latina woman, nine White women, and seven White men. The topic is recruiting and maintaining students of Color as a means of eliminating discrimination. The instructor states that African American men are not successful in your training program and there has been discussion among the faculty about not admitting any more applicants of this type. One of the African American men gets up and walks out of the classroom and he does not return to the course.

DISCUSSION QUESTIONS

1. What are your emotional reactions to the scenario? What kinds of similar or different reactions might the others involved have? What is important about the differences?

2. What kinds of racial power dynamics would you expect in a group with this racial makeup? Are you part of the class' racial minority or majority? Does this position affect your reaction?

3. What are the implications of the power differential between the instructor and the student who left the class? Are there similar and/or different implications of the power differential between Whites and People of Color in the room? Do the implications change if the instructor is White, African American, of another race?

4. What is the issue? Share your thoughts with others racially different from you and seek out alternative perspectives. Did your views change? Why or why not?

5. Do you think discrimination or prejudice is being exhibited? By whom? Are there ethical or legal implications to this scenario? Is anyone at risk of being harmed? If so, who is at risk?

6. What would you do in this situation? What would you like to see others do? Which responses to this situation might cause harm or perpetuate prejudice and discrimination? Which responses from White people maintain or give up privilege?

REFERENCES

American Psychological Association. (1993). Guidelines for providers of psychological services to ethnic, linguistic, and culturally diverse populations. *American Psychologist, 48*, 45–48.

Constantine, M. (1998). Racism's impact on counselors' professional and personal lives: A response to the personal narratives on racism. *Journal of Counseling and Development, 77*, 68–72.

Gazel, J. (1999). Building community through diversity: Theory and practice of the Multi-Racial Unity Living Experience. In R. W. Thomas, J. Gazel & R. L. Byard (Eds.). *Building community across racialized lines: The Multiracial Unity Project at Michigan State University* (Unity Studies Monograph Series, Monograph Number 1). East Lansing: Michigan State University, Urban Affairs Programs.

Katz, J. H. (1978). *White awareness: Handbook for anti-racism training.* Norman, OK: University of Oklahoma Press.

Kiselica, M. S. (Ed.). (1999). *Confronting prejudice and racism during multicultural training.* Alexandria, VA: American Counseling Association.

Ponterotto, J. G. (1998). Charting a course for research in multicultural counseling training. *The Counseling Psychologist, 26,* 43–68.

Steward, R. J., Neil, D. M., Breland, A., & Miller, M. (1999, April). Negative outcomes of diversity training: What can we do? Paper presented at the annual conference of the Great Lakes Region of the American Psychological Association, Columbus, OH.

Thomas, R. W., Gazel, J., & Byard, R. L. (Eds.). (1999). *Building community across racialized lines: The Multiracial Unity Project at Michigan State University* (Unity Studies Monograph Series, Monograph Number 1). East Lansing: Michigan State University, Urban Affairs Programs.

Vasquez, M. J. T. (1992). Psychologist as clinical supervisor: Promoting ethical practice. *Professional Psychology: Research and Practice, 23,* 196–202.

Glossary

Acculturation refers to the process that occurs when cultures come into contact with one another. Acculturation does not presume that one culture will eliminate the other, nor that the two will coexist in harmony, although these are certainly possibilities.

Ageism a form of systematic stereotyping and discrimination against people simply because of their age.

Ally a person who takes some action to oppose oppression of a group of which he or she is not a member. For example, an Asian American who challenges a racist joke that targets African Americans is acting as an ally to the African American community.

Assimilation wherein members of one culture opt to (or are "forced" to) relinquish their own values and traditions in order to adopt those of the new or host culture. Thus, assimilated individuals are not motivated to maintain their original cultural identity.

Aversive Racism (Dovidio, Gaertner, Kawakami, & Hodson, 2002; Kovel, 1970) an attitudinal adaptation that results from an assimilation of an egalitarian value system with prejudicial and racist beliefs. In aversive racism as applied to white folks,

one consciously endorses egalitarian values and denies negative feelings toward People of Color. There is no evidence of blatant discrimination. Racist behavior is often unintentional and attributed to nonracial factors. Despite an absence of racist intentions, racist *outcomes* still occur. Aversive racism results in nondiscriminatory behavior in situations in which doing the "right" thing is obvious, but racist behavior when the situation is ambiguous. For example, Dovidio and Gaernter (2000) found that when both black and white applicants are weakly qualified for a job, there is no evidence of discrimination in hiring practices. White research participants reject both candidates. When black and white applicants are both moderately qualified, there is a slight but nonsignificant preference for whites. However, when black and white candidates are both *highly qualified*, then a strong preference for the white candidate is seen. The term *aversive* refers to the tension and anxiety experienced by whites when they are interacting with People of Color. It also refers to the aversion that whites have to the notion that their thoughts or actions might be racist.

Bisexual term for a person who has orientations for intimacy toward both men and women.

Cisgender a descriptor for those people that experience satisfaction and comfort in their birth assigned sex and the gender roles that are socially aligned with this sex assignment.

Closeted hidden; most commonly used to refer to keeping one's sexual orientation secret; the opposite of *out*.

Core Conditions from Rogers' (1957) proposal that there are three necessary and sufficient conditions for therapeutic change: 1) congruence, 2) unconditional positive regard, and 3) empathy. Generally speaking, congruence refers to one's ability to be authentic and genuine in a relationship. Unconditional positive regard refers to nonjudgmental acceptance of another person. Empathy occurs when one enters another person's frame of reference and uses reflection of feeling to communicate an accurate understanding of that frame.

Ego-dystonic a term used to describe when a person's thoughts, impulses, and behavior are felt to be repugnant, distressing, unacceptable, or inconsistent with the self-conception.

Gay term for a person whose primary orientation for intimacy is toward people of the same sex; progressive literature uses the term *gay* to refer to men and *lesbian* to refer to women, to denote that these are two distinct groups rather than one group being a subcategory of the other group.

Gender the social construction of masculinity or femininity as it aligns with designated sex at birth in a specific culture and time period. Gender identity claims individuality that may or may not be expressed outwardly, and may or may not correspond to one's sexual anatomy.

Gender Variant/Queer people who find other gender categories constraining. Their gender identities and/or expression are consciously not consistent with conventional standards for masculine or feminine behavior or appearance. Some identify as a blend, as androgynous, or as neither gender.

Heterophobia the irrational fear of being perceived as heterosexual.

Heterophobic a person that internalizes and/or externalizes an irrational fear of heterosexuals.

Heteroqueer a person, couple, or multiple partners in relationship that identify and/or are perceived as queer yet, one or more of those partners has heterosexual privilege.

Heterosexism the ideological system that denies, denigrates, and stigmatizes any nonheterosexual form of behavior, identity, relationship, or community (Herek, 1990); the system of values that promotes heterosexual relationships to the exclusion of other kinds of relationships (for example, platonic friendships, gay and lesbian relationships); beliefs, behaviors, or systems that discriminate against people who are lesbian, gay, bisexual, transgender, or queer, based upon a narrow view of heterosexuality as normal and healthy, whereas other sexual orientations and gender expressions are viewed deviant and unhealthy. The norm of heterosexual sexual identity being the dominant socially accepted romantic-, sexual-, or emotional-based relationship that then places all other forms of attraction as subordinate.

Homophobia irrational fear of, aversion to, or discrimination against homosexuality or homosexuals.

Homoprejudice negative judgments and/or stereotypes about gays and lesbians; preferred by some over the term homophobia.

Intersectionality an understanding of identity that recognises the multiple ways in which identities intersect with one another. This approach does not view identities in an additive sense, but rather sees all aspects of an individual's experience combining concurrently to produce a particular position in the world that may involve both privilege and disadvantage.

Lesbian a person that typically identifies as a woman that is romantically, sexually, and/or emotionally attracted to other people that identify as women.

LGBTQ acronym used to indicate *lesbian, gay, bisexual, transgender. and queer. In some cases the Q may stand for individuals questioning their status.*

Meritocracy a society in which people are rewarded solely based on merit. In a true meritocracy, the conditions of one's birth (race, class, sex, etc.) would have no effect on one's chances to succeed.

Oppression (Jaggar, 1983, p. 6) "The imposition of constraints; it suggest that the problem is not the result of bad luck, ignorance, or prejudice, but it is rather caused by one group actively subordinating another to its own interest."

Out open; most commonly used to refer to being open about one's sexual orientation; the opposite of *closeted.*

Privilege a right or immunity granted as a peculiar benefit or advantage, often taken for granted by members of dominant cultures or statuses.

Queer depending on how the term is used, it could be a derogatory word to describe people who are gay; reclaimed by some lesbian, gay, bisexual, or transgender people who self-identify as queer to show pride in who they are, including their differences.

Racism "system of advantage based on race" (Wellman, 1977, chapter 1). "Any behavior or pattern that systematically tends to deny access to opportunity or privilege to one social group while perpetuating privilege to members of another group" (Ridley, 1989, p, 60).

Rheumatoid Arthritis an autoimmune form of arthritis causing chronic joint inflammation, pain, and damage.

Sex the medical assignment of "male" or "female" based upon the external genitalia that an individual possesses at birth. The biological sexes are commonly seen as mutually exclusive, and it is often believed that a person's assigned sex dictates their gender expression, chromosomal, and

hormonal makeup (those born with "male" genitalia should behave in a masculine way and those born with "female" genitalia should behave in a feminine way).

Sexism the socially constructed system that creates a dominant group and subordinated groups based on how one is labeled at birth, anatomy, and other biological factors that then determine social privilege. In the United States culture, men are the dominant group, whereas women are subordinated. Gender queer, transgender, and people during transition are further subordinated.

Sexual Identity a person's self-description of the romantic, sexual, and/or emotional relationships with another or others such as heterosexual, gay, lesbian, bisexual, asexual, etc. Much like gender identifications, sexual identity labels are constantly being created to both unite communities and divide members from others.

Sexual Orientation an inborn, enduring emotional, romantic, affectionate, and sexual attraction to another person; sexual orientation falls along a continuum ranging from exclusively heterosexual to varying degrees of bisexuality to exclusively homosexual (lesbian or gay). Sexual orientation is not determined by behavior (for example, sexual intercourse between two men, two women, or a man and a woman), but by primary affectionate attraction and how one self-identifies.

Stigma (1) a mark of shame or discredit, and (2) an identifying mark or characteristic.

Transformational Learning processes which result in fundamental changes in how people see themselves and the world. "Transformational learning *shapes* people; they are different afterward, in ways that both they and others can recognize" (Clark, 1993, as cited by Merriam & Cafarella, 1999, p. 318).

Transgender an "umbrella term" for someone whose self-identification, anatomy, appearance, manner, expression, behavior and/or other's perceptions of challenges traditional societal expectations of congruent gender expression and designated birth sex.

Transition the period of time where a person is electing to move from one gendered category to another via social expressions, labels, clothing, mannerisms, voice control, as well as but not limited to taking hormones, accessing surgeries, and other such changes until the individual feels comfortable with their body, expression of their gender, and are perceived by others consistently and correctly.

Transphobia the irrational fear of trans and gender queer people by gender conforming people.

Transsexual individuals whose designated sex at birth does not match their personal sex/body identity and who, through sex reassignment surgery and hormone treatments, may seek to change their physical body to match their gender identity. Transsexuals can be male-to-female (MTF) or female-to-male (FTM). Transsexuals' sexual identification can be heterosexual, gay, lesbian, bisexual, etc.

Well-Meaning White Person (WMWP) (Wolfe, 1995) one who consciously despises racism, but possesses hidden racist attitudes and fears, which impede the development of authentic relationships with People of Color. The WMWP has an investment in differentiating oneself from blatant racists and oppressive institutions, to support the belief in oneself as "a good, concerned, altruistic person" (Wolfe, 1995, p. 44). Despite an expressed commitment to equality and justice, there is little evidence of *anti-racist* practices, and rarely examination or ownership of one's own racism and prejudice.

Index